GLOBAL ACCOUNT MANAGEMENT

GLOBAL ACCOUNT MANAGEMENT

A COMPLETE ACTION KIT
OF TOOLS AND TECHNIQUES
FOR MANAGING BIG CUSTOMERS
IN A SHRINKING WORLD

PETER CHEVERTON

KOGAN
PAGE

London and Philadelphia

First published in Great Britain and the United States in 2006 by Kogan Page Limited

120 Pentonville Road
London N1 9JN
United Kingdom
www.kogan-page.co.uk

525 South 4th Street, #241
Philadelphia PA 19147
USA

© Peter Cheverton, 2006

ISBN 0 7494 4538 6

British Library Cataloguing in Publication Data

A CIP record for this book is available from the British Library.

Library of Congress Cataloging-in-Publication Data

Cheverton, Peter.
   Global account management : a complete action kit of tools and techniques for managing big customers in a shrinking world / Peter Cheverton.
      p. cm.
   Includes bibliographical references and index.
   ISBN 0–7494–4538–6
   1. International business enterprises—Management. I. Title.
   HD62.4.C445 2006
   658.8'4—dc22   2005035681

Typeset by Saxon Graphics Ltd, Derby
Printed and bound in Great Britain by Cambridge University Press

Contents

About the author

Peter Cheverton is a founding director of INSIGHT Marketing and People, a global training and consultancy firm specializing in Key and Global Account Management, Leadership, Business Strategy and Value Creation. He has developed an international reputation as one of the leading experts in the challenging area of Key and Global Account Management, working 'hands on' with clients in Europe, the Americas, AsiaPacific and Africa.

He is the author of *Key Account Management (4th edition)*, the seminal work in this important area, and now used as the standard text by several business schools. He is also the author of *Key Marketing Skills (2nd edition)*, and the General Editor of the '*How come...*' series of essential business guides, including two of his own titles: *How Come You Can't Identify Your Key Customers?* and *How Come Your Brand Isn't Working Hard Enough?*.

Peter regularly presents INSIGHT's one-day Key Account and Global Account Management *Masterclasses* in London, and other major cities around the globe.

Prior to establishing INSIGHT in 1991, Peter was the European Sales and Marketing Manager for ICI Dulux Paints.

For contact details please see Chapter 16.

Preface

The aim of this book is to make clear the significant challenges of global account management (GAM), and to guide you through the process of decisions and actions required to make it a success. The challenge begins by accepting that there are no rules of GAM, at least no rules set by anyone except you or your customers, and so this is certainly no rulebook. How can there be any hard and fast rules when every circumstance is different, when every customer is unique, and when every supplier's starting point and ambition are their own alone?

It gets tougher. No rules, but plenty of difficult choices to be made. Perhaps you like the liberating feel of a blank canvas: I hope so. Some of the toughest decisions are about 'who?' and 'how many?', neither question (nor the answers) being as obvious as may at first appear. After that come the actions, and these are no trifling matter, concerning, as they do, organizational structure, levels of authority, and cross-functional and cross-business collaboration. And over and above all this (as if you needed anything more) there is the challenge of cultural diversity. For many this remains the biggest challenge of all, and yet as we will see, the apparent problems of such diverse attitudes and behaviours around the globe can become, in the realm of global account management, a genuine source of competitive advantage.

There is a mountain to be climbed, and with heights come dangers; the implications of getting this wrong are enormous. Not only are you deciding the fate of your relationships with some of your most important customers, you will be committing your business to a series of significant investments. This is the importance of GAM, that it is about securing your future success, and so never was there a better case for taking the time to look, to consider, and to plan with care. That is how this book intends to help you.

GAM OR KAM?

There are, of course, great similarities between the practice of global account management and key account management (KAM). That the challenges of GAM are more complex there is no doubt, and this book will be focusing on those rather than the full nitty-gritty of KAM practice. If you want to read up on this too, then may I point you in the direction of my earlier book (you will see that I started with the simpler of the tasks): *Key Account Management (4th edition), a complete action kit of tools and techniques for achieving profitable key supplier status*, also published by Kogan Page.

A NOTE ON TEMPLATES

Many readers of my *Key Account Management* book asked for prepared templates of account plans and other formats, and I expect similar requests regarding global account management. I should be clear about my views on such. First, the nature of any particular business's challenge is far too particular to itself to benefit very much from any generic templates. Second, the task of designing your own formats is one of the single most important activities to ensure that things are made to happen; it ensures that the format used is appropriate to your circumstances; it avoids the sin of 'box-ticking', a sin almost to be guaranteed when using someone else's format; and, most importantly of all, it forces you to assess the tools and concepts with your own challenge in mind, and to set your own priorities. So I make no apologies for the absence of prepared templates – honestly, it really is for your own good!

Acknowledgements

My thanks to Penny Carté and Chris Fox of Canning for their generosity in letting me make use of so much of their work in the chapter on cultural diversity, and to Kingsley Weber of INSIGHT for his challenging guidance on this same area.

As ever, my thanks go to Irene Larcombe for her alertness on the trail of the aberrant apostrophe, and other abominations committed by me on the English language.

My biggest thanks must go, however, to our clients at INSIGHT, for allowing me to develop my knowledge and expertise in the area of Global Account Management through long and fascinating observation of their own splendid efforts in this field. Needless to say, *almost* none of the 'bad practice' examples in the book are based on them…

1

Defining *'global'*

'Global account management? That's just key account management with time zones…'

Yes, I've heard it said, and if you've heard it said in your company, particularly if it was at the top, then watch out for trouble. Not only is this so very clearly the comment of someone who has never tried it, but as an underestimation of the task ahead it ranks alongside the notion that flying is just walking, with wings.

Global account management (GAM) uses many of the same processes and tools as key account management (KAM), but don't allow that to lull you into any false sense of security: the comfort of familiarity will be far outweighed by the complexity of the new challenge. Taking on the global challenge may prove to be one of the most testing things that your business undertakes; it will certainly occupy large amounts of your time, and it may cost you more than you had ever imagined. This is not something to be entered into lightly.

It may even be that you choose to avoid this particular challenge altogether; you would not be the first to look, and consider it a bridge too far. KAM, as with GAM, has few if any rules, and least of all that you should be obliged to practise it globally.

So to what extent do you have a choice? What if the customer is truly global? Can you ignore such a thing simply because the prospect of genuine GAM seems rather daunting? Broadly speaking, the nature of your account management (whether it be practised locally, nationally, regionally or globally) should begin with the nature of your customer. This explains why KAM and GAM have developed at such very different paces in different industries.

Where you are headed must begin with the nature of your customer

KAM saw its birth among suppliers to the retail trade as long ago as the 1970s when it was clear that consolidation in the grocery sector was going to change the nature of the supplier/customer relationship out of all recognition. KAM had spread to most manufacturing and B2B (business to business) suppliers by the late 1990s, though its practice here was very different to those early FMCG (fast moving consumer goods) pioneers.

For those supplying the retail trade today, the prospect of GAM looms large with the likes of Tesco, Wal*Mart and Carrefour dominating the scene, but it is a new challenge, and the long experience and hard-learnt lessons of national KAM may prove less helpful than many suspect. Supplying Tesco across Europe, compared to the challenge of supplying them across the UK, is a very much taller order than accommodating the extra miles involved.

For new lessons they might look to the very businesses that watched them so closely in years past, the B2B suppliers that have leapfrogged them in their experience of genuine GAM as manufacturing industry has moved away from its traditional locations and national characteristics, looking increasingly to Eastern Europe and the Far East.

In recent years KAM has begun to feature on the boardroom agenda of pharmaceutical and financial services companies; latecomers, but with good reason. While the world of retail and manufacturing was consolidating like crazy, the pharmaceutical and financial service firms' customer bases remained relatively fragmented, but now they see the emergence of new entities and new business opportunities that demand the practice of KAM, though to a different model again. The prospect of GAM is still rather far off for most of the pharmaceutical players, though perhaps a good deal closer for those in financial services.

If the nature of account management practice must follow the nature of the customer, then doesn't it follow that when the customer is truly global the supplier must respond in kind, with GAM? The answer to this is very probably 'yes', but the question brings us immediately to one of the most fundamental issues: define *'truly global'*.

Getting this right could save your business a great deal of time, money and frustration.

TRULY GLOBAL, OR JUST PLAIN INTERNATIONAL?

Let's begin with a simpler definition: the 'international' customer. International simply means that they operate in more than one country; it is about geographical presence. You will doubtless have plenty of customers that fit that bill, and big ones into the bargain. Described as such, there is no burning reason why you should aim to manage these customer relationships in any way other than nationally. Perhaps you sell to them in some countries, and not in others: does that matter? Perhaps you regard them as a key account in one country, but just as an ordinary customer in another, or perhaps even as a nuisance customer: does that matter? Perhaps your offer is based on value and close collaboration in one country, but is a straight transactional 'price for volume' arrangement in another: does that matter? If these things _do_ matter, because they matter to the customer, then perhaps this is something more than a 'plain international' customer, and we have the makings of a truly global customer.

Global means... shrinking the world

'Global' implies something far more significant than geographical presence. Nor is it a question of numbers. There may be customers that operate in just two or three countries and you might consider them global, while others might operate in 20 or more countries and yet still be viewed as 'plain international'.

They may be big, they may be everywhere, but are they 'shrinking the world'? Do the ways in which they behave act to preserve or bolster national or regional boundaries, or do they render such things old-fashioned, even meaningless?

There are three important tests that you should apply to any 'international' customer, before defining them as 'global':

1. Do they have needs that are consistent across different countries, and that require globally consistent solutions, measured by globally consistent standards?
2. Do they have a global structure at some relevant operational level? For most suppliers this will mean that the customer has a global procurement operation, but depending on the nature of your offer, a global structure in the customer's R&D, manufacturing, operations, finance, or sales and marketing organization (or any other for that matter) might be equally relevant.

3. Do they have, and demonstrate, the ability to implement global decisions (and in particular, supplier agreements)?

The first test is to do with the opportunity: is this customer worth pursuing in a global way? There can be significant economies of scale for both customer and supplier if this condition is met.

Suppliers of raw materials to the pharmaceutical industry often enjoy the protective benefit of something called 'good manufacturing practice' (GMP). It means that tough standards are set for their manufacturing processes, but once achieved they are likely to find themselves tied in to supply contracts for some time, and very likely on a global basis. GMP demands strict uniformity and consistency, and those suppliers that can provide this, and on a global level, will be valued by their customers.

The second test is to do with practicalities, not to say realities: is there an organizational structure that you can interact with? Without such a structure, your way ahead will be marked by frustration after frustration as the brilliance of your 'global solution' falls on deaf ears; the ears of those concerned only with their own neck of the woods.

Just because there *is* a global purchasing function doesn't mean it applies to *you*

In the case of the raw materials suppliers to the pharmaceutical industry the structure will exist in most cases through a global purchasing function, and yet we will see later in this chapter another case where a supplier of services to the very same industry found that there was no such global structure for them to work alongside. This comparison makes an important point: defining customers as global or otherwise has to be based on your own circumstances and your own offer.

It might be said that of pharmaceutical firms Pfizer is one of the more centralized, displaying many of the traits of a truly global business, while GlaxoSmithKline appears a much more federally run business, almost a 'plain international' with a good deal more independence granted at local operating levels. It might be said; but if that isn't the case in your own particular experience then don't rely on general observations, go with what you know to be the case.

The third test is a vital one, and is to do with your reward. It is all too easy to make agreements globally – it really is – particularly when they involve suppliers trading discounts for global arrangements or listings. It is so very much harder to ensure that these arrangements are enforced in each and every location. Indeed, it is not unknown for buyers to go laughing all the way to the bank after agreeing such deals, knowing all too well that there is little or no chance of the suppliers getting their side of the bargain. The buyer perhaps has no intention of policing the agreement; it is not their job.

The global 'hunting licence'

The danger for the supplier in such deals is clear; all they have gained is a global 'hunting licence'.

Isn't that better than no hunting licence? Maybe not, if you consider at what cost this licence has been won. The supplier has almost certainly given something extra for the global deal (let's say it was a 5 per cent discount, and extended credit), and yet it now has to do locally what it would have had to have done anyway without such a deal: make it happen. Perhaps if it had pursued the opportunity locally in the first place it might have secured the same ends, and at better terms. Perhaps in some localities it might rightly have avoided giving some unnecessary service, or perhaps it could have avoided incurring some unrewarded expense; but now there is a global standard. Perhaps... there are a dozen such 'perhaps' in this scenario, and most of them deeply unsatisfactory.

TIMING YOUR GLOBAL RESPONSE – _HANDLING THE 'WOULD-BE GLOBALS'_

So, before exposing your business to the significant demands of global account management, it is vital to assess the _true_ globality of your customers. At any given moment in time you will probably be able to place them along a spectrum stretching from plain international to truly global as shown in Figure 1.1.

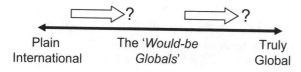

Plain International   The '_Would-be Globals_'   Truly Global

Figure 1.1 _The international/global spectrum_

It is relatively easy to do this 'at any moment in time', but what really matters is in which direction they are moving, and how quickly, because that should determine your response. The two extremes of the spectrum are straightforward enough, and the required response likely to be clear. The truly global, as defined, have probably been so for some time and they are letting you know it in no uncertain terms. For these, if you haven't already, you had best start to bite the bullet, and quickly, before they become terminally frustrated with your fragmented silo mentality and your hopelessly national structures. At the other end are those that remain stolidly international and look to remain that way for some time yet. For these you should almost certainly put aside the challenge of GAM; it is unnecessary, and its practice would be artificial, almost certainly causing you more trouble than good.

The difficult ones are those customers that lie somewhere in between. To leap into a full-blooded GAM approach with such 'would-be global' customers could perhaps be inappropriate right now (more trouble than good again), and yet to label them as 'plain international' might be to consign yourself to missing a very important boat. At best you will be throwing away an opportunity, and at worst you risk disregarding the customer's true aspirations, and we all know where that one will lead.

This isn't just about buyers (*and nor is it just about sellers*)

The creation or development of a global procurement function within the customer is very often the spur towards GAM, but it is far from the only function that might make your customers global. Other functions may have been operating globally for many years, and you may even have been taking notice.

If you sold to a technology-driven customer, your product perhaps being a vital raw material of high specification, then you would have had good contacts for some time (I hope) with the customer's R&D people, and probably with their manufacturing people. If that customer seeks to develop technical and manufacturing uniformities around the globe then you will have found yourself drawn into global relationships within these functions. Strange to relate, but such global developments can often take place without sellers or buyers being interested, or even aware, and this isn't always the fault of the buyers and sellers. R&D folk can sometimes live in a different world…

Global relationships can develop between supplier and customer in any function without there necessarily being any call for global account management (legal people talk with legal people, finance with finance, and the commercial functions may remain unaware or uninterested). The point at which such relationships should spark a call for GAM is when they result in value being delivered by the supplier and received by the customer. Once there is value there is the question of reward, and that should bring us swiftly to considerations of GAM.

GAM: seeking to be rewarded for value given – wherever and by whoever

The second of the three tests applied earlier in this chapter was: do they have a global structure at some _relevant_ operational level? What is _relevant_ could be a dozen different things depending on the particular supplier and customer, but any point in the customer's organization where value is delivered and for which a reward may be expected is usually a good place to start looking. Without such value, there will be no compelling reason to build a global account management structure around what are simply relationships: people who talk to each other.

Reading the signs

Judging the customer's position, and more importantly, their direction of movement on this spectrum is not easy, particularly as different parts of the same organization may be voicing different aspirations, perhaps even behaving in almost opposite ways. This is not unusual in a business undergoing change. We need some touchstones.

For globality…

We might consider some of the factors that tend to move businesses towards true globality, and assess our own customers with regard to those factors. Do we see a fit, or a pattern? This is not to say that the existence of the factors is a sure-fire sign of their intentions, rather it will help us to consider more closely their motivations, and so their _likely_ intentions:

- Businesses faced by global customers tend towards globality – it is why you are reading this book.
- Businesses that seek cost reductions through ever-increasing scale will tend towards globality.
- Truly global brands provide many economies of scale, and businesses dependent on their brands for success will have a tendency towards globality. Of course, this is only the case where the values

that underpin those brands are communicable across national boundaries.

- Businesses dependent on cutting-edge technology (their own) will have a tendency towards globality. The pressure to stay ahead forces such a business to ever-broaden its horizons, looking for new ideas, and looking for new competitors. At the same time, their solutions tend to have global applicability

---

'Technical markets are global'

In 1999 ICI Paints sold its Autocolor brand to long-time rival PPG. Autocolor was the paint brand for the car refinish market, the paint used to respray damaged cars. Some observers were surprised – the business was a success and a technical jewel in the ICI crown, but as a global brand it was a non-starter. John McAdam (at the time of writing, CEO at RHM, but at that time, the executive VP for coatings at ICI) was clear about the sale: *'Technical markets are global... if you are not in the top three – forget it.'*

In the decorative paint market ICI owned the Dulux brand, and then in a quick succession of purchases it acquired Valentine, one of France's leading paint brands, and Glidden, owners of some of America's top brands. The scene was set for a process of *'Duluxization'* – the creation of a truly global brand, but not for long. After failing to get either the French or the Americans fascinated by the idea of an Old English sheepdog running through the houses of their imagination, the strategy was changed, and by the same VP, John McAdam. *'Decorative markets are different from technical ones,'* he said, *'because you can be no 1 in the UK and be nowhere in Italy.'* Instead, the strategy became to use local brands where they had strengths and resonance, and to build a portfolio of strong brands that included Cuprinol, Hammerite, Polyfilla and Polycell, as well as Dulux. John McAdam conceded, *'We thought we could apply a UK solution to the US, without doing regional research.'*

Same company, two very different pressures and aspirations; so different that in the end the solution had to involve the sale of one of them.

If you had been a supplier to ICI Paints at this time, which signals would you have been reading? The problem would have been that some of the signals would have been very clear indeed, but what if they were the ones taking the business in the wrong direction, and quite possibly taking their suppliers with them? Chapter 5 attempts to provide a solution to this dilemma, arguing that the best practitioners of GAM will not simply rely on the signals that come from their customers, they will go one better than that and aim to understand the customer's business for them, perhaps even better than them.

Against globality…

There are also factors that influence a business to shy away from globality: laws, customs, traditions, culture, tastes, climate and geography. This combination of factors is very apparent in the food industry. Of course there are global players, but by far the largest number of businesses in this industry, whether they be producers, retailers or service providers, are national, bound by the customs and tastes of their own culture.

If it doesn't fit, don't force it…

Judging the customer's position and aspirations is just the start; you must also be aware of your own capability to manage a global relationship and to deliver a truly global offer. It takes time to become global, for suppliers just as for customers. Figure 1.2 considers the closeness of fit between the customer's global ambitions and the supplier's global capability, suggesting the kind of actions that might be required, and in what direction.

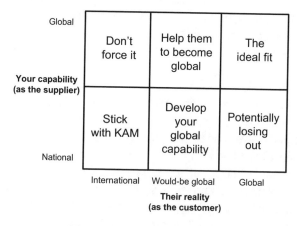

Figure 1.2   _Assessing the fit_

You do… they don't…

If you already have a global capability then there may be a tendency to approach this matter with some aggression, perhaps even trying to push the customer into a global set of behaviours. There is a very simple piece of advice here: don't. If it is only for your own benefit that you are pushing then I hardly need say why this will not work, but even if it _is_ for the benefit of the customer it is still a pretty hopeless approach, like nailing jelly to the wall. How many times have you heard a salesperson complain how their 'splendid idea' for global supply was rejected, despite proving that it was to the customer's benefit? The customer is accused of being blind, or worse. What is not considered is the customer's problem; they are not truly global, and so nobody at any individual location has the authority or power to impose a decision on other locations. They may lobby on your behalf, but we all know how slow and painful such exercises can be. The moral of the story is clear and simple: don't get so far ahead of your customer with regard to global aspirations that you find yourself trying to force the issue on to them.

Forcing it ...
... where it
didn't fit

A supplier of a high-value service (they provide tailored sales teams to the pharmaceutical industry) found themselves in this position when they won a very large contract with the UK operation of one of the world's largest pharmaceutical companies. The contract didn't come out of the blue, but had been won through many years of persistence and steady demonstration of value. The impact of this success on the UK business was so significant, however, that it was not long before noises were being made about repeating the trick but now with each of the customer's operations in France, Germany, Spain, Italy, Scandinavia and the Benelux. The supplier was already based in each of these locations and they had the capability to coordinate their operation globally.

A GAM (global account manager) was appointed and big targets were set. The months went past and nothing happened. The customer's operations in these countries were entirely independent from the UK and were not going to be influenced by what went on there. Moreover, the nature of their markets was very different from the UK's and their needs from the service provider were equally different. Most important of all, why should any of them leap into a contract with a relatively unknown supplier: shouldn't that supplier have to prove themselves over the long term, just as they had in the UK?

The GAM became frustrated, the targets were clearly not going to be met, but a lot of noise and disturbance had been created across the supplier's organization and it left a slightly bitter taste of disappointment. People couldn't help thinking that someone had let them down, whereas in truth this had never been a true opportunity. The supplier had been forcing it where it quite clearly didn't fit.

You don't… they might…

If on the other hand you have no global capability, the tendency is to be defensive about the whole issue, perhaps even to be in denial of the whole question of global customers. If the customer is solidly international then no problem, but it is as they start to shift to the right of our spectrum that the difficulties arise. Saying that you will behave globally only as and when your customers become truly global may save you a good deal of unnecessary effort and expense, but where will such a 'keep up' strategy land you if the customer's move to globality outpaces yours? Indeed it is very likely that it will, given the differences between being a global customer and a global supplier.

Consider a customer with an existing operation 'overseas' that they now require to be serviced by their home-based supplier, but in a new global capacity and working to an agreed global standard. For the customer this may involve changing product specifications or formulations, or changing manufacturing practices or operational processes, but compared to the supplier's lot this is the proverbial piece of cake. The supplier now has to develop a local capability in manufacture, or distribution, or service, and very likely they will have to build this from nothing. Great opportunity, or is it?

Playing 'catch-up'

It is when the customer is clearly making the shift towards globality that the supplier's active response becomes vital. If the supplier has no global capability, then they had best start working, and more than that; they must demonstrate to the customer their intentions. But be warned: this is no place for pretence. No buyer will forgive a supplier that pretends to have a global capability and then lets them down when the test is applied. But to indicate your intentions is a different matter, and buyers will be surprisingly patient with suppliers who show that they are moving in the right direction and give plenty of progress reports and feedback on their experiences and the lessons learnt. Honesty and openness not only improve your chances of 'keeping up', but increase the likelihood of being _helped_ to keep up.

Where the supplier already has the global capability, then their response to a 'would-be global' customer is of the greatest significance; they should of course be actively working to help the customer develop their own global operations. The customer faces no easy task, and positive help from a supplier can only be to the benefit of the relationship, forging a long-term loyalty from the customer.

Timing

Timing is everything, but that is generally easier to see in retrospect. When looking ahead the moment to act seems far less certain. Figure 1.2 is only a guide, and rather vague at that, but I will venture a definition of 'the right time'. The *right* time to behave globally, as a supplier, is when a global aspect of the customer relationship will work to the mutual benefit of all parties.

Jump too early and you will involve yourself in unnecessary hassle, almost certainly losing more than you gain. Jump too late and you will be playing catch-up for ever more – a negotiating stance that always works in the customer's favour. Only you know how long it will take you to develop the necessary capabilities (and be brutally honest over this – no pie-in-the-sky dreams will do in this matter), and so only you can determine how far ahead of things you must be.

The best advice has to be: keep your eyes peeled and your ears working like satellite dishes; watch for all signs of change; and above all, keep close to the customer. Ask them what their ambitions are, globally, and then seek to understand the implications of those ambitions. These implications may not always be as clear and obvious as at first thought.

Does a customer's global ambition necessarily favour their existing suppliers?

In 2005 Tesco, the UK's largest grocery retailer, declared profits in excess of two billion pounds sterling, and announced an aggressive strategy of expansion beyond the UK base. In fact, already one-fifth of revenues came from activities outside the UK, but most of their suppliers still regarded them as 'British'. They also explained a key requirement for global expansion: the need for locally appropriate product offers. So, is this an opportunity for an aggressive global account management approach from the leading UK suppliers, or will it be the local suppliers that enjoy the 'benefits' of Tesco's arrival on their doorsteps? Most suppliers seem to think that the true globality of the big grocery retailers (Wal*Mart and Carrefour are the other two in the 'big three') is still some way off – but what if they are wrong?

Losing out…

What about when the customer has been a local key account, working within a national framework, but now decides to shift a significant part of its operations overseas? Is it as simple as moving overseas with them?

A UK-based manufacturer of packaging for a major brand of toiletries and household goods had for many years prospered through their closeness to the customer. This closeness was quite literal, they lived next door, and this gave them fast access to new opportunities, lower costs than any competitor, and an almost automatic 'first option' advantage. The supplier explained it simply as being local, but the customer valued something else in addition, the supplier's knowledge and experience. Then the customer decided to start moving production from Europe to China, and with a clear indication that volume would rise substantially as costs reduced. A problem? Not at all, thought the supplier, indeed this was an opportunity; they would grow their volume alongside the customer, and ease themselves into the Chinese market at the same time through acquisition of a Chinese packaging firm. Imagine their surprise when instead of signing a global supply arrangement, the customer appointed a new supplier in China. Why? Because the customer valued what they had in the UK, a local supplier with local knowledge and capabilities, and wanted to replicate those things in China, not to suffer the 'new market' teething troubles of its UK supplier's venture into Asia.

Why piggy-backing the customer's global ride is not as simple as it may seem

And the moral of the story? As well as asking the customer to explain their global ambitions, you must also understand clearly why they do business with you now, locally. Then ask, will that same logic apply when they become global? In this case, the answer was yes, but the supplier had not properly understood the full logic of the local supply, seeing only the tangible geographic proximity and underestimating the intangible matter of local expertise.

TAKING THE LEAP... UPSTAIRS...

The ability to identify the customer's global aspirations and to ensure the appropriate fit with their own global capabilities is clearly a prime requirement for any supplier wishing to prosper, and so it cannot be something left to individual national operations, and still less to the sales teams in those national operations; and yet it is precisely there, in the local sales operations, that the big questions of *'should we or shouldn't we'* so often reside.

It may well be that the sales people have the greatest interest (it is almost certainly sales people who buy books like this one and look into the question), the greatest motivation and the most energy, but they cannot be allowed to take this decision alone. The decision to move towards GAM, the assessment and eventual selection of global accounts, these things have to be the responsibility of the most senior management team. Not just because the decision is an important one – that much is obvious – nor that the development of the necessary capabilities must be sanctioned by the senior team – hugely important though that is – but because the difference between the right and the wrong choice may be the difference between the success or the failure of the company's future.

Managing the future

Figure 1.3 shows what is involved in successfully managing the future (with no recourse to tea-leaves or crystal balls), and the strategic role that GAM has to play in that task.

Figure 1.3 *Managing the future*

Managing the future is about getting the right balance between the objectives set, the opportunities available, and the resources deployed. It is not an easy balance because in all but the most boringly stable of markets the opportunity will keep on changing. Resources have a tendency to lag behind to the point that many businesses could honestly say they had the perfect resources... for the opportunity of 18 months earlier.

It is all too easy for objectives to be set without proper consideration of the realities betwixt opportunity and resources. There is a belief in some quarters that tough and stretching objectives will force the resources into the right places. In some circumstances perhaps this is so, but in the realm of GAM it is usually little more than wishful thinking. For GAM to succeed we will need genuine objectives based on the realities of the customer's globality and our own global capabilities. We must aim to avoid on the one hand the dangerous machismo that threatens to bring the issues on too soon, or on the other, the feeble defensiveness that wishes the problem away, or hopes to 'cope' in the unlikely event that it should ever raise its head.

GAM now takes on a strategic purpose, attempting to manage the future through an appropriate match between business resources and the market opportunity. The objectives that flow from this matching process will be all the more genuine for the enhanced understanding of what that match can realistically achieve.

2

The *particular* challenge of GAM

The practice of global account management (GAM) shares a lot of tasks with the practice of key account management (KAM), the following list being just some of them:

- Understanding the customer's market better than they understand it themselves (an unrealistic expectation, or the whole point of the thing? See Chapter 5 for more on this.)
- Penetrating the customer's decision-making process, well beyond the buyer (without alienating said buyer).
- Managing a complex contact strategy through 'diamond teams' of people from diverse functions (and often with diverse opinions).
- Achieving consensus and collaboration across functions and operations, in order to present a uniform face to the customer.
- Achieving key supplier status by making a positive impact on the customer's purchasing strategy.
- Achieving strategic supplier status by making a positive impact on the customer's business strategy (which means you have to understand that strategy, and how it translates into the customer's 'moneymaking logic').
- Developing true, customer-focused, value propositions (which means understanding in detail the customer's *activity cycle*).
- Measuring customer profitability.
- Writing a strategic account plan.

With such an apparent similarity of tasks it is easy to see why so many think of GAM as being KAM, but on a larger scale. My response to that is simple: *'Nay! Thrice times nay!'* (to quote Frankie Howerd, who it must be said is not quoted that often in books of this type). But we only need consider the practice of any one of these tasks on a global level to see straight away how the additional complexities really do take GAM into another league.

There are many such 'additional complexities'; Figure 2.1 and the following list attempt to pin down the most important:

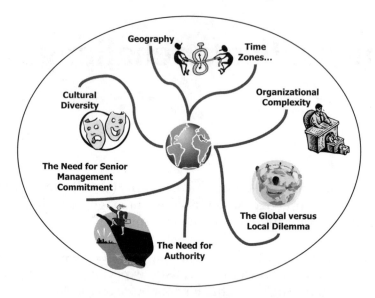

Figure 2.1 *The* particular *challenge of GAM*

- organizational and structural complexity:
  - the fact that the supplier's nationally based organizations are built the way they are for very good reason: meeting local needs, not global ones;
  - the fact (most likely) that performance measures and the related performance rewards are also based on national structures, and may continue to be so based, and again, for the same good local reasons;
  - the fact that a global customer may well do business with you not just across the different regions that make up your own organization, but also across more than one business unit;
  - the pressing need to get it right globally, but without compromising any of the strengths and advantages of the local relationship – the classic 'global versus local' dilemma;

- the need for the GA Manager and GA Team to have real and demonstrable authority that will run beyond a single business unit or territory;
- the need for the commitment and involvement of multiple (and sometimes competing) senior management teams;
- cultural diversity – the supplier's and the customer's;
- geography and time zones (after the last chapter's debunking of the time zone issue perhaps you didn't expect this last to be on the list, but they are a real enough challenge, just not the only one).

The rest of this chapter (and the next) will elaborate on the nature of these additional challenges; the possible solutions will be looked for in later chapters. Problems without solutions can make for a rather pessimistic read, but it is important to know what we are up against, and if the cavalry isn't exactly waiting to come over the hill, I can at least promise you that once we have raised the challenge we will deal _positively_ with each of these testing issues in turn.

ORGANIZATIONAL AND STRUCTURAL COMPLEXITY

Matching two global organizations for the purpose of trading at a profit is no simple task. Having stated the obvious, let's turn to two particular obstacles that have a high probability of existing within your own organization.

First, if your organization has a strong local and national character, then there was probably good reason for that to have been so in the past, and there is probably still good reason for it now, and there may still be good reason for it to be so in the future. The likelihood is that despite your interest in GAM, the majority of your customers are still local (or at least, the national part of a 'plain international' customer), and still require a purely local service. Your nationally based organizations are set up to do just that.

The practice of GAM now calls on members of those local teams to work with 'global customers'. This may mean introducing new customers to them, perhaps even ones that were avoided in the past, or they may be just the same customers as before but now the relationship is managed to a different set of values, principles and practices, and of course, largely managed 'elsewhere'. The potential for conflict between GA manager and local team is huge, and not only conflict; does the local operation have the capability, do they even have the desire?

Don't be suprised if local sales teams prefer local customers ...

Many years ago I was responsible for launching a UK consumer goods brand into the Dutch market. Straight away I wanted to target a particular multiple retailer that also operated in the UK and was a good customer of ours there. Nothing like an easy start, I thought. I soon discovered that the local sales team, which had been working with other brands for some years, was hugely reluctant even to speak with this customer. They were regarded as the bad boys of the Dutch retail scene, using aggressive tactics that threatened to put out of business the very independent retailers on whom the local sales team depended. Conflict? Just a little, and it was due to this as much as anything else that that our launch was not a great success, but I am ever grateful for the learning!

With buckets of hindsight I can see that I was in fact right to want to work with the global retailer – the multiples were a force that meant to stay and the independent's days were numbered, but without that vision at the time it was all too easy for the status quo to be maintained and the notion of GAM to be ridiculed – a classic case of denial.

This brings us neatly to the second of the internal problems. Why should anyone in a local operation do anything to support a global customer, if the measurement of their own performance is based on the local business, and if the particular action required of them doesn't enhance that local business? Because it's for the good of the company? Because it will enhance shareholder value? (If you believe that either of these will make them jump through hoops then this isn't the book for you: perhaps you should try something by Hans Christian Andersen, or the Brothers Grimm.)

... particularly if that's how they get paid

You would expect an international paint company specializing in the marine market to have offices in all the major ports of the world – it's where their customers gather, of course, and where they have their ships repainted. Their customers are as global as they come, moving their fleets around the world, expecting the same service and attention wherever they go. Each time a ship comes into port there is the chance of a sale. Now you might expect that the local staff of this paint company would have a global outlook, striving to win contracts with any ship that berths at their port, not caring where the ship was actually going to be painted, provided the contract was won for their product. You might expect; but unfortunately the people in this company are measured and rewarded on the basis of their own port's P&L, and that only includes work done at that port. Sad to say, but if they know the ship is moving on and not stopping for a paint job, then it becomes a bottom of the list priority – somebody else's opportunity, wherever it may be headed.

Just change the scope of the P&L, you say… just try that one on the barons sitting at the top of each local and regional hierarchy…

The cross-business challenge

Global customers are no respecters of a supplier's internal structures whether they be based on national boundaries, regions or business units. The only structure that matters is their own, and if they happen to do business with more than one of your business units then expect them to be interested in your ability to collaborate internally. Unfortunately, it is rarely as easy as the customer might imagine. Companies divide themselves into different business units for very good reasons, and most usually because the nature of those units' operations and moneymaking logic is so different. To expect them to snap into collaborative mode in front of a common customer, without a great deal of time spent on preparatory spadework, and without overcoming a number of genuinely testing obstacles first, would be another case for the works of HCA and the Brothers Grimm.

Let's consider a manufacturer of food ingredients that through acquisition has also found itself in the business of selling food additives, food flavourings, fragrances to the household and toiletries industries, and fine fragrances to the perfume and cosmetics trade. Each of these five activities has been organized into a separate business unit and for all the right reasons of market focus and core competency development. Now let's suppose that there is a customer that deals with each of these five businesses, some locally and some globally, but is frustrated at having to manage five separate relationships with five different standards of performance. The customer wants to see some benefit from a truly global relationship and presses the five suppliers to 'get their act together'. Some of the five see the opportunity and the benefits more clearly than others, and there is reason for their variable focus. The secret of success in the food ingredients business is the handling of large orders that fill their production capacity, allowing them to quote the very best prices on the market – this is their 'moneymaking logic'. The secret of success in the fine fragrance business is the cherry picking of contracts suited to their particular expertise, which is in the provision of bespoke solutions. The fine fragrance business makes margins on these deals that would have the food ingredients people dancing in the street if they could match them. The food

How far would _you_ go to make this supplier think 'customer first' and 'own business second'?

ingredients business makes margins on their deals that would put the fragrance folk out of business.

How then to build a global offer around such different propositions? To each part of the supplier the prospect looks as much a threat as an opportunity – the fine fragrance manufacturer fearing that they will be dragged into low-margin business, and the food ingredients manufacturer fearing that their costs will be set to soar, not to mention three other business units watching this debate from their own perspectives. It would come as no surprise, then, if the component parts of this business were to choose to go their own way...

(To see how this case develops, see Chapters 4, 8, 11, and 12.)

The global versus local dilemma...

In theory, if the customer were a truly global customer, then their needs would be consistent across countries, and so the solutions to their needs would be equally consistent. Unfortunately, life rarely gets as simple as that. It is far more likely that products and services (*especially* services) will vary to some degree by each location. Each 'local solution' will have its own cost structure and so each local operation will work to its own profit level. Global solutions that move towards global consistency will change those cost structures, often putting a burden on local operations, which *at best* could damage their own profitability as the cost to serve rises. If that is the 'at best' scenario, just wait for the 'at worst'.

No customer would thank you for your global solution if the result was a diminished local service. But this is just what can happen, and very frequently, if you ask local operations to change their working practices as part of a global package. In pursuit of the global good, it is quite possible to compromise the existing strengths of the local operation, and to lose the advantages that have been gained over many years of a strong local relationship.

None of this need happen if sufficient consideration is given to the issue well in advance, but so often the problem only arises *once it has become* a problem and the customer is starting to complain. What happens next is that the local operations realize what's going on (they're not stupid), and react by resisting what they are being asked to do by the global account manager; they want to revert to how things were, before the complaints started. They might go further, perhaps even raising doubts as to the whole notion of GAM as a workable mechanism. So now must come the reaction of the global account manager. What would you do?

Most will jump on a plane and 'go out' (the terminology itself expresses where the GAM thinks the real problem lies) to make a 'forceful' presentation or two, and when these are not listened to, make them louder, and to lecture, and to lay down the law, and ultimately to appeal to some higher authority to knock these local operations into shape. The reaction of the local operations (and would you blame them?) is to dig their heels in even further…

The real answer is not to get into this mess in the first place, and for the global account manager to consult with the local operations _before_ making the global deal. If they had bothered to find out what _can_ be done locally, and how much change might be required, and what should not be changed, and so on and so forth… but who has the time for all of that? There is a very simple answer to this one: the global account manager _must_ have the time. If they don't, then something is very wrong with the practice of GAM.

AUTHORITY

The global account manager has one of the toughest management tasks going: managing a team of people who in all probability do not work for them directly, where several members of that team might very well be senior to them, and where all the members of that team will be 'cleverer' than them, at least in their own individual special-izations. This is a challenge shared with any nationally based key account manager, but on the global scale there is an additional twist raising it by a factor of 10: this management task has to be achieved through a team spread around the globe, a virtual team managed for a great deal of the time by remote control.

What they need, of course, is authority, and not just over the people in the same business unit as them, or in the same country, but authority worldwide. That is an awful lot of authority to give to any one individual. Perhaps too much? (We will return to this question.) How many management boards are brave enough to give such largesse? How many so reckless?

To give any individual such authority, with such breadth of appli-cation, would surely be to make them the equal of the most senior managers in the company? And to handle such authority, wouldn't they need to have had a very broad experience of the business, and over some period of time? In many cases this will in fact be just what it takes to make GAM happen – a senior appointment, and of someone able to work as a business manager. But if we look at the majority of cases in current practice this is *not* what happens: the global account manager comes from a lower middle management level, almost certainly from a sales background, probably still reports to a sales director somewhere in the business, and will face the challenge of their lifetime.

THE IRRATIONALITY OF SENIOR MANAGERS
(NO, REALLY...)

The global account manager must build a consensus across the organization, a consensus that supports the aims and activities of their global account plan. That means winning the hearts and minds of people at all levels in their own business, and most importantly the hearts and minds of those right at the top. The nationally based key account manager had much the same task, but for them there was probably only the one management team to engage, while for the global account manager there will almost certainly be many more, at functional, business, national, regional and global levels.

Winning over one team might be easy enough, but what about winning over all of them? Perhaps you start on your home turf, and given that they are people you know well, and that they appointed you in the first place, you probably stand a good chance of success. The perfect start, you think, but is it? This might seem a rather strange question; surely winning over one team is simply the first step on the way to winning them all? Enter stage left, rivalry. Enter stage right, jealousy. Enter downstage, upstage and any other stage, competition. In many businesses the different national or regional management teams are in competition with each other, sometimes deliberately (and even formally), in order to inject an extra pulse of energy. If you have ever attended one of those global business conferences where the managers of each region present to each other then you will know what I mean. Behind the smiles and the hail-fellow-well-met bonhomie there lies a desire to win, often manifested by the attempt to outshine their fellows. It's a circumstance that makes many a global business tick, a kind of motivational fuel that comes largely free of charge. It may not say as much in the constitution of the company, or in the job descriptions or performance objectives of individual managers, but it is there all the same.

I have seen at least one global account manager, flushed with their success at convincing their own head office, commit a kind of suicide by announcing this support to the regions. And they actually expected such support to ease their way… Call me a cynic, but isn't it one of life's 'great lies' (alongside _'the cheque is in the post'_) to say: _'I'm from head office and I'm here to help'_?

CULTURE

A popular theme among advertisers of global services (particularly banks – and I refer to the high-impact campaign by HSBC) has been to argue that a truly global supplier must offer their clients a good deal more than geographic presence; they must also understand the impact of culture on the world of business, and act on that understanding. HSBC in particular offers to escort its clients through the potential minefield of cultural differences, so saving them embarrassment as they go. The adverts show how simple ignorance of local customs can lead to great offence; the showing of the soles of your feet in parts of Asia, for instance, or the ever-present perils of misunderstood eating habits. The implied advice is the need to adapt to the local culture if you wish to succeed.

My own favourite is the advert where two businessmen are meeting to sign a major contract, surrounded by their armies of assistants and the press photographers. One is Japanese and the other is European. At the critical moment the European makes a low bow, just as the Japanese stretches out a hand for shaking. It is a touching moment of both consideration and flexibility, and we are left to assume that all is well from that point onwards.

When East meets West … things can go fine!

It is of course sensible advice, but the real businesspeople involved in such relationships must take care to avoid what may be seen as tokenism. Tokenism is possibly more offensive than plain ignorance or clumsy misunderstandings. The latter can be forgiven, but it is hard to forgive someone who patronizes you. Donning the national dress of your customer for a day is hardly the way to demonstrate sincerity and flexibility, especially if it is backed up by a complete intransigence on more important issues. It is the 'Black and White Minstrel Show' approach to bridging the cultural gap.

Patronizing behaviour raises a significant obstacle to progress. It begins with an assumption, usually false, that those of other cultures to our own are not smart enough to realize our predicament, cannot see our clumsiness for what it is, and will not make allowances accordingly. If we would only recognize the arrogance of the view that says *'we must conform entirely to your culture for fear of upsetting you'*, then we might all proceed apace without so very much damage being done.

What makes the question of culture so particularly challenging in GAM is that the diversity of attitudes and behaviours exists on *both* sides of the supplier/customer relationship. This is a veritable melting pot of complexity that cannot be ignored, but neither should it be agonized over as some blot on an otherwise simple exercise. Making a meal of such things, indulging in a forced kind of political correctness, will slow you down to the point of immobility. The only proper response is to see it for what it is, and seek to turn it to the advantage of all parties.

Chapter 15 aims to show how the cultural diversity within your own GA team can be harnessed as a source of competitive advantage. That people are different is undeniable, and that businesspeople around the globe have different preferences for working and relating is equally undeniable. Starting from that basis the only intelligent thing to do is to forget the stereotypes, suspend all judgements (and especially prejudices), observe, aim to understand how culture determines behaviours and attitudes, and case by case select those behaviours and attitudes that will work to best effect within the team and with the customer. Where there are differences of opinion you will need to agree the rules, and again, case by case.

Appreciating cultural diversity doesn't mean that there are no rules

Let's just invent a whole new nation for a moment – Barbakuairia – with its attendant cultural preference with regard to time – they always like to be late; they believe that it is the only polite thing to do. You have two Barbakuairians on your GAM team and they are vital players, not just in their own country, but also in forging the relationship with your global customer in Europe, who happens to be headquartered in Germany. I'm sure you can see the problem looming.

Some things are not up for compromise. If the Barbakuairians on your team really are always late (and we are not just labelling them because of some stereotype), then there is little use agreeing with them that they should be 'just a little less late', as a gesture to their cultural background. That would be both silly, and actually quite offensive if you think about it. In this case the rule must be for punctuality, and it is made all the better as a rule by being based on the cultural preference of the customer, not the supplier.

But that isn't the end to it. Simply laying down such a rule would just make the two Barbakuairians uncomfortable, perhaps resentful, and almost certainly less effective as a result. The secret of such things is to discuss openly the needs of the customer, and to recognize the possible conflict of cultural values, and the need for a modified behaviour in this case. That way everyone gets to understand why the rule exists, and that it wasn't imposed as some sideways knock at their background.

Global account teams will sometimes require global rules, regardless of local sensitivities, but will then be very wise to recognize where latitude should be given for local flavour, local appropriateness, and so local competitive advantage. Knowing where the lines should be drawn is, of course, the sixty thousand dollar question (or should that be sixty thousand euro, or yen, or rand…?).

GEOGRAPHY AND TIME ZONES

Much of this book is based on the premise that the world is shrinking and that the barriers of nation states are of diminishing importance. That may be so in the big picture but the miles are still miles and distances remain a practical issue. The physical separation of global account teams, often meeting as little as once a year, and plenty of teams not even managing that, has to be a problem. Such remoteness from each other is not to be cured entirely by videoconferencing and e-mails, and I have to say that to practise GAM without 'regular' physical meetings of the team is a tall order, and a high-risk strategy. (Don't ask me to define 'regular', that one is for you to decide.)

Similarly, time zones are not just a practical issue; they also carry cultural and political baggage. Anyone who has worked for an internationally spread business will recognize the following syndrome.

If you work at head office, time zones are of no problem at all, to you. They are somebody else's problem. Imagine that your HQ is in London, then to have tele-conferences between the hours of nine and five is no great issue – it is up to the Americans to get out of bed early, and it is for the Japanese to stay at the office late (and please don't pretend it isn't so!). I know of offices in Eastern Europe that have starting and finishing times of 11:00 and 19:00, so that the London head office crowd can find them, at their convenience, nine to five. Don't imagine that the customer will be so accommodating. Be prepared to be talking on telephones when you should be in bed, at both ends of the day. If you make yourself unavailable at the customer's peak hours then it should be no surprise if after no great amount of time they start to look for some more approachable supplier.

Unlike the other issues discussed in this chapter, where we have simply laid out the challenge but not moved towards any kind of solution, let's get the problem of time zones dealt with here and now. The fact is that they are there, so we had best make the best of them, which is actually not so hard as it seems. Time zones are not all pain. One of the joys of global customers is that you can be working while they sleep, presenting them with the answers to their questions of only the day before as they come into work the following morning. Worked skilfully, time zones can sometimes give you a positive advantage over the local suppliers who like to go to bed at the same time as their customers...

3

Innocents among wolves, and other deadly sins...

In life, there are seven deadly sins (pride, covetousness, lust, envy, gluttony, anger and sloth), but global account management (GAM) is a thing much tougher than life and the list of *its* sins grows a little longer. (I leave it to you to decide whether it also includes the original seven.)

The list divides into two parts: the first finds those things shared in common with the practice of key account management (KAM); the second contains those things particular to GAM.

The 'deadly sins' of KAM and GAM

- Silo mentality – managers as 'barons'
- Multiple or competing supplier business units
  - Whose key/global account is this anyway?
- Failure to measure the impact
  - Inadequate measures of account profitability
- Resistance from the sales team...
  - A preference for 'hunting'
- Inappropriate people or skills
  - A non-'streetwise' supporting team

- Too many key / global accounts
- No plan for freeing up the energy from non-key / global accounts
- Top management short-termism

It can be readily seen that the addition of a global aspect would make each of those listed here yet more sinful. Taking just one example: a *silo mentality* is where individual functions see the world solely from their own vantage point, driven by their own values, seeking their own goals. In GAM, these silos are most likely to be in the form of country-based structures as well as functionally based, so presenting two lines of inward-looking obstacles. When these silos are driven by conflicting goals and measures – one country seeks to win the customer with the lowest price supported by the lowest costs, while another aims for an added-value proposition with a value-based price – then the prospect of a truly global offer is remote. Where these silos have no opportunity or desire to speak with each other, then the innocent attempt by one silo to practise GAM opens up a road to chaos and confusion. The problem lies in structure, and with the 'barons' who head up their 'baronies'. Don't underestimate their determination to protect what has perhaps been built up over a whole career. Too often it takes a disaster – the loss of a customer – before such barons will sit up and listen, by which time, of course, it is all too late.

(Anyone interested in further explanation of the other sins listed here might like to refer to my earlier book, *Key Account Management*, 4th edition, published by Kogan Page.)

The additional 'deadly sins' of GAM

- Practising GAM with any but truly global customers (see Chapter 1).
- Winning global deals that are in fact no more than global hunting licences (see Chapter 1).
- Ignoring the imperatives of cultural diversity (see Chapter 15).
- Winning global deals that work out fine in the 'home country' (for both parties) but backfire in the 'overseas' operations (see the case study below – *'But it worked in the home market…'*).
- Agreeing 'apparent' global supplier requirements and activities that become an 'unnecessary' burden on the local 'cost to serve' (see the case study below – *'Just too big a cost to serve'*).
- Being in denial of the need for GAM, often at a local level (see the case study in Chapter 2 concerning the Dutch multiple retailer).

- Allowing politics (head office and local) to hamper GAM operations, and in particular the development and delivery of value propositions (see the case study below – _'Politics and the destruction of value'_).
- The removal of support and resources for GAM, by local operations, when 'the going gets tough' on their own patch (see the case study below – _'Pulling the plug'_).
- Global account managers, and their teams, becoming a separate or elitist body (see the case study below – _'Doing their own thing'_).
- Being an innocent among wolves (see the case study below – _'Innocents among wolves'_).

A supplier of fragrances to the cosmetics industry had built a substantial business in the United States through one customer by taking on a range of tasks and operations that were usually handled in-house by such customers. Over the years this policy of outsourcing had worked to the advantage of both parties, though in truth it had been rather less of a policy and more a matter of 'just how things worked out'.

But it worked in the home market …

The customer had been an international company for many years and was just beginning to show signs of a true global nature, so what if they could be persuaded to repeat this outsourcing policy around the globe? The proposal was made, and accepted; the advantages to the US company were clear enough and they would be prepared to follow suit elsewhere. But then came the problem: 'elsewhere' had not been outsourcing to anyone all these years; 'elsewhere' still had a full in-house capability. To take on the supplier's offer would entail closing that down, and at a significant cost. They would do so, they said, but only if the supplier paid for the costs of the closures – which ran into the hundreds of thousands for each location.

What worked fine for both the supplier and the customer in the United States was going to cost both supplier and customer dearly in the other locations. Too dearly, and the idea was dropped, but not before a lot of expensive 'trials and pilots', and not without a substantial loss of face all round…

I don't want you getting the idea that I was a poor salesman in my youth, but here is another example of a great 'training event' that I was lucky enough to 'attend'.

Just too big a cost to serve …

Many years ago I was a keen young salesman working for a UK paint company, so keen that in return for my positively effervescent energies I was given the responsibility for a number of 'development accounts'. Now we all know about 'development accounts', don't we? These are the customers that the company sells nothing to, and remains unlikely to do so for the envisaged future… but I got lucky.

One of those customers was BP, and I acquired the account just as they decided to make an alteration to their corporate colour scheme. What an opportunity! The décor of every BP petrol station across the UK would need to be changed, and that would be an awful lot of paint.

Thinking back, I can see that the opportunity clearly went to my head and I came up with a plan so ambitious that it frightens me to think of it now. We proposed to the customer that we could transform each and every petrol station in the space of a month, and with a guarantee of an absolute colour match on all surfaces – no idle claim. And you know what: they liked it, and they promised us the business. I saw rapid promotion ahead. In fact, they liked it so much that they asked if we could do the same for them across Europe; they knew that we had a European capability. If things carried on like this, I thought, it could only be a matter of time before I made the board.

So, a few telexes (for that is how long ago it was) to my opposite numbers in our French and German operations and I sat back to watch the orders coming in. You can perhaps guess the answers to my telexes:

1. Who is BP?
2. Why should we go to such efforts for a customer that is a very small opportunity for us?
3. Do you realize what a proposal like this will do to our local costs?

Needless to say, we didn't win the European business, and indeed our failure to do so also cost us the UK business. Also, needless to say, my fondly expected promotion was a long time in coming…

A global training company wishes to offer its customers access to a purpose-built intranet where delegates can find additional information and help, can network with other delegates, and can suggest their next requirements. I say a global training company; rather I should say _one part_ of the global training company wishes it, the AsiaPacific team, because this is the brainchild of that team. The management of websites and e-business is not the responsibility of the AsiaPacific team, however; that sits in the United States, and there they have different ideas. They have different ideas in the United States not because they don't like the idea, indeed they had wished to do something similar themselves, but because it was NIH (not invented here).

At this point things become silly. The AsiaPacific team say they will get on with it themselves, and the US team forbid them on the grounds of possible infringements of IT policy. The AsiaPacific team make a start in any case because they have a customer waiting to use the service, and willing to pay. The US team gets heavy and sends the VP of IT to read the riot act.

Meanwhile, the customer who wanted the service has decided that they would also like it in their other locations outside AsiaPacific, including the United States. Before the AsiaPacific team have chance to shout _'told you so'_, they are stunned to discover that their US colleagues have told the customer the service is not to be made available, due to technical problems. It would seem that having taken the stance they took, too many people in the United States couldn't face a change of heart. And so value was destroyed, and _is_ destroyed, every day.

Politics and the destruction of value

Pulling the plug

Acme Mouldings was a UK-based firm growing fast in a number of new locations in Europe and the Americas. One of the smaller locations was Mexico and the global account manager from one of its suppliers had just managed to persuade their own sales team in Mexico to recognize that Acme, though perhaps not the biggest customer in Mexico, was in fact a very important global customer, and so deserving of their time and attention. This was important because although it was true that the Mexican operation was small, it also happened to be where the son of Acme Moulding's CEO had just been sent to head up the business.

Things went smoothly for a while, and then one day the GA manager received an e-mail from the CEO at Acme asking, well... basically, _'what the hell...?'_. The supplier's Mexican team had pulled the plug, refusing to supply the customer. When asked why, they said at first that the customer was not paying its bills. While this was true, it soon transpired that they did in fact pay their bills as well as any other customer in the territory (credit control was not a strong suit of the Mexican team, it would seem!). Finally, and after much pressing, the truth came out and the GA manager was informed that the Mexican team had serious supply chain problems and was having to ration its customers. This was simply a case of 'last in, first out'.

What seemed reasonable to the Mexican team was now a disaster for the GA manager as they watched the orders decline from the US, UK, French, Spanish and German operations. The CEO had not taken kindly to their son being 'dumped', and had decided to do some dumping of their own...

The very title 'Global Account Manager' has a ring of superiority. Surely it is a position more important than a humble key account manager? Perhaps it is, but allowing the practice of GAM to develop into a separate or elitist function will be a fast road to nowhere. The global account manager requires the full support of local operations, including the sales teams, and to appear to float above them on a cloud labelled 'cuckoo land' is unlikely to get them very far in that pursuit.

Doing their own thing

A 'would-be global' supplier was having problems getting its local sales teams to cooperate, and for pretty much all the reasons already discussed in this chapter, but the GA managers did not read it that way. They believed that it was a question of competencies, and that quite simply the local sales teams were not up to the job. As a group they decided that they must create a new sales team, to be based locally but responding directly to the GA managers, to provide the local sales support required by their global customers. The local sales teams would remain unscathed, and unused by the GA managers, so what problem could that cause?

Two sales teams, both based at local operations, one responding to one boss, the other to another, both doing much the same job but with different customers, one called sales representatives, the other called senior account executives, and on different terms and conditions – so what problems could that cause?

The dust never really settled on the rows that erupted, and the only option was to backtrack and re-engage the original local sales teams in the task. It took an investment in training and coaching but the results repaid that investment in no time at all.

Global account teams *include* the local personnel; they shouldn't try to supersede them, and to build additional structures above or around them is not only expensive but also likely to be destructive.

This is related to the hunting licence issue… only it gets worse. Imagine that your company has been doing business for some time with a customer in a number of different countries, but in each case the business is on a purely local basis. It would be no surprise to find that different terms and conditions applied in different locations, or that there were different pricing structures and service packages.

Now comes the rush of blood to the head, and the surety that dealing globally would be a good thing. Imagine the meeting at the buyer's office. They hadn't thought of you as such a very big supplier before, but now that they add each individual country's business to the grand total their eyes roll like the lemons in a fruit machine, only these lemons have _'big percentage discount'_ written all over them. As they examine each different set of terms and conditions they carefully extract the best characteristics from each, best of course for them.

At the end of the meeting you leave with your precious global agreement, and the right to put 'Global Account Manager' on your business card. But what price your fanciful ego? You have maybe done no more than confirm the status quo as far as volume and distribution are concerned (valuable, you convince yourself, as a defence against the competition), but find yourself tens of thousands short in additional discounts and stretched terms.

Did you really need to dress up in red and walk along the top of the trench?

This last case study raises some important questions about timing. What was the motivation behind the move? Was it a genuine attempt to block the competition in advance of the customer becoming a truly global customer, or was it a misplaced pride that drove an innocent enthusiasm?

There is a dilemma to the timing of GAM, as shown in Figure 3.1.

On the one hand you should aim to avoid rushing into GAM before you have to, but having said that, you must also aim to be ready, and to be ready in advance of your competitors; but then, to be ahead of the field, and even ahead of yourself, could just render you an innocent among wolves…

There is no easy answer to 'when?', but there is some advice on how to proceed towards an answer. Begin with careful observation, maintain a steady discipline, identify your genuine value as a global supplier, and develop relationships and processes that ensure your just reward. That is in essence the subject matter of the rest of this book.

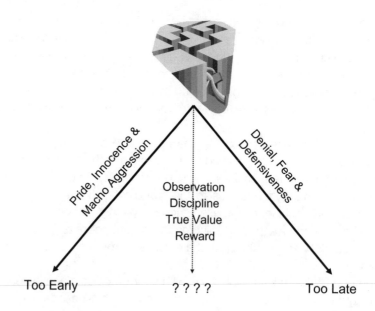

Pride, Innocence &
Macho Aggression

Denial, Fear &
Defensiveness

Observation
Discipline
True Value
Reward

Too Early   ? ? ? ?   Too Late

Figure 3.1   *Timing your move*

4

The critical success factors – *making it happen*

From here on, I intend to focus more on the solutions and the successes than the problems and the disasters; we probably need some assurance at this point that GAM (global account management) *can* actually work.

In discussing the issues, obstacles and sins, we have already begun to point towards some possible solutions, but only in a rather philosophical way. What we need now are some very tangible and practical things that can and must be done. In this chapter we will consider these things as a set of *critical success factors (CSFs)* for GAM.

These CSFs are not listed in any order of importance, nor does the list represent a chronological plan of action that you should follow (the idea of a chronological process will be considered in Chapter 11). They are not in fact separate and individual tasks but a series of activities that overlap and build on each other as the journey progresses.

It is another of GAM's challenges that so many things (analysis, plans, actions, responses) must happen all at the same time, and that is simply because this is how the world throws them at us. If any reader really does have the chance in their business to suspend the movement of time and bring customers to a halt, then please could they let me know as I would love the chance to walk through this process in a neat logical order!

It is for ease of treatment more than anything else that I have broken these CSFs down into the chapters that form the rest of this book. Here we will summarize the work ahead.

- **Getting the big picture** *(Chapter 5)*:
  To manage a global account successfully you must understand their market, their business, their drivers, and what I will call their 'moneymaking logic', and then act on that understanding to achieve some form of preferred, key or strategic supplier status. That you must also aim to understand all of this *better* than the customer understands it for themselves is part of GAM's Holy Grail. Is it possible? Ask yourself the following question: can *your global team* understand the customer's global ambitions and requirements better than any *nationally* based or *functionally* based entity in the customer? If the answer to that is 'yes', then you are well on the way to that strategic supplier status, and your chances of *managing* the account, as opposed to reacting to its demands, will be dramatically enhanced.

  We can see here one of those chicken-and-egg conundrums: which comes first, the strategic or the global supplier? We have already seen that being a strategic supplier in one location is no guarantee of the same success in others, yet how can you hope to become a global supplier without demonstrating your value and importance *somewhere*? And looking from the other side of the conundrum: it is only through an investment of time and effort on a global basis that a supplier can hope to understand the customer sufficiently to become a truly strategic supplier. I suggest that you don't worry over much about the conundrum – you will be starting where you start – but do recognize that the activities and the outcomes go hand in hand.

- **Understanding the global buyer** *(Chapter 6)*:
  The global buyer has a difficult task, and one in which they are not always helped by their own local operations (so mirroring exactly the challenge for the global seller). Take great care not to become an additional obstacle in their way. Suppliers might not always rush to help the global buyer, partly from fear, partly from misapprehension, but also because they are so often in collusion with those self-same local customer operations, trying hard to maintain their local business. Such attitudes have to go if

you wish to become a genuine and valued global supplier. The more help in their task that the global buyer receives from the *potential* global supplier, the more likelihood there is of that supplier becoming an *actual* global supplier.

To become one of the *favoured few* you must get fully underneath the skin of the customer's purchasing strategy, which almost certainly means getting beyond the smokescreen of pricing. Sure, pricing matters, but it is rarely the only concern of a global buyer, and if it is, then you must find those that *do* care about more…

- **Understanding the customer's decision-making process (Chapter 7):**
  'Penetrating the customer's snail' is a phrase with which you will become quite familiar. This is about recognizing that while the global buyer may be the point at which you negotiate the deal and receive the order, your chances of success and your likely level of reward were determined a long way further back, inside a snail-like decision-making process (the phrase refers to the spiral shape of the snail's shell, but sometimes it can be just as apposite to their speed). Properly understanding where your value impacts in the customer's operations, and how the people on the receiving end of your value influence the final decision to buy or not buy, is another part of GAM's Holy Grail.

- **Managing the global *touch points* (Chapter 8):**
  Influencing the customer's decision-making process requires a careful management of contacts and relationships, but managing the global touch points goes further than influencing skills. One of my customers once described GAM as being: *'all the things that go on between the supplier and the customer when the sales folk are not around'.* I like that, as it expresses well the task required: to manage every point of contact with the customer to ensure consistency of approach, consistency of quality, and consistency of outcome.

  To do this effectively will require a wide range of skills, and some vital disciplines and processes. We describe it as *'building diamond teams'*, a concept well entrenched in the practice of KAM, but with GAM we are sometimes called on to build these diamond teams on a truly grand scale.

- **Getting the board *on board* (*Chapter 9*):**
  Senior management must be fully engaged for GAM to happen. There are so many obstacles, and most of them internal, that the management team must take on board their responsibility to 'clear the way'. They must also champion the cause, develop the capabilities in the business, coach the participants, and take up their own role as members of global account teams. Not every business is blessed with a management team capable of taking on this responsibility; the ones that are, are the ones that will prosper.

- **The global account manager (*Chapter 10*):**
  It is the responsibility of senior management to appoint the right people, and to provide them with the right skills and resources; but what does it take to be one of this *rare breed*? The global account manager must have a range of talents, but most important among them is what has been called *'political entrepreneurship'.** This is the ability to see and develop the commercial case, but also to manage the competing interests (and egos) encountered on the way. They must be confident leaders and skilled coaches, and their ability to plan, persuade and motivate will be tested to the full. They must demonstrate authority but should not expect to have that authority handed to them as a badge, recognizing that the best kind of authority is the kind that is earned. They will have to manage diverse and virtual teams with the challenge of cultural diversity in particular ever at the forefront of their mind.

  They are indeed a rare breed, and from this description maybe a non-existent one, which brings me to another quality – their ability to extract from their GA Team the capabilities and the competencies required for the GAM task: they must *not* be loners.

- **Structure and the *persuasive process* (*Chapter 11*):**
  Building an organizational structure that supports GAM, without creating a bureaucratic hierarchy, and without detriment to existing local capabilities, is such an individual task for each

---

* My thanks to Kevin Wilson, Nick Speare and Samuel J Reese for the creation of the splendid term *'political entrepreneur'* in their book *Successful Global Account Management*, published by Kogan Page, 2002.

business engaged in GAM that this will not be the place for templates. Perhaps the most important 'rule', as far as any rules apply, is that GAM structures should aim to merge with local structures, not replace them or supersede them.

Successful GAM structures are not just diagrams or organigrams; they contain common sets of skills and processes that bind together the constituent parts, so ensuring the consistency of approach demanded by global customers.

The _wrong_ structure can kill GAM, but unfortunately you cannot rely on the _right_ structure to guarantee success. There are limits to structural solutions and more often than not it will be the ability of those involved to persuade and influence that really makes things happen, not the rewriting of those organigrams. A _persuasive process_ (an example of _political entrepreneurship_) will rank high in the list of capabilities required to make GAM happen.

- **Performance and reward** *(Chapter 12):*
  Without doubt this is one of the toughest of the CSFs, so let's at least start with a simple principle: the methods of measuring performance and rewarding that performance must match the globality of the challenge.

  So long as your customers are only just emerging from 'international' status, than locally set objectives and locally based reward schemes may still work, but their days are numbered. So long as they deal only with single business units in your company then unit-specific objectives and rewards will be fine....

  First and foremost will be the need for a global profit & loss account for each global customer. It is a sin (you will recall from Chapter 3) to make such large investments as GAM will involve and not measure their impact.

  As well as the global measure, those involved in servicing the customer (whether business units, functions or local operations) will need to be aware of the value of their contribution, which will bring us on to the question of reward.

  None of this need replace what happens locally or in individual business units. Any individual country will still want to know how a particular customer contributed to their national picture, and the same will go for an individual business unit. There is no reason why either should not measure that in any way they choose. As time goes by, however, perhaps the fascination with the local or the business unit measure will diminish and a desire to be part of the global measure will become more important. The patience required to manage this kind of transition, and the ability to force the pace where necessary, will be another example of the *political entrepreneurship* already mentioned.

The true *political entrepreneur* knows just where the 'greater good' stops and the 'local interest' starts

You will recall the supplier to the food, household, toiletries and cosmetics industries introduced in Chapter 2. They were struggling to find common ground between their five very different business units in order to supply a global customer, and to do so as a truly global supplier. Their problem was that with each unit having such a different business model and moneymaking logic, for any one of them to measure success by the standards of the other would have been the fastest way to ensure 'no go'.

The need to measure the contribution to the *greater good* of the whole business will be vital to any hope of progress, but just as importantly, each business must feel that an adequate reward is available for their own efforts, and is allocated to their business accordingly. This may sound a little like a silo mentality, but unless you plan to combine the businesses as one unit (and probably lose the very strengths of their independence) then this is very likely the way it will have to be.

Again we are looking at *political entrepreneurship*; the recognition of the realities of existing business structures and so the nature of rewards expected.

(To see how this case develops further see Chapters 8, 11, and 12.)

- *Getting IT right (Chapter 13):*
  The complexity of the challenge demands that a number of robust processes and support systems will need to be in place. It is here that we will see the vital role to be played by the information technology (IT) department, another member of the global account teams. In particular there must be systems for data capture, for analysis, and for sharing of information. Communication tools will be vital (attempting GAM before the era of e-mail would have been a mighty task indeed!), but even more important than the tools must be the disciplines required to see them used – in the end this is not about software: it is about people.

- **The global account plan** *(Chapter 14)*:
  Could you believe that there are firms with individual global customers worth in excess of 10 million pounds sterling that have no written strategic global plans and rely on a consolidation of the many local plans already in existence? How about your own?

  I said in my introduction to this book that there were no rules of GAM, but here is an exception: there *must* be a single plan that identifies the opportunity, sets the direction, and establishes the rules of engagement.

- **Harnessing the strengths of cultural diversity** *(Chapter 15)*:
  Cultural diversity is a factor that can make or break the whole GAM edifice. Handled badly (which usually means ignoring it and hoping it will go away), cultural diversity will be a source of frustration that can exhaust the most committed enthusiast. Handled well (which means being open-minded, observant, and discussing things openly), the diversity of your team can be harnessed as a source of competitive advantage.

  Perhaps the key is in setting the rules; which parts of the relationship are best left to local treatment and local norms, and which parts must follow a uniform global approach? Don't forget that the customer has just the same anxieties as you over this matter, and a supplier that demonstrates its ability to work globally without setting off cultural 'bombs' at every turn will be welcomed. More than that, a supplier that manages its diverse team to ensure that its global and local resources are deployed in the best interests of the customer will very likely be viewed as a key supplier, a strategic supplier, and a truly global supplier.

5

Getting the big picture

'So much to know – so little time to know it.'

Knowing about your own products, your own services and your own proposition is what I call the 'little picture'. The 'big picture' is knowing about the customer, their products, their markets and their customers, and for a global account it is a huge task. Any global account manager that attempts the big picture 'solo' just makes the task all the harder still. It is the GA *team's* job, from the very outset, and throughout its entire existence, to gather information, to analyse that information, and to build an increasingly better picture of their customer.

But will the picture become better over time, or will it simply become more complex? Like the peril of analysis paralysis, knowing more and more 'facts' can sometimes obscure rather than illuminate, and the bigger the picture becomes the more blurred are its outlines. With so much to know, and so many different ways to both know it and interpret it, a little order and method is called for.

The *big picture* is a great deal more than a lot of little pictures thrown together in a communal database. There should be three large ambitions: to understand the customer's markets, to understand the customer's business, and to assess the potential for genuine partnership between global supplier and global customer. This chapter provides some of the tools for realizing those ambitions, built around three pieces of analysis, each one complementing and building on the other:

- **opportunity chain** analysis – *the customer's markets*;
- **business driver** analysis – *the customer's business*;
- **the shared future** analysis – *the prospects for partnership*.

In each case we will consider the purpose of the analysis, discuss its form and how best to go about making it, and most importantly of all, ask: what are you going to do with its conclusions?

OPPORTUNITY CHAIN ANALYSIS

Purpose of the analysis

We start with the ambition to understand the customer's markets, and to go further than that, to understand those markets *better* than the customer understands them themselves. This is an entirely realistic ambition *for your team* if we remember the circumstances and complexity of a global customer. It is also a vital ambition, for at least two reasons.

I am assuming that you are not interested in being a key or strategic supplier 'just for a moment' but wish to maintain that status over a considerable period of time. To achieve that you must be in tune with the customer's 'pace'. How do they progress towards their market opportunity? Is it a sprint or a marathon? Is it a hop-skip-and-a-jump, or a measured plod? It is about their speed and their length of stride, and only when you understand both these things can you hope to meet and *continue* to meet their needs.

The customer's pace is determined, to begin with at least, by the pace of their own market – is it experiencing growth, maturity or decline; is it stable, changing, or experiencing disruption? It is, of course, their response to these different scenarios that will determine their needs from suppliers. While a customer operating in just one country may face just one of these scenarios, a global customer is likely to be facing a mix, and the global supplier must be able to match their offer to that mix. Any supplier that does not recognize the variation of need based on these factors is unlikely to keep up with the true pace, whether globally or locally.

Understanding your value

The second reason that your understanding of the customer's global markets must be superior to their own is bound up with getting your just reward. Your reward will depend on your value, and value is a complicated concept.

First, value is only to be seen through the eye of the beholder, the customer. What you say or think is valuable, in your brochures and in your sales presentations, is only valuable if the customer regards it as such.

Second, value has to be measured and quantified (if you are to get a measured and quantified reward), and that means measuring it in the customer's terms. Telling me that a certain grade of petrol is kinder to my engine is of no value to me if I'm driving a hire car. Telling me that a higher grade of petrol will improve my fuel economy is interesting, but if it costs more in the first place and I can't work out the trade-off then I'm no further forward and will probably stick with the lower grade.

Third, value received by a customer is very often defined as being the impact made on their ability to compete in their own markets: _'What it does for me is defined by what it does for my customer.'_

Taking all of this together, it is easy to see how failing to understand _their_ market can easily result in you failing to understand _your_ value. And we don't expect them to tell us any of this: _'Thank you so very much Mr Key Supplier for helping us to reduce our costs and secure our customer's loyalty, please put your prices up...'_; these are things that we must know for ourselves.

A supplier of ink to the printing and packaging industry was asked to develop a new grade of ink that would glow with a neon-type quality on cardboard cartons. It was an interesting request technically, and one well within their capabilities, and so they got on with the task without asking many questions. Compounding that sin, they made plenty of assumptions, biggest of which was that the deal would hinge on price. The customer had a reputation for tough negotiations, the result of their own slim margins when selling into the highly competitive household and toiletries markets.

The ink was developed and delivered on time and at a price marginally below their standard inks. The supplier justified this discount on the grounds that they had received the bonus of orders to supply the customer's sites in the United States and Japan as well as the normal UK site. Indeed, their technical services manager was delighted at the chance to fly out to both the United

Your true value may make its impact a long way down the 'customer chain' ...

... it pays to 'sniff it out'

States and Japan to provide support on the presses; 'another bonus', he said to the Sales Director.

Several months later the ink supplier's MD purchased a bottle of perfume for his wife, a new perfume that caught his eye at the airport duty-free shop because of the way its packaging glowed out at him; indeed, the new perfume was called 'Glow'. He had heard of 'project Glow' in his own company and was impressed by the result.

'Glow' went on to be a huge success, winning international awards for the perfumer, the product designer and the advertising agency. All the awards commended the new brand's global appeal, something of a relief to the marketing team as this had been their first genuine global launch and supported by their largest ever promotional spend.

Noting all of this, the ink supplier's MD raised the question of their price with his sales director. Why was it so low, in fact it represented rock-bottom margins, when they had clearly contributed so substantially to the success of a major global brand?

'We thought it was for a soap powder packaging project, that's what our customer usually works on,' answered the sales director.

'But didn't you wonder about the US and Japanese orders?'

'They were just a bonus.'

It was a short meeting and at its close the MD made a mental note to look for a new sales director.

Of course, if the ink supplier had known something of the use that their ink was being put to; if they had known something of the importance of their customer's customer's product launch; if they had appreciated the globality of the opportunity; if they had appreciated the importance of their technical support in the United States and Japan; in other words: *if they had properly appreciated their value*, then they might just have been able to realize something better than the rock-bottom margins achieved. But they didn't. They had no ambition to understand their customer's markets; they just wanted to make a good product.

The analysis

The analysis takes the form of a picture, or what we will call a 'chain' and some call a 'map', as shown in the example in Figure 5.1.

In this example we consider the market described in the ink supplier's case study: the packaging industry. It is, of course, something of a simplification, but the full story would occupy a wall.

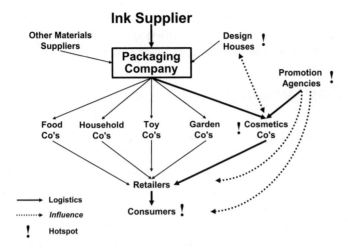

Figure 5.1 _The opportunity chain_

There are some chronological steps to the exercise:

1. The first task is to make sure that the opportunity chain contains two important elements:
    a. the flow of products, or what we will call the _logistics chain_ (solid lines);
    b. the points of influence on the decision to purchase (for both the customer's product and so also your own), or what we might call the _influence chain_ (dotted lines).
2. Next, note on the chain where you consider the market's 'hotspots' are to be found. A 'hotspot' is where a significant decision is taken that will influence the decision to buy or not buy (our product, or the customer's, or even the customer's customer's product), and where any of those products do, or could, add value. These hotspots are indicated by ! marks in Figure 5.1.
3. Next, note on the chain those places where you currently have good understanding and knowledge. Where do you have contacts with people? Do they help you to understand the dynamics of both the logistics and the influencing processes?
4. Now comes the potentially uncomfortable part of the exercise: Are you lacking contacts, knowledge, or understanding, at any of the points that are important in the total opportunity chain, ie the hotspots? To what extent therefore do you understand the full and true opportunity? To what extent therefore are you likely to understand your own true value?

Frequently there is a bias in understanding towards the logistics chain, and equally frequently the hotspots (and so the opportunities for value) are biased towards the influencing chain…

Expanding the analysis

There are several further steps that you might like to add to this analysis, depending on your circumstances:

- Indicate the volume and value flows at each point in the chain. This might help you to identify under-exploited opportunities.
- Note the market shares of players along the chain. This might help you to understand the balance of power in the market and so the likely pressures that will be brought to bear, on your customer's customers, your customer, and so ultimately on you.
- Note the presence and impact of competitors – yours and the customer's. The latter is, of course, something of extreme interest to the customer, and by understanding the pressures that result from the activities of the customer's competitors the supplier takes a huge leap forward in understanding the customer.
- Identify the boundaries of the customer's target market segments. To understand the customer's basis of segmentation is to be able to speak their language, and to identify with their ambitions, which will take us on to the second analytical tool – their business drivers – to be discussed later in this chapter.
- Identify whether the market at each point in the chain is growing, maturing, or declining. In mature markets you can expect customers to care more about costs (total costs, not just prices). In declining markets expect them to just want lower prices.
- Look out for examples of 'disruption' in the market. A disruption is more than just change; it is something that affects the balance of power and the moneymaking logic of customers, and so the roles of suppliers. New technology can disrupt a market; for example, digital photography changing the whole map of suppliers and channels of supply as consumers shift from photographic prints collected in albums to digital files held on PCs. New business models can disrupt a market, the arrival of easyJet and Ryanair on the European air travel scene being one of the more significant examples.

Priorities, investment, and rewards

For a global customer an analysis of this type will be a very big task indeed, and you must decide just how far to take this particular investment of time and effort. A good sense of priorities will be vital: how far down the chain must you look, and how many hotspots can you hope to understand or influence? A useful question that will prevent you getting sucked into *'interesting but so what?'* territory will be: how would better understanding or influence at any given point impact on our own success, or the success of our customer?

Some suppliers may find it too daunting to consider. Perhaps it is a task so daunting that even the customer has not undertaken it? Surely that makes it all the more important that you take it on, and all the more likely that the insights it provides will give your global team a superior understanding to that enjoyed by any one person or function or unit within the customer?

Using the conclusions

Throughout the exercise the ambition should be to see and understand the world through the customer's eyes, looking, as they would look, for new opportunities. This is the 'opportunity analysis' part of the exercise; where can you help the customer to do a better job; how can you reduce the impact of their competitors; how can you increase their value and reward, and so by implication increase your own value and reward?

You may be looking for points of similarity between markets, perhaps comparing different regions to see whether solutions already provided by you in one situation will be transferable to others. The greater the similarities, the more truly global the customer (using our definition from Chapter 1).

You may even be looking for inconsistencies in the customer's own approach, always a sensitive issue to raise, but a highly valuable opportunity if you can persuade them to conform around your solution.

You will be looking for ways in which you can deploy your global team to better effect, perhaps by developing contacts in parts of the chain relatively unknown to you.

And if you find that your analysis really does put you one step ahead of the customer, aim to use that to your advantage. It will help you play a better hand of poker when faced by price-obsessed buyers who deny your value. It will put you in the position (if you choose) of consultant rather than plain supplier. It will help you to plan and forecast more effectively. It will help you to find synergies and so reduce costs, and so it goes on.

Perhaps your ultimate goal should be to conduct this analysis *alongside* your customer. Customers will be impressed by your interest (though expect them to be suspicious of your motives at the start), thankful for your help, and as the picture builds will be pleased to be collaborating with such a knowledgeable supplier.

Thinking on behalf of your customer is 'a good thing' ... (but see page 63)	Your customer is a global supplier of fresh-packed salmon to the retail trade, and you supply the packaging material used in moving the product to the retailer and on to the consumer. By examining the opportunity chain through to the consumer you have found an important 'hotspot': consumer inspection in store. Consumers like to be able to *see* the fish, distrusting too much packaging, and this need appears to be a global characteristic.

Your customer knows this, but has been more focused on solving the logistical challenge of shipping fresh fish than on the aesthetics of in-store presentation; and here is your opportunity. By suggesting a see-through packaging you can add substantially to the value given by the salmon supplier, and as this is an issue that you know to be consistent in every national market, it is a solution that can be applied globally.

BUSINESS DRIVER ANALYSIS

Purpose of the analysis

The customer's 'pace' is defined *only to begin with* by the pace of their market; it is then modified by the nature of their ambitions within those markets.

How do they plan to operate in those markets? What is their business strategy? What drives their business, or, as many people would put it: what makes them tick?

Assessing a customer's business strategy is another big task with plenty of questions that *could* be asked. There are textbooks full of models and tools, but this is not to be an academic process, it is to be about drawing practical conclusions from a manageable analysis. The following four questions will not tell you everything you could ever know about the customer's business strategy, but they will point you in the direction of helping them to realize their ambitions. It is of precisely such stuff that strategic global suppliers are made.

The four questions are:

1. How do they plan to grow?
2. How do they plan to compete?
3. What are their value drivers?
4. What is their moneymaking logic?

1. How do they plan to grow?

The analysis

Figure 5.2, the Ansoff matrix, shows the four options for growth that exist for any business if we consider the two variables of their products and the markets into which those products are sold.

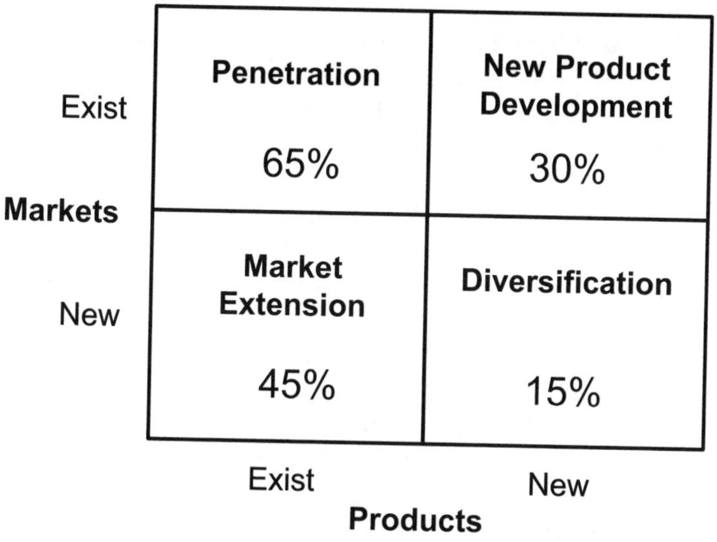

Markets	Products Exist	Products New
Exist	**Penetration** 65%	**New Product Development** 30%
New	**Market Extension** 45%	**Diversification** 15%

Figure 5.2 _The Ansoff matrix_ – growth and risk

Our first purpose is to identify the customer's growth strategy, which may be one or more of the following:

- A penetration strategy is one where the customer seeks to sell more of its existing products into existing markets.
- A market extension strategy is where new markets (territories, applications, groups of customers) are sought for existing products.

- A new product development (NPD) strategy seeks to launch new products into existing markets.
- A diversification strategy involves new products *and* new markets.

Our second purpose is to understand the level of risk that is involved in their chosen growth strategy. The percentage figure in each box indicates the likelihood of success of each growth strategy. In other words, the risk of failure increases as a business moves around the matrix. This is not overly surprising: leaving the security and familiarity of home usually increases the level of risk.

Using the conclusions

Let's begin with two hugely important observations:

- The nature of the customer's growth ambitions will determine to a great extent the *nature of their demands* on suppliers.
- The level of risk involved in their growth strategy will determine the *significance* of those suppliers.

Risk is necessary in business, but most people wish to minimize it, or act to manage it in some way. Customers often elect to manage their risk by passing it back up the line to suppliers; global customers even more so.

Is this a problem or an opportunity for the supplier? The answer really depends on whether that supplier is able to help their customer to reduce their risk. If they can, then this is a splendid opportunity to demonstrate value, to be regarded as a strategic supplier, and to be rewarded appropriately.

In a **penetration strategy** the customer is taking very little risk; they are in control of their own destiny and their expectations from suppliers are simple: *'more of the same, but at a lower price please'*. Proving your worth as a strategic supplier has definite limits in this scenario. It is when the customer chooses to 'leave home' that the opportunity to shine as a supplier increases.

In a **market extension strategy** the customer may be looking for suppliers with experience in these new markets.

We have already asked (see Chapter 1) whether Tesco's growth ambitions outside the UK might be good for existing UK suppliers, or not. Theirs is a *market extension* strategy and they will be looking for suppliers who have experience in these new markets, suppliers whose presence in those markets provides Tesco with an easier, less risky entry. Suppliers new to those markets themselves and hoping for a piggyback ride may find themselves disappointed.

If the customer is pursuing an **NPD strategy** then their requirements from suppliers will be along the lines of innovation, shared development costs, and speed. If you can provide any of this, then expect to be welcome. Speed is perhaps the most important of these requirements; the success of NPD is so often down to being first. On a global stage the stakes are raised even higher, and if you wish to impress your customer with your ability to respond swiftly, make sure that you impress them first with your global capability.

One of the world's leading high-tech communications firms surprised many commentators by electing to work on a new global NPD project with what most players in the industry regarded as the 'second best' choice supplier when it came to technological solutions. They discounted what would have been other's 'first choice' on the grounds that they were too nationally based and would be hard to work with on a truly global NPD project. The global capability of the chosen supplier was more important than their technical credentials.

In some markets, being the best, but local, isn't being the best

Where the customer is following a **diversification strategy** then they will need as much help as they can get from suppliers with knowledge, experience, creativity and speed. Sir Richard Branson's advice to any business in diversification mode (and he has more experience of this than most – record label to airline to cola producer to personal equity seller to mobile phone provider, to credit cards...) is to work with expert suppliers.

Risk is good?

It would seem that customers indulging in risk are good for suppliers; so global customers indulging in global risk must be wonderful news? True in as far as that the customer's risk provides an opportunity for suppliers to provide and demonstrate value, but let's not forget that the greater the chance of customer failure, so the same must go for their suppliers. It is the classic investment decision, balancing risk and return, and the GA team must be able to make such investment assessments.

Infinite variability – global or not?

It is quite likely that a customer's growth options will vary around the globe and this will place a limit on the true globality of that customer, and so the true globality of any supplier solution. For such as Cadbury's or Nestlé, Tesco may be in penetration mode in the UK and market extension mode in other parts of Europe, so where does that leave their own relationships and propositions – local or global?

2. How do they plan to compete?

The analysis

It may seem that there are a hundred ways in which a business can choose to compete, but many years ago Michael Porter identified that there were in fact only two broad choices: competing by having the lowest costs of supply, or competing by finding a point of differentiation, whether that was the product, the brand, the people, or whatever else.

Step one in this analysis is to determine the customer's choice, a task that will almost certainly require you to enquire well beyond the purchasing office. This is where life can get complicated: a business with more than one market and with more than one market segment and with more than one product may make this choice differently by each product/segment/market. This you need to know, because the customer's expectations will therefore vary by product/segment/market.

A further complication is that the customer may claim to be making both choices – reducing costs (usually meaning *your* price) and improving their product (meaning *your* quality), but in most realities it will be one or the other that dominates in their competitive strategy, and this you also need to know.

Step two of the analysis is to identify the customer's position on the product life cycle.

Figure 5.3 shows the classic progression through introduction, growth, maturity and decline, with the related impact on profits. Aim to understand where the customer lies. If they have several products or activities in which you are interested, understand where each one of them lies, as the 'stage of life' will very often determine the competitive strategy chosen by the customer, and so their requirement from suppliers.

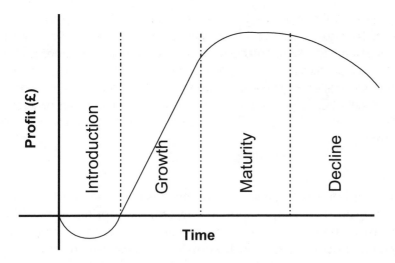

Figure 5.3   *The product life cycle*

Using the conclusions

This is about making appropriate responses, so take care not to leap to inappropriate conclusions. First, some conclusions regarding the customer's choice between lowest cost and differentiation.

The 'lowest cost' option

A customer that chooses to compete by having the lowest costs of supply will have some very clear expectations from its suppliers, but they are not always to do with price. Sure, the easiest demand for a buyer to make is for lower prices, but in fact they might be much better helped in their ambitions by suppliers who are able to help them reduce their *total costs*, even where this involves paying a premium.

A manufacturer of confectionery products needed to respond to some very heavy retail pressure to reduce its prices. In order to maintain profits it looked to reducing its own costs and asked the buyer of ingredients and additives to play their part. The buyer took the easiest option and made some quick changes to their supplier list, swapping some longstanding ones for new and significantly lower-priced alternatives. Patting themselves on the back for a job well done, they reported their actions to 'them upstairs' and waited for the praise and the promotion.

Almost immediately the problems began. First, manufacturing reported problems with the new materials; they took longer to mix with existing recipes,

Never confuse 'lowest cost' with 'lowest price'

slowing down the line. The buyer suggested that R&D might rework the recipes. Then there were problems with supply, and the line was halted on more than one occasion. The buyer rang around and found some short-term alternatives, another job well done, they said to themselves. Then came the product recall after consumer complaints of 'bits' in their previously smooth confectionery treats. It was the phone call from the marketing director that finally persuaded them to get back in touch with the recently sacked suppliers…

A premium product that saves time, speeds processes, and so reduces costs may be of very high value. The test for the supplier is their ability to measure these things; how much time, how much faster, and how much are costs reduced? Such knowledge doesn't come from sellers talking to buyers; it comes from the many interactions between members of the GA team and members of the customer's team; technical, operational, R&D, and all the rest. We will return to this is Chapters 7 and 8, penetrating the customer's decision-making process and answering the crucial question: who cares about your value?

The 'differentiation' option

The options for differentiation are many and you must be able to recognize those that work best for your customer and then aim to make a positive impact on those things. If you can help them to distinguish their product, or their service, or their people, or whatever it is, then you will be a valued supplier. If you cannot make such an impact then expect the buyer to be putting pressure on your price.

Knowing you are touching a nerve helps you play a better hand of poker

A management consultancy firm identified that their single most important point of differentiation was their people, or at least it should have been, only morale was in decline and staff turnover was increasing, and there was a danger of that differentiation disappearing out the door, quite literally. They approached a training firm and asked them to develop a series of workshops designed to improve morale, focus people's minds on the customers, and improve skills of rapport building.

The events were designed, but shortly before delivery was due to start the buyer met with the supplier and demanded a significant discount on the basis that the supplier was more expensive than any other training supplier ever used. To sweeten the pill they offered the prospect of global delivery, if the supplier played their cards right. The supplier refused to give the discount, adding that if indeed the workshops were to be delivered overseas then there would be some extra design costs to ensure that they were appropriate to the new audiences. The buyer threatened to cancel the workshops and the meeting was adjourned.

The workshops went ahead, there was no discount, and they were so successful that they were run overseas after suitable modifications, for which an additional charge was raised. The supplier understood the value of what they were providing by knowing how their product impacted on the customer's biggest challenge and biggest ambition. Such knowledge enabled them to play a better hand of poker with the price-obsessed buyer.

The product lifecycle

The second step in this analysis concerned the customer's product life cycle. Figure 5.4 suggests some typical expectations from suppliers by a customer at the different stages of this life cycle.

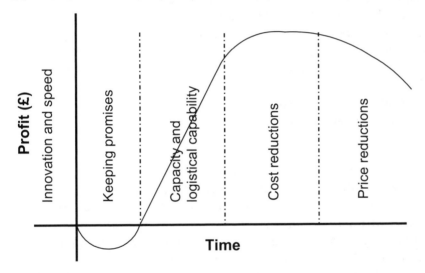

Figure 5.4 _The product life cycle_ – the requirement on suppliers

By understanding the customer's position the supplier can predict the likely requirements even before the customer is aware of them themselves. Being proactive is almost always better than reactive; it is so much easier to get a premium reward for proactive solutions than reactive ones.

The supplier can also predict who they will need to be speaking with in order to discuss those requirements and to demonstrate their own value. In a typical B2B manufacturing environment there might be a sequence of contacts running something like the following:

marketing (interested in speed and creativity), followed by R&D (interested in technical ability and reliability), followed by manufacturing and operations (interested in capacity and logistics). The buyer (interested in price) might come next, and rather later in the sequence than they themselves may have indicated.

3. What are their value drivers?

The analysis

What makes the customer's business hum? What 'values' distinguish it, and 'drive' it? How does its staff know what to do each time there is a tough decision? What broad values guide them in making those decisions?

In their book, *The Discipline of Market Leaders* (HarperCollins, 1995), Michael Treacy and Fred Wiersema identify three such value drivers. All are likely to be present in any successful business, but in *really* successful businesses, one or other of these drivers tends to stands out, distinguishing the business for its staff, for its investors, for its customers and for its suppliers. The three value drivers are:

- operational excellence;
- product leadership;
- customer intimacy.

The task of the GA team is to identify the customer's mix of value drivers, identify the lead driver, and so identify the nerves that must be touched if they are to be considered as strategic suppliers.

Operational excellence (OE) is about doing things well, whether purchasing, manufacturing, selling or delivering, and in a business driven by OE, very likely *all* of these. Supply chain management is likely to be a well-established discipline and process, indeed effective processes will lie at the heart of the firm's success. Uniformity and conformance are important to such a business, bringing the economies of scale on which their moneymaking logic rests.

IKEA and operational excellence

IKEA achieves huge efficiencies through its logistics chain from manufacture to store, and in store the 'self-selection self-collection' formula completes the operational excellence of their supply chain. Global uniformity (Swedish product names like 'Gutvik' and 'Sprallig' make it all the way to Australia), modular ranges, and a carefully honed offer are some of the key ingredients.

Product leadership (PL) is about producing the best, leading-edge, or market-dominant products. In a business driven by PL, high rates of innovation and NPD are likely, and the R&D department will be to the fore. Such a business will continually push the boundaries of performance.

It is hard to imagine a successful ethical pharmaceuticals company that is not driven by this value; the market for *'nearly there'*, or *'almost as good as the best'* drugs is rarely good. The reliance on successful NPD is huge; witness the concerns voiced by investors should the pipeline of new products appear to be drying up, and then the search for another firm's pipeline to acquire by purchase or merger. (Of course, the supplier of generic drugs, on the other hand, might be driven far more by operational effectiveness.)

Pfizer (or GSk, or AstraZeneca etc) and product leadership

Customer intimacy (CI) is the ability to identify with specific customer needs, and match products and services accordingly. In a business driven by CI you are likely to hear a good deal about the importance of developing close customer relationships, and the determination to act on the resultant knowledge at all levels of their operation. They will perhaps have a wide menu of products and services, and the ability to mix and match these to suit individual customer requirements, or go one step further and offer a totally bespoke service. There is a limit to how many customers this can be done for, and a CI-led business will probably think carefully about segmentation and key account selection.

My own business, INSIGHT Marketing and People, has very few off-the-shelf products and can only be of use to its clients if it understands in some depth the nature of their challenges and ambitions. No two GAM training workshops are ever identical because no two GAM challenges are ever identical.

INSIGHT and Customer Intimacy

Using the conclusions

At first sight the use of this analysis is clear: tailor your proposal to match the customer's lead driver. As well as the obvious advantage of speaking their language, you dramatically improve your chances of being regarded as relevant, in tune, and so of value.

If the customer is driven by *operational excellence*, focus on propositions that impact on their supply chain, that reduce costs, and that improve efficiencies.

If the customer is driven by *product leadership*, focus on propositions that impact on their product, that improve quality, and that enhance their leading-edge ambitions.

If the customer is driven by *customer intimacy*, focus on propositions that impact on the customer's customers, that increase their ability to respond, and that enhance their flexibility.

These are, of course, only indications, not absolute rules, but they show the way forward for any prospective key supplier: tailor the message, target the right value drivers, and target the right people.

Great ideas only look that way to people who think like you ... ... remember who the customer is ... ... start trying to think like *them*

A friend of mine once worked behind the counter at McDonald's. McDonald's is one of the very best examples of an operationally excellent led business; their ability (and determination) to replicate the product unfailingly, on every continent, is a remarkable achievement. My friend was young and keen to make a good impression and so one morning, as a sign of his initiative, he took a bottle of his mother's best homemade pickle in, and placed it on the counter. Each customer was offered a free scoop from the jar, to add to their burger.

My friend did not last long with McDonald's. This was the wrong kind of initiative. Now, if he had found a way to improve the uniformity of the buns, or reduce the cooking time of the fries by 5 per cent, and had he kept up the pace with those kinds of initiatives, then perhaps by now he would be on their board.

And what if you sell to McDonald's? Would you tell them that you had a great way to improve the taste of their burgers, or might you tell them that you could help them to make them even more uniformly? The gap between these two approaches, from the supplier's side, is not so very far apart, but I'm sure you can see the huge chasm between success and failure viewed from the customer's perspective.

So far so good, but it is time to add a little complexity. Imagine I was to ask all my contacts at a particular customer to help me by explaining their lead value driver, and assuming of course that they recognized these terms and used this language, how might I fare? If I were to ask a group of production people I would not be surprised to hear them say operational excellence. If I asked the same question of a group from R&D I might hear them say product leadership instead. And if I asked a group from sales and marketing, might I hear them say customer intimacy? Very likely, and the point I am making is that while the business might be driven by (or attempting to be driven by) a uniform lead driver, each function within that business might have their own ideas.

Remember, we are selling to a complex global customer, and the chance of encountering different answers across different functions and then across different regions and countries is high. So how to make sense of it all?

- First, don't attempt to be too precise about this. Any business has a mix of drivers, and different circumstances will bring one or the other to the fore at different moments.
- Second, recognize that the art of using this analysis is not to be found in a box-ticking or template-style response, but in your sense of awareness and flexibility of mind.
- Third, recognize that times change, and that however clear the customer's drivers might be right now, it may not always be so.
- Fourth, identify where in the customer's business your offer has the biggest impact and delivers the greatest value. What is the lead driver in that part of the business?
- Fifth (and here we stand foursquare in the world of reality), what does the buyer say?

Let's return to the case study concerning the salmon supplier discussed earlier in this chapter, and observe a potential problem with our 'transparent packaging' solution. The salmon supplier was focused on issues of logistics, suggesting that perhaps their main value driver was operational excellence. And our solution, to provide transparent packaging; isn't that one that would appeal more to a business driven by product leadership, or perhaps even customer intimacy? Indeed, our solution might even have a negative impact on operational excellence.

So, a great idea, but it leaves the customer cold (perhaps as cold as a fish?). In such a case there are usually two choices:

Thinking on behalf of your customer is 'a good thing' ... ... but make sure that _your_ type of thinking is _their_ type of thinking ...

1. Find the people in the customer who _are_ driven by product leadership or customer intimacy and sell them your solution. The danger of this option is that you are forcing _your_ idea on to a customer who is looking at other ideas for their salvation. You may find the people who are interested, but are they the ones that make things happen?
2. Reframe your proposal to hit on their 'operational excellence nerve'. In this regard, issues to do with the consistency of packaging, or the ease of packaging, might have more resonance. Unless transparent packaging can be argued in these terms, it is an idea unlikely to fly.

4. What is their moneymaking logic?

The analysis

Alvin Toffler said: *'Profits, like sausages, are esteemed most by those who know least about what goes into them.'* He had in mind the world of financiers and investors, but he could so easily have been speaking of the majority of people who work as small cogs in large corporations. Profits and their make-up cannot and must not be a mystery for those engaged in GAM. GA teams must understand the drivers of their own profitability to ensure that they chase the right opportunities, and they must understand the drivers of their customer's profitability to ensure that they make the right propositions.

There are, of course, many routes to profit, and Figure 5.5 shows some of the choices available to a manufacturing company.

Each customer will have their own unique twist to the 'standard options' shown in Figure 5.5, and across a global customer there may, of course, be a number of such twists, or variations on the 'head office theme'. It is the detail of these twists that the GA team must aim to understand, for that way lies competitive advantage.

Asking the buyer is almost certainly not enough. They will tend to emphasize whichever part of your offer is the weakest; a standard negotiating ploy, but one that could seriously mislead you. Asking buyers the essence of their moneymaking logic tends to reveal no more than that buying at the lowest price is the secret…

There are clues everywhere: annual reports, press statements, announcements to the City. Speaking with the customer's sales professionals can tell you a lot in this respect, for if they are to make the right deals they have to understand their own money-making logic; do they pursue volume with generous discounts in order to fill the factory, or do they cherry pick the high-margin opportunities?

Using the conclusions

To be viewed as a strategic supplier on a global level you had better be very sure that your proposition touches the customer's money-making logic nerve. You will need to be able to demonstrate how your proposition enhances their profitability, in line with their objectives, and described in their terms. Anything less than this will have you pushed down the supplier pecking order. The prospect of true global supply will either recede, or become simply a matter of price: a brutal basis for any global relationship.

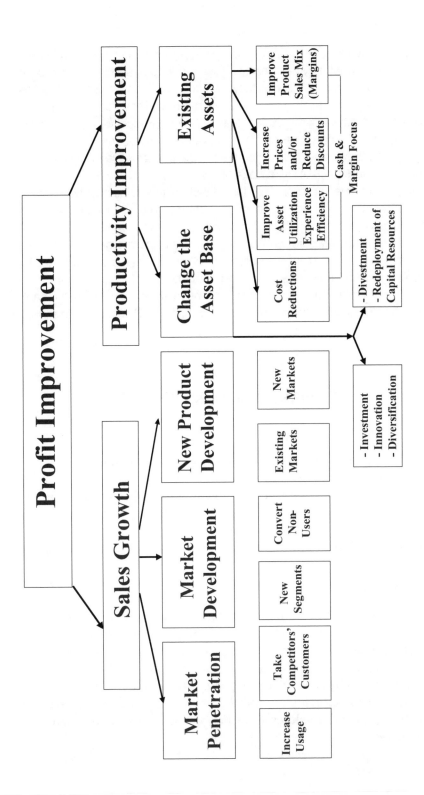

Figure 5.5 *Some options for improving profitability*

Moneymaking logic – a prime basis for segmenting your customers

Wal*Mart and Tesco share a similar moneymaking logic. They both need scale, they both need what they call 'velocity' (high stock turn, and the healthy cash flow that should come with it), and they are both happy to work on low margins to ensure they get the scale and the velocity required. They also tend to regard individual products as less important than the wider product categories; Heinz baked beans is simply one of many products in the canned vegetables category, and they are far more interested in the performance of the category than in the performance of Heinz baked beans.

Trying to enthuse Tesco or Wal*Mart to work with you as a global supplier based simply on promises of enhanced profit margins by individual product lines would not get you very far.

There are other retailers who *do* look to the profit margin on individual products as the source of their success, this being typical of a specialist retailer and even more so if they are a small independent.

Trying to argue that a zero margin will be fine as the cash will be in the bank before the supplier's bills are paid is unlikely to thrill many independent specialists.

THE SHARED FUTURE ANALYSIS

Purpose of the analysis

This analysis asks the sixty-four thousand dollar question: is this customer worth the effort, or if there is any doubt on that, can it be made worth the effort? It forces us to consider the customer's hopes and fears, and to ask how well we relate to those as a supplier. A good match suggests a promising future, while a poor match shows us what must be done to improve.

The analysis

The analysis is completed using the form shown in Figure 5.6.

It is a kind of SWOT (strengths, weaknesses, opportunities and threats) analysis, but used with a good deal more analytical rigour than the usual SWOT (which too often tends towards wishful thinking and an internal focus), forcing us to make the link between the customer's opportunities and threats (the external focus) and our own strengths and weaknesses *as they are perceived* by the customer (the true reality).

+ sign(s) we make a positive impact on their ambitions or reduce their worries	- sign(s) we detract from their ambitions, or compound their worries	What future issues _excite_ the customer?				What future issues _worry_ the customer?			
		1	2	3	4	1	2	3	4
What are we perceived as being good at?	1		+++		+			+++	
	2	+++	_'Attack' these issues_		++	_Help resist these issues_			
	3								
	4					++			+
What are we perceived as being poor at?	1		_Ensure these_			- - -		- -	
	2		_don't cancel out_			_Resolve, or_			
	3	- - -	_the 'attack'_	- -		_withdraw?_			
	4		_issues_			-			

Figure 5.6   _The shared future analysis_

Their ambitions and fears

Start by putting your own business out of your mind and putting yourself entirely in the customer's shoes. This is vital. Now try to identify the things that excite the customer about their future, their ambitions, their hopes. Remember, keep your own business out of your thoughts; these are the customer's own ambitions, not yours, and nor are they the ambitions you would _like_ them to have because they match with your own!

Next step: what are the things that they fear, that they worry about, that they lose sleep at night over?

It is possible that you will not know the answers to these questions, and if that is so your next course of action is very clear: find out. Ask the customer, and have all the members of the GA team do the same. Read the customer's annual report and their in-house newspapers; these can be goldmines for learning about their current ambitions and fixations.

To some degree this analysis summarizes many of the questions we have been asking throughout this chapter: how do they aim to grow, what are the market pressures, where do they see the opportunities, how mature is their product offer, how do they wish to drive their business? As such, the tool is an excellent one to consolidate a good deal of complex analysis already undertaken.

Their perceptions of you – good and bad

Now turn to your own organization, but keep yourself in the customer's shoes. What do they like about you? What are your strengths, in other words; what do they see in you that will help them achieve their dreams? Equally, what do they not like about you? What are your weaknesses, in other words; what do they see in you that turns their worries into nightmares?

Again, there is no substitute for talking with the customer, but this takes some subtlety. The aim is not to get them focused on a long list of complaints.

Before moving to the next step, stop for a bout of honest reflection. Are these really the things that excite and worry them, or just what *you* would like them to be excited and worried about? Are the listings of our good and bad capabilities as seen through their eyes and not through yours? If they don't know about your particular brilliance, whatever it might be, then you can hardly list it here as a good capability. Why this pause for reflection? We are about to use this analysis to determine our direction for the foreseeable future – it will be as well to have it right.

Scoring your contribution

Now consider each vertical column (their ambitions, excitements and their worries) in turn, working down through your capabilities, good and bad. At each junction indicate with a plus sign where a strength makes a positive contribution to an ambition or helps to relieve a worry (use a scale of one to three pluses to represent the size of the contribution). Do the same with minus signs where a weakness either detracts from an ambition or makes worse something that worries the customer already.

Using the conclusions

Do you help or hinder their progress? Do you reduce or exacerbate their concerns?

Where you show minuses, you must ask whether these can be resolved, and at what cost. It is one of the facts of life in business that no amount of pluses will work in your favour so long as there is one significant minus blotting your copybook. The actions required will involve correcting the weakness, but just as importantly you must give time to letting them know the weakness has been corrected. This is an area where perceptions can be more important than fact and memories of bad performance are long.

Where you show pluses, aim to talk these up. Pluses where you help them with their ambitions are obviously good news, pluses where you relieve them of worries can be even better news; it is much the same principle as regards blots on copybooks. In the final analysis, does the balance of pluses and minuses argue for a shared future based on mutual respect and partnership, or does it suggest a long battle over shortcomings? We come again to the question of GAM as an investment. You will wish to invest in customers where there is a good potential future, but you may also need to invest in the rectification of weaknesses. There are no easy choices here, but the analysis will help you to identify them, and to establish some priorities for action.

A French-based food manufacturer was looking to expand their operation into the UK. This was a very clear and publicly stated ambition, but they also had a major concern, and one that they didn't shout from the rooftops. They were worried by what they saw as a continual series of food scares in the UK market, and worried that becoming involved in any such scares might have a negative impact on their home market.

You are only 'good' if it matters ...

They were looking for a UK supplier of some vital materials and services, and arranged a number of supplier presentations. One of these potential suppliers also had some business with the customer in France, and so was able to learn something of the customer's concerns from their French colleagues.

The UK supplier assessed its strengths and weaknesses, as they would be seen through the customer's eyes. High on the debit side was their price; they had a reputation for being top of the market. High on the credit side was their own track record on health and safety; they were spotless. Their analysis of the correlations between their own various strengths and weaknesses and the customer's ambitions and worries encouraged them to major in their presentation on their health and safety record as being the most relevant to the customer's biggest concern. Needless to say, they won the contract.

... but if it matters, you can be 'very good' indeed

Knowing the competition

There is one last factor that will help determine your likely future together, and that's the competition. A shared future analysis full of pluses and very few minuses is a great start, but what if the customer is in the pocket of a competitor? Perhaps a Chinese customer has a preference to work with Chinese suppliers, or perhaps there are long-term contracts in place with other suppliers, or a history of affiliation with one in particular? There are a dozen such 'perhaps?' and we can only hope to sort our way through them by making sure that we understand who we are up against.

So, here's a question that would rattle a good many account managers, whether local, key or global: 'What share of your customer's business do you have, who are your competitors, and what share of the balance do they each have?'

I have known account managers who thought they had over half the business only to discover that they had less than 10 per cent, and others who were equally misinformed in the other direction. And you don't have to look far for the reason for this poor intelligence – it is the seller's rule: never talk about the competition. Unfortunately, the buyer has a very similar rule (unless it is to exaggerate their charms; an equally misleading situation), and so it is all too easy to be ignorant even of the names of the competitors, let alone their shares. I've been there myself, as a seller, and discovered that an innocent question often overcomes the problem: *'Who else are you working with on this? I hope you don't mind me asking?'* It's the second part of the question that is the secret, of course, for only the toughest-minded customer will be steely enough to say that, well actually, they do mind.

There are some serious implications to this lack of understanding. How about calculating the investment required to grow your business? We all know that in most cases it is a much easier task to grow from a 10 per cent share to a 15 per cent share than it is to grow from 90 to 95 per cent. It's the same volume difference, but the investment required to make it happen is usually out of the question at the 90 to 95 per cent end of the spectrum.

In the global context you need to know a lot more than percentage shares. How does the customer position the competition (see Chapter 6), and what do they think of their capability as a global supplier? From that analysis: what are the obstacles to your own progress, or what gaps are there to be exploited? Only then can you calculate the real opportunity and appreciate the nature of the task ahead.

Knowing your enemy isn't even half the story – far better to know your customer's friends (and enemies) ...

A global supplier wished to increase their share of business with a global account, and identified that the best immediate opportunity was in rooting out small pockets of competitor business in relative backwaters of the customer's operations. Why they considered this the best opportunity was simple; these local suppliers were operating beyond the global buyer's control, and were infringing corporate purchasing standards. By rooting them out the supplier was actually doing the buyer a favour, and could certainly expect to get a good deal of help for their cause.

There had been an alternative. They knew that they were the number one supplier already and that they could take on the number three supplier by arguing various advantages to their own offer. Why they didn't go that route was equally simple; the global buyer wished to maintain a three-supplier strategy and to actively replace the third supplier's business would not be helping the buyer's cause.

A POSTSCRIPT

This has been a very long chapter with many questions to be asked of your global accounts. Will you have the time to answer these questions? If not, then not only do you severely reduce your chances of success, but you should be reflecting on whether you are being allowed to practise GAM properly in the first place.

I would not be surprised if some of you were thinking that this kind of analysis is a little over the top. I don't suggest that you need it all and in every case, rather it is a set of tools to be selected from depending on the circumstances. Are there even some circumstances in which you don't need any of this stuff? What if you sell a simple commodity but on a global basis? If your offer _really is_ such a simple commodity, then maybe much of this analysis is academic – there's a price and just get on with it – but be warned: the easiest way to condemn yourself to the world of commodity selling is to convince yourself that you are in fact a commodity; and don't expect the price-obsessed buyer to argue with you…

6

Understanding the global buyer

Are global buyers good for you? As a supplier, dealing with someone with the authority to make deals with global application certainly has its good sides, *if they are genuine*. This is a vital caveat; nobody that *pretends* to be a global buyer, but has in fact no authority to act, will bring you any of these benefits.

The good sides of a genuine global buyer might be seen in the speed with which they help you to realize the full global opportunity, and at much less effort than it would take you with a range of local sellers and buyers. They can give you access to parts of their business that you might not otherwise have been able to reach, and they bring the prospect of scale. If you are 'in' with a global buyer, life can be just fine.

On the debit side, however, the global buyer will almost certainly demand a discount for the global deal, and their focus on price and terms may be detrimental to your attempts to argue a value-added offer. Very few global buyers can actually *promise* you global distribution, so what you get in return for the cost of the global deal is usually less than you anticipated (unless you have long experience in this and know about such shortfalls). They can sometimes lead you astray by taking you into places from which you might well have preferred to steer clear, and their knowledge of local circumstances might sometimes be poor, which can result in you encountering problems once the deal is done. If you are 'out' with a global buyer, then getting 'in' can be a monumental task (especially if a competitor is securely 'in'). And worst of all, if you were once 'in' but subsequently fall 'out' with a global buyer, then you can lose the whole business at a click of their mouse.

Draw up your own list of pros and cons, test the authenticity of their global credentials, judge the impact of that on their global status, and determine your resultant intentions. But may I suggest that if as a result of all this you *do* decide to consider the customer a global account, then put aside the list, for by this point the question, *'Are global buyers good for you?'* is no longer the one to be asking.

The problem with getting too fixated by the downsides of the arrangement is that you will tend towards a defensive approach, possibly even resisting the global buyer's requests, and that can only lead one way. If the customer presents you with a global buyer then you really only have one choice: aim to understand them, and from that understanding aim to make it work to your best advantage, which usually means making it work for them.

(If the downsides are so bad that you feel you must adopt a defensive posture for your own good, then you had best seriously reconsider whether the practice of GAM (global account management) is right for this customer.)

THE GLOBAL BUYER'S AMBITIONS AND PURPOSE

A business may have many motivations behind their decision to appoint a global buyer:

- to improve purchasing power;
- to reduce the power of dominant suppliers;
- the pursuit of better prices – by increasing the size of the order, and by securing better prices for granting global access;
- the pursuit of greater efficiencies in the purchasing operation;
- the reduction of staff in local purchasing operations;
- the pursuit of supply chain efficiencies;
- the pursuit of uniformity, perhaps something vital to the development of a global product offer, and particularly so with a global brand;
- better management control over their own operations;
- to weed out undesirable local purchasing practices;
- to rationalize the number of suppliers and so better manage the remaining list;

- the desire to work more closely with a small number of key / strategic global suppliers;
- to develop the capabilities of those key / strategic global suppliers.

Viewed from the supplier's perspective this list might appear as a mixture of good and bad, creditable and discreditable, but we should remember that from the buyer's perspective there is _only_ good and creditable. There is a vicious circle to be wary of here. If a supplier only sees the global buying role as an exercise in price negotiation then they are likely to misunderstand or underestimate the customer's broader motivations; they will see only the tip of the iceberg. This failing will lead to the wrong responses, and the more they get it wrong the more the global buyer _will_ focus on price; it is all that is left to get from a disappointing supplier.

Let's consider this list, consolidated into four main motivations, with the attendant interests shown in italics:

- buying power – _price, terms, leverage_;
- operational efficiencies – _organizational structure_;
- supply chain management – _making it happen_;
- supplier management – _positioning, rationalization, and key/strategic suppliers_.

BUYING POWER – _PRICING AND TERMS_

Of course, the buyer will take the opportunity of a global deal to negotiate your prices down; not only is it their job, but often there will also be a good case to argue. In some instances there will be genuine increases in scale (not just the apparent growth by lumping all local orders together in one). There may be genuine cost savings for the supplier – no need to take orders locally, perhaps a central delivery as well as a central order – and any good buyer would expect those kinds of savings to be shared. It may be that a single global payment from a reliable head office is much to be preferred to the chasing of monies from a variety of less reliable local operations; in effect you will have gained an improvement in your payment terms. In each of these cases you would happily discuss price as a genuine issue in seeking to make the arrangements work for both parties.

But then there are those instances when it is just a game, or a ritual, and your response can only be as good as your knowledge.

Do you know the scale of the business by each location so that you can make proper comparisons to what you are being offered centrally? Have you worked out the costs of supplying locally versus globally? Most importantly of all, do you know what gross margins you are achieving, and what impact price reductions will have on them?

Know your margins

Figure 6.1 shows the relationship between your gross margin, discounts given, and the increase in volume required for your cash profits to *stand still*.

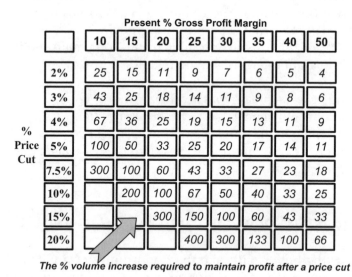

Present % Gross Profit Margin

% Price Cut	10	15	20	25	30	35	40	50
2%	25	15	11	9	7	6	5	4
3%	43	25	18	14	11	9	8	6
4%	67	36	25	19	15	13	11	9
5%	100	50	33	25	20	17	14	11
7.5%	300	100	60	43	33	27	23	18
10%		200	100	67	50	40	33	25
15%			300	150	100	60	43	33
20%				400	300	133	100	66

The % volume increase required to maintain profit after a price cut

Figure 6.1 *Trading volume for discounts – the impact on profitability*

(Example: a 43 per cent increase in volume is required, to stand still in cash profit terms, if a business making a 25 per cent gross margin reduces its price by 7.5 per cent)

Simply *stand still*, mind; anything less than this increase in volume means that you are less profitable from the deal. Of course, if you don't know your gross margins in the first place (and *do* you know them, globally?), but the buyer knows very well what they can offer you in terms of volume, then the trading of volume for price is likely to go badly for you: knowledgeable buyers have a tendency to do better than ignorant sellers.

Know your costs

Beyond gross margins, do you know the real costs of dealing with the customer, and so their actual profitability to you? GAM can be an expensive activity and while the buyer will not be interested for a minute in those costs, they must be weighed against the benefits promised by a global deal.

Know their capabilities

As in any negotiation, knowledge is power, so what do you know about the buyer's side of the fence? What do you know of the reach and ambition of their global purchasing organization? Is it empowered to act? Will it be effective and reliable? All of this is important preparatory homework before plunging into any negotiation on price and a global deal.

Managing your prices (whether global or local)

If getting the best price really _is_ the only thing that matters to the buyer then they might actually be better off using a different tactic. Rather than arguing for discounts on a global deal they could just allow the supplier to trade locally for a while, from each of their local operations, and then pool the information on prices received at each of their own locations. It would be no strange thing if they were to discover a broad range of prices, terms and conditions, and a simple enough task to identify the best/lowest and demand that as the going rate across the whole global business.

If you were caught in this way you might find yourself arguing that this 'lowest price' is, of course, in a market where your own costs are very much lower... and now the buyer really does have you where they want you: discussing _your_ costs. It is always wise to try discussing the _customer's_ costs; from there you can so often find opportunities to add value by reducing those costs. Discussing your own costs is a very different matter, for so long as your price is related to your costs you will be on the defensive, often trying to justify the unjustifiable, in grave danger if you should fall into the hands of a skilled and unscrupulous 'unbundler' of a buyer, and it will not be long before you arrive at discussing your margins...

Keep a close eye on the breadth of prices quoted around the globe, even when the customer is a 'plain international', for the times they have a habit of changing. What you might regard as a 'dumping market' today can so easily become the buyer's delight tomorrow.

Price or value?

Buyers are people who know the price of everything and the value of nothing. That's old-fashioned buyers. New-fashioned buyers are much keener to look for value received, and this chapter looks at some of the ways they might go about this. It is excellent news, of course, if you are a good, added-value supplier. The bad news is waiting for the cowboys and the 'low price, low quality' merchants.

That's all fine and dandy, but the lessons in value learnt by new-fashioned buyers can sometimes be forgotten in the heat of their global challenge. Buyers who genuinely sought best value when working in the simpler environment of a local buying office (with the opportunity to discuss with their internal customers the impact of their purchasing decisions) can suddenly find themselves going back to a much cruder measure when plunged into the complexity and relative 'anonymity' of the global task. That cruder measure is, of course, price.

The response of a good global supplier should be to recognize the buyer's predicament and aim to help. Help reduce the complexity of their task by being a provider of local knowledge. Help them to make better decisions by providing them with options. Most importantly of all, if you wish them to buy on value rather than price, provide them with the means to measure that value.

Figure 6.2 shows how value differs from price, and how the supplier can provide the customer with a means of recognizing this truth.

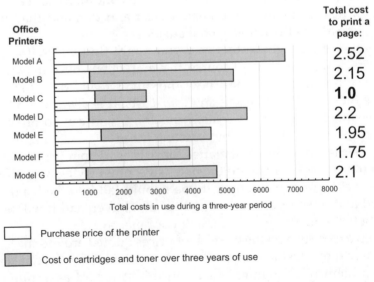

Figure 6.2 *Measuring the value received*

The buyer who buys on price is likely to choose Model A from this range of office printers; it is the cheapest and let's suppose that it is a recognized brand. We all know that buying the cheapest can bite back in the long run; think about cheap shoes, a cheap bed, or a cheap car. It is in fact the second most expensive printer, Model C, that provides the best value, in the long term, because the cost of cartridges and toner is so much lower. Perhaps the sales professional for Model C has been arguing this case for a long time, but the buyer needs something more than assertions if they are to commit to what looks at first glance a much more expensive option. The secret is in the column of figures to the right; the calculation of what it costs to print a page of paper using each printer. The beauty of this example is not just its simplicity, but that it provides a measure of value received that is relevant to the customer. The seller does not need to discuss the price of the printer, nor even the cost of the toner, but only the cost of the output: the customer's output.

Out of complexity you can offer the buyer simplicity, vital in a global context. The measure of value has, of course, to be globally relevant. If in this case we imagined the customer to be a global hotel chain, then I think we can show how it would work. Here is the proposition: '_How many hotels do you have around the world? What is the average number of bedrooms per hotel? What is your percentage occupancy rate? How many sheets are there to the average customer bill?_' A few simple sums and you have the number of customer bills printed a year across the chain, and an easy calculation to show how much your product can save compared to the incumbent printer.

OPERATIONAL EFFICIENCIES – _ORGANIZATIONAL STRUCTURE_

Buyer's heaven is not the place where sales representatives stand with palm fronds and grapes at the ready, jumping at a click of the buyer's fingers; it occurs, and somewhat more prosaically, when the prospect of enhanced buying power merges with the prospect of increased operational efficiencies. Combining a series of local purchases into one gives them the buying power, while centralizing the administration of such a purchase on to one global purchaser gives them the operational efficiencies.

Sellers often forget that it costs money to buy; buyers have to be employed, purchasing offices have to be maintained, and just as sales teams have been slimmed down in order to save costs, and key accounts identified to focus the seller's attentions, so the same has happened with buyers. If suppliers can be rationalized, and if the management task can be centralized, then there are huge cost savings to be made, as well as increased leverage.

But it is a strategy that comes with its own problems, foremost of which is knowledge, or rather, the lack of adequate local knowledge on the part of the centralized, global buyer. I recall that when one of my customers of many years ago was globalizing its purchases, they chose to centre the operation in Italy. Their UK-based buyer was on the list of redundancies, and at my last meeting with him, he finally 'snapped': *'For heaven's sake, the man doesn't even speak English, and they expect me to send him everything he needs to know. Well, they can forget that for a start. If they expect me to…'.* Global buyers often have a tough remit, considering such circumstances, and the seller should not ignore the internal politics that will have surrounded their appointment and might still bedevil their attempts to get on with their job.

The more specialized the purchase, the harder it is for the global buyer to understand the local idiosyncrasies, and so it is no surprise that they start their work by focusing on the easier options, the commodities and near commodities. This is not to say that if you supply a speciality product you can heave a sigh of relief and carry on working with your local contacts. The buyer *wants* to include your product, but it is a challenge, and they need help. Who would you rather gave them that help: their locally based colleagues, your competitors, or you?

Even the most basic of products sometimes come with a twist…

A bad global purchasing decision

A bulk chemical company with manufacturing sites across Europe purchased a huge number of 205-litre barrels for the shipment of its products. Each site handled its own purchase of these barrels and there was a great variety of prices and terms across the group. It was an expensive activity for what was surely such a simple purchase, and 205-litre barrels was just one of many similar examples.

The appointment of a global buyer was intended to cut right through all of this, and the 205-litre barrel was seen as an easy case on which to cut their teeth. And so it seemed when a deal was struck with a brand-new supplier to service the whole European group, and at a price that put tens of thousands of euros straight on to the bottom line.

Now you might think that 205-litre barrels are always the same size. They are always 205 litres, of course, but, rather like people, sometimes they are taller and thinner and sometimes they are shorter and fatter. Each site was geared to receiving a barrel size that they knew; their loading bays and storage areas were designed for stacking four barrels high to a perfect fit. This new barrel just happened to be of the taller and thinner variety, and straight away several of the sites had a problem: they didn't fit. Ingenuity is a great thing, however, and they muddled through, but after six months of muddle a bright spark in the internal audit group reckoned that the extra storage and handling costs involved in these new barrels far outweighed any saving they had made on the global purchase. In short, they had made a bad global purchase.

A good global supplier will work to help their customer make a good global purchase, and in this case it will be their knowledge of local circumstances that makes this possible. Rather than fearing the change and keeping their heads down, the good supplier will recognize the customer's ambition and rise to the challenge. There are several options, of course:

- Use your local knowledge to advise the buyer on their choice of barrels.
- Agree a deal that allows for a central purchase but involves you the supplier in ensuring the right barrel type gets to the right location (such a service deserves a premium, and you also get the global deal).
- Advise the buyer that before making this change they should aim to modify local loading bays and storage areas, so as to be able to take advantage of a great central purchasing opportunity.

This is a great example of how a global account team really can understand the customer's circumstances better than the customer does themselves, and use that knowledge to propose genuine solutions that work to the advantage of both parties. There is an important moral to this story: centralized global purchasing does not mean abandoning your own local contacts. It is the knowledge gained from these contacts that puts you in a position of strength to work with the global purchaser. What has changed is the role to be played by those local contacts. They may not be scratching order pads anymore, but now they have a much more important task; they are the eyes and ears of the GA team.

Structural options

Figure 6.3 shows four options for structuring the purchasing operation, and there are many more besides. Each has its own pros and cons for both buyer and seller.

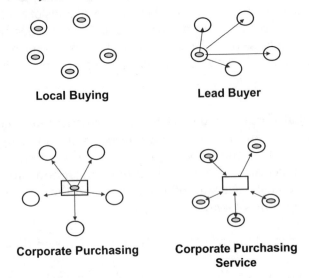

Local Buying   **Lead Buyer**

Corporate Purchasing   **Corporate Purchasing Service**

Figure 6.3   *Purchasing organization* – some options

Local buying

This is the most traditional model – simple local autonomy. For the buyer, this can be good for accommodating local needs, but buying power is fragmented and operational costs are high. For the seller, this can be good for building local loyalties, but selling costs are high and winning all the business is very hard work.

Lead buyer

One site takes on the responsibility for all. For the buyer this brings cost savings and ensures that an expert is involved in the purchase, though local bias can, of course, colour the picture. For the seller, this is great news if the chosen lead is one of their good contacts, but fairly disastrous if it is one they have ignored!

Corporate purchasing

A central body is established to run the show. Substantial cost savings and good purchasing power are the main advantages, but local knowledge can be poor, and inappropriate decisions (from the local unit's perspective) may be made. Sellers will face tough negotiations and may find it harder to argue a value-added case, but they are given access to the whole opportunity with its promise of scale.

Corporate purchasing service

A central body carries out the administrative task, to 'instructions' or 'requests' from the local units. The buyer has all the advantages of purchasing power while taking care to respect local needs. The downside is the need to maintain local operations, with their attendant costs. The good seller will have to balance local influence with central management, but this can work to their advantage if they have a good added-value case to argue.

These are just four of many options, with plenty more variations possible on each theme. Aim to identify your customer's ambition, recognize that getting things in place may take them some time, try to assess the motivation behind their choice, assess the likely pros and cons for them and for you, and seek a line that makes the best of it for both parties.

SUPPLY CHAIN MANAGEMENT – _MAKING IT HAPPEN_

Buyers tend to be more interested in supply chains than sellers, largely because of their greater ability to look along them in both directions, though this two-way observation is something of a recent development. Figure 6.4 shows what I mean.

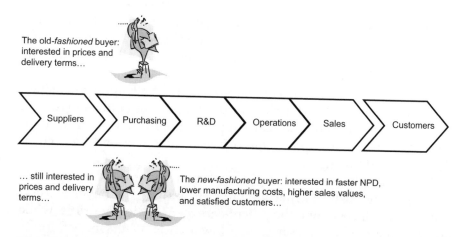

Figure 6.4 _Buyers old and new, and their perspective in the supply chain_

The buyer has always had to look backwards towards the suppliers, aiming for the best purchase in terms of price, delivery, etc. The new-fashioned buyer, in pursuit of value as well as price, has been encouraged to look in the other direction at the same time, towards the customer, aiming to make sure that their purchasing decisions are of benefit to the whole chain. Perhaps they can speed new product development by sourcing innovative materials, or by securing the active assistance of suppliers in testing and piloting. Perhaps they can reduce manufacturing costs by buying raw materials that reduce rework time, or maybe they can speed throughput by buying materials of higher quality and faster processing time. Perhaps they can help to raise sales values through better quality, or greater consistency. Perhaps they can help to make customers more satisfied by reducing product failures, or by buying what the end customers actually want to see in their products.

It is a bigger challenge to be sure, and not every buyer will rise to it, and certainly not with every supplier. Some suppliers are more able to impact on the customer's supply chain, and these are the ones that will be engaged in such conversations. It is, of course, music to the seller's ears, if they can tune in to the right signals. Once on the same wavelength the supplier can share the buyer's more ambitious perspective, and this should be a relatively easy task because the buyer's new perspective is now so much more like the seller's. At last, buyers are no longer people who know the price of everything and the value of nothing...

We see the buyer becoming more like the seller in at least two ways. First, they must identify the needs of their internal customers along the supply chain, whether that might involve research & development, manufacturing, distribution, sales or marketing.

Second, their job no longer finishes with the signing of the supplier deal. For their purchases to have the desired effect in the supply chain they must ensure that they are used as intended, a role not unlike the sales professional in after-sales mode.

That's the theory, but in a global context the challenge is intensified because of physical distances and the number of entities involved. This is where the good global supplier should be leaping to their buyer's aid, providing a bridge between the buyer and their client locations and functions.

Too often the seller is frightened away from this crucial role because they mishear what the buyer is asking. The buyer is interested in lower costs, and the seller hears them say lower prices, while all the time they *really were* saying lower costs. We have seen in the office printer case study how price and costs are not the same thing at all, and the buyer focused on both ends of the supply chain will be less likely to make the mistake (intentional or otherwise) of confusing them. Take full advantage of this new enlightenment (but don't expect them to make the price negotiation part of the equation any easier for you!).

SUPPLIER MANAGEMENT – _RATIONALIZATION, POSITIONING, AND KEY/STRATEGIC SUPPLIERS_

Buyers face much the same problems as sellers: 'so many options and so little time to choose'. For the seller those options are the customers, and the key question is: who should get my attention? For the buyer it is the suppliers, and it is much the same question.

The late 1990s was a great time for purchasing organizations in all industries to reassess their 'supply base' with a view to setting some clear priorities. It was common for them to discover that well over 80 per cent of a buyer's time was spent 'policing' numerous small suppliers whose products were far from significant in the grand scheme of things. A small fraction of their time was left for what they really wanted to do: manage their larger and more significant suppliers properly, so as to extract more value.

Three important concepts and ambitions emerged from such studies:

- supply base rationalization;
- supplier positioning;
- key/strategic supplier management.

What lies behind these ambitions is something that any prospective global seller should be deeply interested in, because they determine to a very great extent the global buyer's strategy and tactics.

Supply base rationalization

Many years ago, buyers had to ask their suppliers to give them details, monthly, of what they had sold to them, this being the best way of knowing what they had bought. Today, at the touch of a mouse button the global buyer can tell their suppliers what they have bought that very morning, and where, and for how much (and many a seller has been subjected to the embarrassing question that follows on from such knowledge: _'and why was it so much cheaper there than here?'_).

With such information to hand it is no surprise that buyers begin to wonder if they have too many suppliers for what look like very similar products and services, and so is born *supply base rationalization*.

Buyers have always tried to limit the number of suppliers that are dealt with, and for all the obvious reasons: having a list of alternatives keeps the incumbents on their toes, being on the alternative list tends to get the pencil sharpened, and I don't have the time in the day to see them all.

While in the past the choice of who was in and out might have been made for reasons that included familiarity, old loyalties, and personal likes and dislikes, increasingly they are made by reference to data, and in particular, *spend maps*.

Spend maps

A spend map lists all the suppliers for a particular product, around the globe, ranked by size. An example is shown in Figure 6.5.

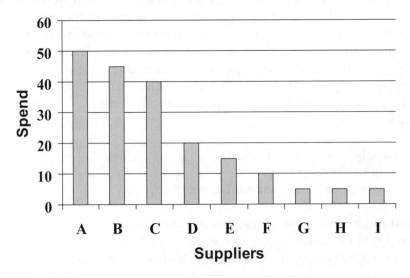

Figure 6.5 *The buyer's spend map*

Armed with such an analysis, the buyer will commence with step one of what is a long-term strategy, perhaps in the form of a three-year plan.

Year one: cut out all the small fry, aiming to end up with four global suppliers: A, B, C and D. This saves a great deal in transactional costs. Give the small fry's business to C and D, the numbers three and four, and deliberately *not* to the biggest suppliers, for two very good reasons. First, suppliers C and D, being smaller, will be hungrier for the extra business. What might have been a 5 per cent increase for supplier A may represent a 25 per cent increase for supplier D, and we can guess which supplier would give the bigger discount for their respective opportunity. Second, by building up C and D the buyer prepares their case for year two: the open tender.

Year two sees an open tender between four equal players, and the buyer will have taken great care to make sure that each player _knows_ that they are one of four equals. Each time they are met they will be reminded of their status: buyers call it _supplier conditioning_. Everyone gives it their best shot, something that might not have happened only a year ago because the big ones would have been fat and lazy and the smaller ones would have reckoned they had no chance; now everyone is in with an _equal_ chance. Let's suppose that supplier C loses and that their business is given to A, B, and D, again for substantial discounts and improvements to terms and service.

Year three is the exciting year. The global buyer does not wish to go down to two suppliers; that puts too many eggs in too few baskets, so increasing their own risk and exposure. Perhaps it is not even possible to satisfy their global requirements with just two suppliers. In any case, they have a better tactic to keep their supply base 'honest': reintroduce supplier G, one of the companies that got dropped in year one. Supplier G will of course be very keen to get back in and will offer its best price, its best terms, and its best every- thing for the opportunity (wouldn't you if you had been out of it for the last two years?). I said that this was the exciting year, and that's because of what happens next. The buyer approaches supplier A and asks: '_How is it that although we give G only a tenth of the business we give to you, their price is better, their terms are better, and their service is better? Quite frankly they smile more nicely than you do, and we're thinking of giving them some of your business… quite a lot actually…_'.

It is a game of course, and one that only the buyer wins.

The process works in cycles: rationalize, followed by reintroduc- tions, followed by more rationalization; the aim, to keep the suppliers 'honest'. And it works, and technology has meant that it can be worked ever more effectively. It used to be that the more suppliers there were, the greater would be the transactional costs, which provided a limit to how ruthlessly the buyer might go around this cycle; reintroducing suppliers for the expansion phase could be expensive. Now, by using the tools of e-purchasing, large numbers of suppliers can be approached, considered, worked with, and discarded with relatively low impact on transactional costs.

So, if it is a game, how can you avoid being the victim? The clue to this lies in the second concept to be considered: *supplier positioning*.

Supplier positioning

If buyers made decisions armed only with data on supplier size, they would make a lot of unfortunate errors. How would it be if, in the rationalization strategy described in the preceding section, they rationalized out supplier F, but supplier F was the only one in the world who could provide them with a particular service that they valued? What if supplier H had a unique capability that was now lost to them (and all the more available to their competitors as a result)? And what if suppliers A, B, C and D, as well as being big, were also dull and uncreative?

This is why the modern buyer will take care that data about size is only a part of the equation. Most large purchasing organizations will use an analytical process similar to the one shown in Figure 6.6.

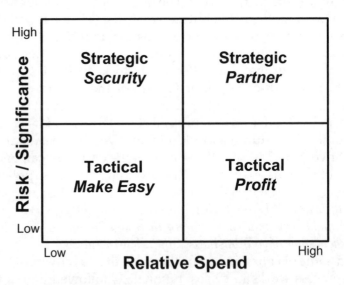

Figure 6.6 *Supplier positioning*

Some will use different words, some may arrange the axis the other way around, but the principle remains the same: an attempt to categorize suppliers in order to determine the buyer's priorities, and their management approach to those suppliers.

Suppliers are positioned based on two considerations. The horizontal placement is the simpler of the two, ranking suppliers by size. Sometimes this will be all suppliers, sometimes suppliers of a particular product type, sometime suppliers involved in a particular project or customer product. In the latter case we can see how a small supplier in the grand scheme of things might actually appear to the right of the line because they represent a relatively large part of a particular project or product.

The vertical placement is a more subjective matter, ranking suppliers by their significance. All sorts of factors may make up this judgement: geographic proximity, the number of suppliers, how long it might take to change a supplier, their use of brand names, the supplier's financial strength, the supplier's level of innovation, particular aspects that represent value, etc. Judged from the buyer's perspective, higher significance often means higher risk, hence the use of the alternative word by some. If it might take a full year to change a supplier, then the significance of that supplier is high (and positive if they perform well, but very negative if they perform badly), and so is the risk of relying on them.

The labels in the four boxes are suggestive of the buyer's expectations from those suppliers, and also their management approach.

Bottom left – tactical make easy

These are the smaller fry, and the less crucial to the business. This is precisely where the buyer used to find themselves trapped for 80 per cent of their time. Now they seek to escape by rationalizing such suppliers ruthlessly, perhaps even down to a sole supplier. Sure, sole supplier status raises the level of risk, but this was a low-risk area in the first place.

As well as rationalizing, the task of purchasing is often outsourced, or handed to a corporate buying group. There is an irony in this box with regard to global purchasing. The suppliers may be small and relatively insignificant, but it might have been here that the move towards global purchasing began, the customer motivated by a desire to remove the local buyer and the complex mass of local suppliers.

For a supplier to succeed in this box the task is clear: make it easy for the customer to do business with you, perhaps even to the extent of performing the purchasing tasks for them.

Bottom right – tactical profit

These are big players, but each is of relatively low significance. Commodities commonly sit here, or products that have a simplicity for the buyer perhaps because of their universal applicability. This is the terrain of the old-fashioned buyer with their finger on the price pulse (the pulse in question probably being the one in the seller's neck). Loyalties are as nothing compared to a 5 per cent discount and money is the watchword. Global purchasing is big business in this box, perhaps its most commonly found manifestation, where big deals will be made for big discounts.

For a supplier to succeed in this box the requirement is the same as it will be in any of the boxes: be appropriate, which in this case means having a low price, and the ability to reduce it further in return for more business.

Purchasing strategies of the 5:5:5 or the 7:7:7 kind have been common in recent times, the numbers representing the percentage reduction in price required, with the number of figures being the number of years the requirement will run. Such strategies work most effectively with suppliers positioned in this bottom right box.

Top left – strategic security

This suggests that suppliers placed here are important to the business, perhaps providing some unique product or service, perhaps having some value-adding impact on the supply chain, but because the amount of money is not high (relatively speaking) the watchword for the buyer is security.

As a private and domestic buyer, what products might you put in this box? How about toilet paper? What kind of inventory control do you have for this in your house: enough to last the day, or enough for the month? Because it is important that you should not run out, you keep plenty; that's security. And I won't be surprised if you are fairly particular about what type you use, probably loyal to a brand, and you won't risk a week of discomfort by switching to a cheaper alternative, at least not without thinking about it.

This can be a good place for a supplier, of course. They are less at risk of the rationalizer's knife, and they can probably secure a premium for their offer, but only if they behave appropriately to their positioning, which means they must never let the customer down.

Contracts tend to be long-term in this box, with carefully thought out provisions should things go wrong; customers do not wish to be left high and dry.

Suppliers in this box will be managed with some care, with the emphasis on performance and reliability rather than pricing and terms.

Top right – strategic partnership

This is where the buyer would like to spend 80 per cent of their time, and not just because they are clearly important suppliers, but because they wish to actively manage them to contribute to their business in an ever more positive way. The contribution might come in many ways; price reductions for sure, but more likely some form of added-value offer. They are not inevitably global suppliers, but if they have that capability there is a very good chance they will become so. Buyers have to make a significant investment of their time in such suppliers, and will expect a reciprocal investment from the seller.

Some conclusions for suppliers

- Behave appropriately to your positioning and you will be welcomed.
- Fail on the watchword given and you will be short-lived.
- Globality can be achieved in any of the boxes, but for very different reasons:
  - Bottom left – make it _so_ easy for the customer that they ask you to solve the problem of 'small fry complexity' worldwide (though it should be said that this is a tough one to pull off).
  - Bottom right – satisfy their need for falling prices.
  - Top left – prove your indispensability.
  - Top right – build broad and deep relationships.
- Don't make the propositions suggested in the last bullet point in any but the box that they relate to, or you will be behaving inappropriately.
- If you wish to raise your status (move vertically in the positioning matrix), start by being appropriate to your starting status, and only when the 'givens' of that status are secure should you move towards more ambitious 'differentiators'.
- Buyers have a preference for keeping suppliers to the bottom two boxes; too many high-risk suppliers will make them nervous. Ultimately, raising your status may involve going beyond the buying office (see Chapters 7 and 8).
- In markets and industries with an overabundance of suppliers, all are pressed down towards the bottom of the matrix. But is this true in the global context? Many buyers have great difficulties finding suppliers with true global capabilities, and even when they do find them, those suppliers can seem strangely unwilling to commit those capabilities (for all the fears we have discussed). Because genuinely capable and genuinely committed global suppliers are rare, it is possible to raise your status by raising your global commitment.

Key/strategic global suppliers

Are these the favoured few? Few, certainly; but favoured? It is an accolade with mixed blessings; along with the scale of business and enhanced access to the customer come responsibility and exposure. Expect to be under the spotlight, which if you are up to the challenge is of course a splendid place to be.

You might imagine that key/strategic suppliers are to be found exclusively in the top right box of the supplier-positioning matrix (Figure 6.6), that being where the buyer wishes to spend the bulk of their time. It is possible, however, to be viewed as a key/strategic supplier in other boxes, simply by providing in spades what is expected of that particular positioning (though in the bottom two boxes probably remove the word 'strategic'). In practice, however, the truly key/strategic suppliers *are* most likely to find themselves in the top right box.

How many?

The number of suppliers considered to be key/strategic is necessarily very small, and on a global level smaller yet. It is the same for buyers as it is for sellers. A key account is an investment of time and effort, and spreading that time and effort too thinly will damage the returns. A key/strategic supplier is similarly an investment of time and effort, and typically they represent less than 1 per cent of the customer's total supply base.

How are they chosen?

On what basis are they chosen? Sometimes it is simply scale (right-hand side of the supplier-positioning matrix), just as key accounts are sometimes simply the biggest, but it is a dangerous methodology. Much to be preferred is some assessment of value received (upper two boxes of the supplier-positioning matrix), and the more measurable the better.

How are they managed?

In Chapter 8 we will look at the building of *diamond teams* (see Figure 8.4), with multiple links across and between functions and locations. Our perspective there will be managing the customer, but very much the same model is used by customers managing their key/strategic global suppliers (and just as well they do because the outcome has to be a mutual team!).

Such teams require management, and usually by an individual. In the case of the supplier it is the global account manager (GAM), matched on the other side of the diamond by the global supplier manager (GSM). Just as GAMs are usually professional sellers (though the rightness of this will be discussed in Chapter 10), so GSMs tend to be professional purchasers.

If GSMs do not appear to exist then perhaps that suggests the customer has not yet developed a genuine key/strategic supplier management strategy, but be careful that their *apparent* absence is not simply because you yourself are not one of those key/strategic suppliers! If they really do not exist then this will slow down the development of genuine diamond-team relationships and it is probably in the interests of the global supplier to encourage the global buyer to develop their role into that of a genuine GSM.

PROTECTING YOUR INVESTMENT

Once you have secured the global deal, and your whole business is tied up in one order, how do you take steps to protect it? There are several options. You can police the deal through your local contacts, reporting to the global buyer where the deal is not being implemented. Some buyers will regard this as a valuable service, while others might regard it as an intrusion on their patch. Agree in advance what you both plan to do in this regard. It is, of course, expensive in local resources, but may make the difference between a secure long-term arrangement and a leaky bucket.

Only you can decide whether such things should be the result of a nod and a handshake or a written contract. It is sometimes said that the minute either party has cause to pick up the contract then the relationship is over, so what value contracts? The value is in the discipline of getting such things clear from the start, a formalized way of making sure you discuss the 'what ifs', and we have seen that in matters of global supply the 'what ifs' can be many and complex.

POSTSCRIPT – *SOME DEADLY REALISM*

A buying director, whose opinion I greatly respect, scanned this chapter and said to me: *'There is nothing that I actually disagree with here, but you do hold a rather optimistic view of our profession.'* So is all of this talk of value and partnership and key/strategic suppliers rather idealistic? What about those buyers from hell (and my buying director friend confessed to employing some of them) who only seem concerned to squeeze a lower and lower price out of you, regardless of your value, regardless of your strategic importance, and regardless of your efforts at relationship building? In the bottom right-hand box of the supplier-positioning matrix this is an entirely fair game and to be expected, but what of those buyers who haven't been on the training course, don't appear to recognize these four boxes, and treat you quite unfairly as a result? It puts me in mind of the words of a very old-fashioned buyer that I once had the pleasure of selling to, when I suggested that he might be behaving a little unfairly with me: *'Unfair?'* he said, *'I'm entirely fair, I regard all suppliers with the same equal contempt.'* (He was the same buyer who also said to me: *'Ethics? Don't give me ethics. Ethics is a county south of Suffolk...'.*)

If such behaviour is coming your way and you are convinced that you are in one of the upper two boxes, then I can only suggest that you may be failing in one of the key tasks of any global account team, the task of getting *beyond* the buyer, of penetrating the decision-making unit (DMU) that lies behind them, selling your value there, and bringing the views and influence of those so impressed to bear on the buyer. In short, failing to gang up on the purchasing department. This is, in part, the subject of the next two chapters.

7

Understanding the customer's decision-making process

Anyone who has worked in a business with more than one site will know that the process of making decisions is slowed by the simple fact of that physical separation. Sometimes the same syndrome can even be observed in businesses that occupy more than one floor of a single building. I once worked in a business with a main road cut through the middle of the site, dividing the manufacturing plant and R&D block from the administrative offices, and I reckon that road added at least a week to most decisions.

Decisions that have to be taken on a global basis, and especially those concerning global suppliers, will be affected by this syndrome, but ten times over. And it isn't only the geography that adds to the complexity but also the fact that buying on a global level is a higher-risk activity than leaving it to the local operations. Any customer that increases its dependence on suppliers by making them fewer, and more global, is raising the stakes for itself (remember the discussion around the supplier-positioning matrix (Figure 6.6) in Chapter 6). The customer will doubtless have concluded that the gains outweigh the risks, but it will be no surprise if the checks and balances on such decisions work to make the decision-making process more extended. We have long since left behind the simplicity of an all-powerful buyer determining their suppliers' fates in isolation.

The global supplier must sell to a DMU, a decision-making unit. In some cases these will be quite formal, with known members: project teams, sourcing teams, tender committees and the like. In others they may be so informal as to be unidentifiable, but they are there all the same, working by inference, by nods of the head and the raising of eyebrows.

THE TYPES OF DMU

Decision-making styles differ hugely from company to company and around the globe (see Chapter 15 for more on the cultural aspect of this) but we might identify three principal approaches:

- authoritarian
- consensus
- consultative.

The authoritarian DMU

An *authoritarian* approach is where decisions are taken at the top, with little or no consultation with those below, and once made it is expected that those decisions will be acted upon and adhered to without question. This might appear an easy one for the supplier with the need only to make contact at the top, and the rest is done for you. Maybe, but there is one drawback of this 'easy option'. This may be the way the customer wishes to make its decisions but only in the rarest of cases is such authoritarianism absolute. In a global business there will always be restive elements, and the further away from head office you get the more restive those elements become. Any global supplier that ignores such local issues is riding for a fall. The global supplier must walk a narrow path, working with the authoritarian central office, while maintaining relations with the local businesses. If they fail in the latter it may be no surprise to discover that a groundswell of opposition is building against them, and who knows, when times change and the global buyer gets promoted, might their replacement come from one of those restive and discontented elements?

The consensus DMU

A _consensus_ approach is where all interested parties to the decision must agree, or at least a majority must be in favour. This is potentially hard work for the supplier, meaning that they must aim to successfully persuade what may be a very large number of people, and in a large number of locations.

The consultative DMU

A _consultative_ approach is where a nominated individual will make the decision after consultation with the interested parties. This is possibly the hardest of all cases, and also the most common. Its challenge is that the supplier has to know so much: who is the appointed decision maker, what are their own views and motivations, who will they consult with, and what is their opinion of those people's views?

Matching the DMU type to the customer's cultural preference

Chapter 15 considers a range of 'cultural preference scales', tools that can be helpful in coming to an understanding of how your customer behaves. One of them concerns hierarchy, and whether a culture prefers the idea that those at the top are there to rule (authoritarian), or are there to consult with and empower those below them (consensus or consultative). Be aware that there will be a tension in any global organization between the organizational culture (which may be any of these three) and the national cultures that make up the business (which may also be any of these three). Those businesses that handle this tension well will not only succeed, but will help their suppliers to succeed by making their global decisions more efficiently and more effectively. Those that get bogged down by the tensions may also drag their suppliers into that same bog, something to watch out for if you intend a close relationship.

DMU ANALYSIS – THE TOOLKIT

Whichever the style and approach (but especially for the consultative DMU), the supplier will need the help of some analytical tools to make sense of the complex internal relationships, and then some action tools to plan their resultant contact strategy (see Chapter 8). In this chapter we will consider the following analytical tools:

- organigrams;
- the decision-making *snail*;
- the *stage-gate* process;
- the buyer's interest and involvement;
- the *user/specifier/economic/sponsor* analysis;
- the *receptive/dissatisfied/power* analysis;
- adopter types;
- management levels.

The aim with each of these tools is to seek for opportunities to penetrate the customer's decision-making process, in order to enhance your influence and to build your security.

Organigrams

The customer's organigrams (those charts that show business and departmental structures) can be a good starting point, even though they do tend to be pretty much out of date almost as soon as they are produced. Perhaps their biggest deficiency is not so much their inbuilt obsolescence but the fact that they do tend to show hierarchies, which is not necessarily the same thing as the decision-making process, although as we will see in Chapter 15 there are some cultures around the globe where the hierarchy and decision-making process do present a very close match.

Using the analysis

Armed with your detective's magnifying glass you might be able to make a number of broad but valuable conclusions from a study of such charts:

1. Comparing charts over a period of time, how fast is the customer's organization changing?
2. Does it show signs of movement towards a global organization, or does it remain a collection of local ones?
3. How far do the charts represent a cross-functional organization, or is it presented to you (as a supplier) as a purchasing-led operation?
4. Given your understanding of the customer's decision-making style, how 'high up' the chart must you aim to get?

The decision-making *snail*

What we really need is a way of tracing the lines of influence and control within the customer, across functions, across territories, and, where it is the case, across hierarchical lines. We need to build a picture, quite literally, of how they make their decisions, and that is the purpose of our next tool, shown in Figure 7.1: the decision-making *snail*.

Figure 7.1 *The decision-making snail*

While undoubtedly a simplification of a more complex reality, the idea of the snail can help us to understand the nature of the challenge ahead. As a supplier we are interested in all sorts of customer decisions; to buy or not to buy, to launch or not to launch, to work on project x or project y, to be local or global, to work with one supplier or multiple suppliers, and a whole lot more in similar vein. All of these decisions have to start somewhere. The snail model is an attempt to identify that starting point and then track the route of the decision-making process through the customer's organization. Each customer will be unique in this regard, so each snail is different; the example in Figure 7.1 is a much simplified example of the typical order of events in an FMCG (fast moving consumer goods) company, where it is the marketing department that tends to set the ball rolling for new products, and so for new supplier opportunities. We see that the purchasing department is some way out from the centre of this decision; not unusual, but a fact that should be raising some obvious questions in the supplier's mind: are we speaking with the right people, are we hearing about things early enough, are our competitors getting in before us, and who really is making this decision? We will return to these questions in Chapter 8 when we will revisit the snail, using it as a guide for how to 'manage the global touch points'.

Finding the centre of the snail

The task of identifying the centre is rarely easy. I have had GA managers tell me that the buyer really *was* the centre, and in such cases I ask a simple question: *'But who asked them to buy?'* This is a question that you must ask repeatedly in your search for the centre, and don't be misled, to mix my metaphors, by false summits. It can be rather like climbing a steep hill where each time you think the particular rise you are on will finish at the summit there turns out to be another just beyond, and then another...

The global snail

All of this is challenge enough with a customer based in one country, but add the global dimension and the difficulties increase exponentially. It is unlikely that you will be faced with anything as simple as one snail; there will be several overlapping snails representing global, regional and local decision-making processes, with a series of feedback loops between them. The task of the GA team is to identify the links, to avoid getting trapped in the loops, and to identify the centre. The centre is key to any hope of achieving global supplier status. Are the real decisions made at a corporate head office or locally? Is this in fact a global account or a 'plain international'?

In the FMCG example shown in Figure 7.1, let's suppose this represents the decision-making process for launching a new product; it may be standard practice for the business to launch in one country only, as a test market. The immediate impact on the global supplier will be local, but this is far from a purely local issue. Every other country will be watching with interest to see if and when they should be following suit. Where does this leave the global supplier? The task will be to work through the process as it unfolds in the test market country while keeping close to the early stages of the decision-making process (ie the centre of the snail) in all others. If a supplier can do this it may even find itself acting as a valuable conduit of information and influence. Simply hanging on the coat-tails of the purchasing people would be to underplay your opportunity for competitive advantage.

Look both ways

There are important influences to be found in the snail *after* the buyer's involvement as well as before, influences that will have great bearing on the customer's decision to repeat an order, or to seek a change. How satisfied are those receiving your products or services? What value do they perceive, and are those perceptions being fed back to the buyer?

Even with the most centrally controlled of global customers, understanding the local snails remains vital to a proper understanding of your value: the deal may be done at head office, but your value will very likely be delivered locally.

It is in working to manage such influences that we will see the role of the GA team rise to its most significant, but this takes us into the territory of Chapter 8. For now, let's turn to an understanding of how the customer might try to manage their own decision-making snail, through the *stage-gate* process.

The stage-gate process

In a complex business where many different ideas and projects may compete for attention and support, some order and method is required. Many businesses will operate a form of the stage-gate process illustrated in Figure 7.2, shown here mapping out a typical process for developing and launching new products.

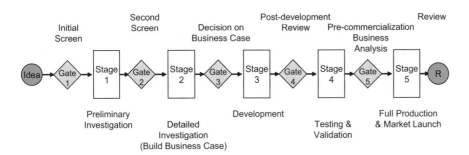

Figure 7.2   *The stage-gate process*

Decisions are put through a series of formal assessments, with a stop, go, or recycle at each stage. The benefits of such a process are to be found in the weeding out of inappropriate ideas, the provision of disciplined checks, the prevention of overload at the implementation stage, and the clarity it gives to all involved. On the debit side, should the process become bureaucratic then it will slow things down, and it can be rather heavy handed with simple ideas that should just be got on with. The secret is in how the process is managed. Done well, it will actually speed NPD (new product development) by eliminating the fluff, focusing on priorities, and avoiding unnecessary errors.

For the supplier, an appreciation of the process, and who controls it, is paramount. Ask to have it explained to you; I have never had a customer refuse such a request. Then, rather than suffering those long weeks of hearing and knowing nothing, when bosses ask what the chances are and your answer of 50:50 means, in truth, 'I have no idea', instead you can observe progress more formally, perhaps even becoming engaged in it, and so continuing to bring some influence to bear throughout the decision-making process.

The buyer's interest and involvement

The *snail* and *stage-gate* models tell us that there will be plenty of other people involved in the decision both before and after the buyer, but given that the reality for most suppliers is that they start with a buyer, we had better consider their role and involvement next.

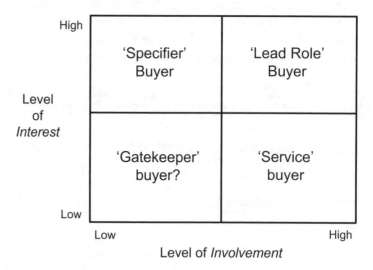

Figure 7.3 *The buyer's interest and involvement*

We see from the matrix in Figure 7.3 what we might call four buyer 'modes', each resulting from the mix of their interest and involvement in your supply proposition. By level of *involvement*, we mean things like how much time they spend on the proposition, whether they are present at every meeting or do they delegate to others, and so on. By level of *interest*, we mean something a little harder to pin down; is your proposition important, or perhaps even intriguing for them?

The lead role buyer

High levels of interest and involvement suggests that they are taking a *lead role*, which is good for you in as much as they will tend to keep you well involved in developments and possibly actively introduce you to others in the snail, before and after their position. They are probably working to engage their *own* involvement earlier in that snail, and you can take full advantage of this in building your own contacts.

The gatekeeper buyer

At the opposite extreme, the *gatekeeper* buyer has neither interest nor involvement and is a classic problem for any supplier. The only good news here is that as their interest is so low they may have fewer problems with you talking to others in the snail, but please don't take that as read! The best option for the supplier is patience and persistence, and to encourage your team to keep their eyes and ears open for opportunities to make contacts elsewhere.

The service buyer

The *service buyer* is to some extent a reluctant role: '*I have to do this, but I'm not thrilled by it…*'. They are performing the task for somebody else's benefit, and we all know the burden of that. The good supplier should be thinking about ways to make the buyer's forced involvement easier. A common problem here is that the buyer's easiest tack is to talk price, while their internal client may well be interested in something else, such as quality. Getting to those interests and having them discussed is important to your goal as the seller, but you can become an additional burden on the already pressed buyer if you are then seen to be complicating their life. If there are lots of nitty-gritty details with your proposition that require end-user evaluations, perhaps you could try suggesting that you relieve them of this kind of detail by talking direct to the end user. Whatever you do, keep things simple for a service buyer.

The specifier buyer

The *specifier buyer* is potentially good news, as they have high interest but want others to handle it, and provided they encourage you to have contact with those 'others', you may be on your way to good penetration. This is a big 'provided', of course, and if you *are* lucky in this way be sure to keep the buyer fully informed of all your activities.

Using the analysis

Use the matrix to answer the two big questions: 1) Must I go beyond this buyer? 2) And will they help me if I do?

The *'user/specifier/economic/sponsor'* analysis

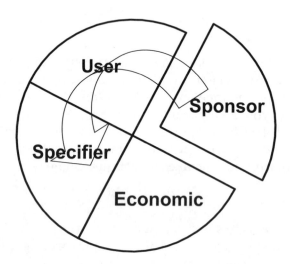

Figure 7.4   *The* 'user/specifier/economic/sponsor' *analysis*

Once beyond the buyer there will be a complex mix of reasons for the involvement by the other members of the DMU. The analysis shown in Figure 7.4 looks at four such reasons (which can, of course, overlap in any individual's own case). The purpose is to decide how to approach the different interests, and in what order. Here we are starting to put some actionable flesh inside the shell of the decision-making snail.

The economic interest

There are those whose principal interest is money – the *economic* interest. Very often they are the buyer, or perhaps someone in the finance department, maybe even the CFO (chief financial officer). At first sight these always seem the most important people; they hold the purse strings and so have the power, but you will do well to pay attention to others in the DMU before attending to them. The real difficulty of speaking with such an interest without having canvassed the others is that when they say you are too expensive you really have no idea if they are right!

The specifier interest

Specifiers will give you clarity on the requirement, and to those eager to have such detail they are an early port of call, but rather as with the economic interest there is a danger of seeing them too soon. When they tell you that it must be black, with green spots, and two metres by three metres, how do you know that they are right?

The user interest

The _users_ are those that will either physically use your product or service or will be direct beneficiaries of its solutions. These are very important people as it is most likely to be here that the value of your proposal will be most appreciated. They also provide you with the reality of the need. Seeing these people before specifiers and before those with an economic interest will help enormously when you come to tailor your proposition and calculate your reward.

The sponsor interest

It would be great if _sponsors_ always existed, but they don't, hence the slightly removed slice in Figure 7.4. These are people who for various reasons may wish you well, or even wish you to succeed, but may not want to take an active part in the decision (too junior, too senior, too remote, etc). They might coach you, or advise you on who you should be getting in front of, and why. Ask them to help you identify the users, the specifiers, and the economic interests, and so guide you around the circle. Of course, if they advise you to go to the economic interest first then you may be wise to take their advice and ignore mine – such is the power and value of a sponsor!

The perfect sponsor – local or global?

Sponsors can turn up anywhere in the customer's organization but, in a global account, is it better that they come from the central or the local part? Frankly, they are rare enough that you should welcome them wherever they come from, but it is wise to be aware of the pros and cons with regard to their 'base'. Centrally based sponsors can probably get more done for you, but they can have the disadvantage of identifying you in local eyes with 'head office'. Local sponsors, very often recently satisfied customers, ought to be splendid points of reference, but here we encounter one of the unfortunate truths of global businesses: 'head office' is not always great at listening to what they think of as 'abroad'. Yes, I know that this runs against the whole principle of being global – there should be no 'home and away' – but people remain people, and businesses retain their national home for a long time after becoming global in most respects. Take care before putting too much weight on the kind words of someone from 'the sticks', and certainly don't base next year's forecast on them.

Beware the 'not invented here' syndrome	My own business has a very successful operation in AsiaPacific and for many years we were frustrated when discovering hugely impressive examples of good practice in the Asian operations of European-based companies only to find a wall of silence when feeding those examples back to the European head office. It was as much our failing as a supplier, not recognizing the NIH (not invented here) syndrome. Nowadays we would be a good deal more subtle, but also more persistent, in our use of 'overseas' sponsors.

Using the analysis

Use this analysis to help answer three vital questions:

1. Where do these interests sit in the global structure? It will be quite usual to find the economic and specifier interests at a central 'head office' while the users are to be found more locally. This is another case for using your full global team to make sure that you cover all the bases. Sponsors can pop up anywhere, and while anywhere is good news with sponsors, note the caveats above.

2. Should we approach them in the order indicated by the arrow in Figure 7.4? In theory, yes, but is this the way that the customer makes its decisions? Do they consult with users to determine a specification and then see what it costs, or is a budget set first by the economic interest, the specifier asked to work within it, and the user expected to be happy with what they get (you will see that I have bias here...)? I stand by my arrow in most cases, but

with a customer operating with a strong 'budget culture' you may often do better to follow the decision-making route travelled by the customer.

3. Do you need to expose yourself to the economic interest? Some will argue that if you do a good enough job with the sponsor, user and specifier then you never need encounter the economic interest, leaving the weight of internal persuasion to do the job for you. It's a nice idea, and often works that way in practice, and you should certainly plan for the internal persuasion to work that way (provide people with the evidence they need); but I'm not sure that I would want to rely on it entirely in a global scenario: _'there's many a slip twixt cup and lip…'_.

The _receptive/dissatisfied/power_ analysis – managing change

The interests looked for in the previous analysis were probably related to the individual's job function; users are users because of their job, people who manage the money are likely to have an economic interest, etc. The analysis illustrated in Figure 7.5 seeks to understand some broader motivations of each individual in the DMU.

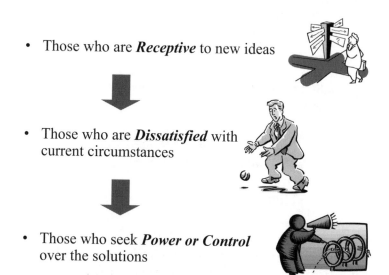

- Those who are **_Receptive_** to new ideas

- Those who are **_Dissatisfied_** with current circumstances

- Those who seek **_Power or Control_** over the solutions

Figure 7.5 _The_ receptive/dissatisfied/power _analysis_

Are they involved because they are receptive to you as a supplier and your ideas, because they are dissatisfied with how things are right now, or because they wish to have power and control over the outcome (or the consequences of the outcome)?

The essence of this tool is in how it helps us to *manage change*, by giving each contact what they want, and so helping us to advance our own position.

People who are receptive…

They like us already (or at least they like our ideas), and may want our support in getting their views a wider hearing. We should provide them with information and with evidence, helping them to develop their case, and perhaps even helping them with the presentations they need to make internally. Such people are often enthusiastic and eager to get on with it – a joy to work with, but take care that they are not innocent of the task ahead. Help them to realize that to get things changed as *they* would wish, they must help *you* to satisfy the needs of two key groups: those who are dissatisfied with current circumstances, and those who want power and control over the solutions.

The change equation

As your allies in promoting change (almost members of your team), it would be no bad thing if they were to share with you *your* understanding of the change equation.

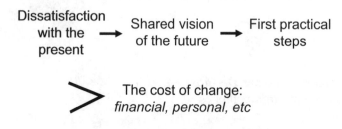

Figure 7.6 *The change equation*

People change (and make decisions that bring about change) only when the string of requirements shown in Figure 7.6 is in place. We need to be dissatisfied with what we have already, or what's the point? Next, we have to have a vision of how things *could* be (perhaps a vision provided by a supplier, but phrased in our terms). Next, we have to be able to get things moving without too much upheaval: some first practical steps. None of this will result in change if the costs involved are too great, and those costs may be measured in terms of money, they may be time, they may even be psychological, such as prestige or 'face' (hugely important in many Asian cultures, as we will see in Chapter 15).

People who are dissatisfied with current circumstances

The change equation makes clear why this group of people is so important; in fact, without them there would be no change. _'Discontent is the first necessity of progress'_, so said Thomas Edison, a realization fundamental to any persuasion task. What these people want from us is our understanding, and our help in designing a solution. I don't go as far as saying the 'whole solution' just yet, that may be too much to take on board, rather that we should aim to share a vision of how things could be, and move towards some practical first steps.

People who seek power or control over the solutions

Give them what they want. Don't expect these people to vote in favour of your solution if it takes away from them their ability to be in control. They will want some first practical steps that _they_ can instigate, and some means of reducing the cost of change (which is where any good supplier comes in).

Using the analysis

Use this analysis to help you:

1. manage change inside the customer's organization;
2. enhance your research into the customer by talking with those who are already receptive to your ideas (ask them to help you identify the decision-making hotspots: those with the dissatisfaction);
3. get in front of those with the current dissatisfaction, and so determine the nature of the desired solutions;
4. identify those people, functions or regions where your solutions make the most positive impact, either by removing dissatisfaction, providing a practical way forward, or reducing the cost of change;
5. identify the true worth of the value that you bring, and so determine the reward that you will expect;
6. make sure that those who want control over the outcome are able to exert that control.

Adopter types

Figure 7.7 takes a tool from the marketing textbook and puts it to use in identifying how decisions percolate through an organization, and how the supplier can help speed their progress.

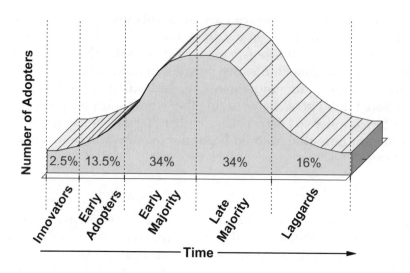

Figure 7.7 *Adopter types*
Source: From Everett Rogers, *Diffusion of Innovations* (New York: Free Press, 1962)

People take up new ideas at different rates, and sign on to decisions that involve change in much the same way. Some people like anything that's new – we might call them 'innovators'. Others might be last in line for change – we might call them 'laggards'. We can then identify a spectrum of attitudes between these two extremes. Everett Rogers even went so far as to identify the portion of any target audience that might fall into each attitude (the numbers shown in Figure 7.7).

We might expect that the impulse to take decisions involving change will start towards the left of the adopter types, while the obstacles put in the way of those decisions tend to become more resolute as we progress further right. Within an organization where the two extremes are well represented, perhaps split between a 'go-ahead' centre and a 'stick-in-the-mud' local organization (and it could easily be the other way around), we will often see acted out the sub-optimizing tragedy of 'the irresistible force met by an immovable object'. This next case illustrates a typical such outcome, here involving the supplier's own decision-making process.

A would-be global business appointed a bright and enthusiastic lady to head up a new global accounts function that was intended to work across the existing local organizations, acting as a catalyst for change. The case was put together well, so well that it would have been hard for anyone to refute it; there were some genuine global customers and some of them were being let down by the supplier's inability to recognize their global needs. Opportunities were being missed and the competition were seizing on them. Everybody could see that something had to be done.

When an 'irresistible force' meets an 'immovable object', too often the immovable force wins ...

The answer was not to be a revolution or an organizational upheaval, it was simply to appoint a few GA managers and have them supported by existing staff within the local business units, to ensure that local requirements continued to be met.

Unfortunately, despite this clearly articulated dissatisfaction and vision, and despite a relatively painless set of first steps, the decision was blocked by the heads of the regional business units, largely because they could see the erosion of their own local power that would result over time, and in truth because they felt guilty at not having done something about it themselves already. Anxious not to appear as laggards, however, the local managers suggested a compromise scheme where one global account manager would be appointed, with a brief to target _new_ global customers only, so keeping them clear of awkward entanglements with current local customers. That done, the local managers would sort out between themselves how to service the existing global customers.

... don't allow your laggards to rule the roost...

Not surprisingly, the bright and enthusiastic lady resigned and is now being even brighter and more enthusiastic working for a truly global business that doesn't allow its laggards to rule the roost.

People to the right of the spectrum (the late majority and the laggards) need more persuading, and want more proof. Those furthest right, the laggards, may not move whatever the proof, at least not until they are the only ones remaining... People to the extreme left of the spectrum, the innovators, enjoy change and newness for its own sake, while the early adopters and the early majority are open to sensible persuasion.

The bright lady from the case study did make one mistake when presenting the plan to the assembled regional managers. Being an innovator herself, she used the language of someone at that point of the spectrum and spoke of 'challenging ideas', the need to 'lead the field', to 'push the boundaries', to be 'entrepreneurial' and to 'take some chances'. Given that her audience were largely laggards, she would have been better to speak of 'measured steps', of 'checks and reviews', and to have given examples of others who had succeeded with similar ideas.

She would have also have been wise to have spoken beforehand with the one regional manager who did sit just slightly left of centre, and might have supported her, but could not do so once part of the regional manager's 'collective'.

Needless to say, she has learnt from these lessons about using the tool to pitch your message appropriately, and to pick off likely supporters and use them to build momentum. Her manager also learnt that to send an out-and-out innovator to tackle such a task, while easy at the outset, worked against the project in the long run. Innovators are not always the best people to swing opinion in a team that sits centre or centre right.

Using the analysis

Use this analysis to:

1. understand the decision-making style of the whole business; where does it sit on the spectrum, and how might you expect it to behave?
2. understand how decisions may be pushed through, depending on the number of people positioned towards the left of the spectrum;
3. understand how decisions may be held up, depending on the number of people positioned towards the centre and the right of the spectrum;
4. identify where you will have to work hardest to make an impact on the decision-making process;
5. build momentum for a decision by gaining support from left to right;
6. identify a preferred order for penetrating the DMU;
7. ensure the right messages are delivered and using the right style and language when talking to people at different points along the spectrum;
8. take care not to let your own position on the spectrum (particularly if it is far left) be used against you.

Management levels

How often have you made what you thought was good progress with a customer only to discover that the person you are in contact with was too junior to effect the decisions required? And how often have you managed to go beyond them, to their boss, without leaving behind a bitter and twisted opponent?

To spare you the pain of such disasters, our last tool will look at the roles played by different levels of management in an organization. Figure 7.8 illustrates the typical pyramid, with three broad management levels.

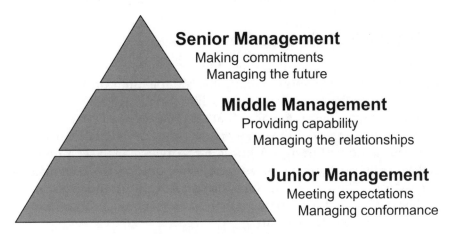

Figure 7.8 *Management levels*

It is easy to start at a junior management level, particularly if you already have some kind of activity with the customer, but very hard to build beyond that base. Junior managers are there to meet expectations and manage conformance, which usually means keeping the status quo the status quo.

Moving up to middle management may be possible, but is not actually the leap required, because the managers here are concerned with managing relationships – the existing ones – and providing capabilities, which are very likely based on decisions taken some time in the past.

It is the top level that you must aspire to if you wish to really influence change and secure commitment, but how to get there from your lowly starting position?

'*Well sir, I wouldn't start from here*' is the famed response to such questions, and in this case it probably *is* the best advice, but what if we really are stuck with the wrong starting place? The answer is, don't attempt this solo. To reach senior managers in the customer you will need to utilize senior managers in your own team, but make sure you give them something to say, and not just something to give. Senior managers should meet to discuss the future, not to haggle over this year's rebate payments.

Using the analysis

Use this analysis to:

1. note your starting point;
2. identify where you need to be;
3. identify who will be required in your team to get you there.

Using the tools in practice

There is no need to use all of these tools for every case; you will find that some are more helpful than others depending on the circumstances. They all have their use, and while you may decide one or two to be your favourites, remember that the analysis of a DMU is a team effort and that others in the GA team may pick different favourites to you. This is no bad thing, encouraging a diverse analysis, provided that you can be uniform on what follows: putting the conclusions into action. Chapter 8 will take these tools and build from their analysis a practical plan to manage the contact strategy, or as I prefer to call it, the *global touch points*.

8

Managing the global *touch points*

I particularly like the phrase *touch points* because it suggests something more than a list of contacts. *'Who sees whom'* is obviously vital to the management of any global account, but the idea of *touch points* goes so much further, including *all* of the occasions that the supplier and the customer interact; whenever, wherever and however. Not just physical meetings; this includes all of those occasions when there is interaction between systems, logistical operations, even the everyday exchanges of letters and e-mails. Such interactions are both observable and recordable, but then there are those events that we cannot log, because we are unaware of them even happening, and yet these might be the most important of them all. How about when the customer is thinking about us: good or bad; or when they are discussing us in their own team: positive or negative? Each and every one of these occasions is a *touch point* that should be the interest of any supplier, whether seen or unseen, simply because they can go well, or badly. They have been called the 'moments of truth', and it is the total experience of all of these 'moments of truth' that ultimately determines the customer's regard for the supplier, and we all know from our own experiences as customers that it only takes one bad experience for the whole relationship to be destroyed.

There are three broad categories of touch point, each with its own requirements on the global account team:

1. Those that are a part of our **influencing strategy**; mainly based on personal contacts, and requiring a dynamic approach to management. Here we will look at three tools designed to help with that management: the diamond team, the contact matrix, and the idea of GROWs.
2. Those that form our **service provision strategy**; largely concerning those regular interactions of day-to-day business, with systems and processes at work as much as people, and requiring a management approach that focuses on stability and consistency.
3. Those **invisible interactions** that happen when we are not there, and require a much more subtle form of management. Here we are less concerned with doing things and far more concerned with ensuring that the customer gets to know what *has* been done.

INFLUENCING STRATEGY

Most successful companies make good products, and most have good services, and in competitive markets there is barely a gnat's widget between their prices; so why does one company win the business and one lose it? More often than not the answer lies in who they got to speak with. If I look back at the contracts my own company has lost I can almost always explain our failure in terms of who we *didn't* get to see. Of course, on a global stage it is so much easier to miss crucial points of contact, when they might be situated thousands of miles from your own home base. Using a global team to manage those touch points is going to be vital. In Chapter 7 we used a range of analytical tools to examine the customer's decision-making process, helping us to identify the targets and determine how those targets should be approached. Here we move on to planning the subsequent contact strategy, using three *action tools* as shown in Figure 8.1.

The *diamond team* model, with its attendant contact matrix and GROWs, is a direct response to the challenge inherent in the customer's decision-making *snail*, a concept introduced in Chapter 7 (Figure 7.1) and revisited here.

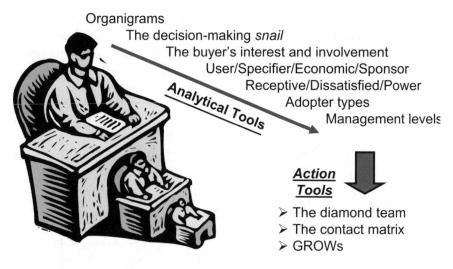

Figure 8.1 *DMU toolkit – analysis into action*

The snail revisited...

Figure 8.2 shows a typically 'shallow' penetration of the snail, resulting from the use of a traditional sales-led customer relationship strategy. I call it 'traditional' because it represents what has been the norm for most sales professionals for such a long time: a simple 1:1

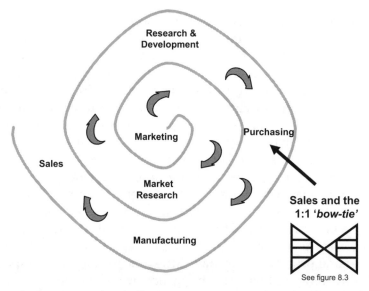

Figure 8.2 *The shallow 1:1 penetration of the 'traditional'*
bow-tie *sales approach*

relationship, like a bow tie. Figure 8.3 shows this bow-tie relationship, a model with some benefits to both parties, but plenty more downsides for a supplier contemplating GAM and a customer seeking a global supplier.

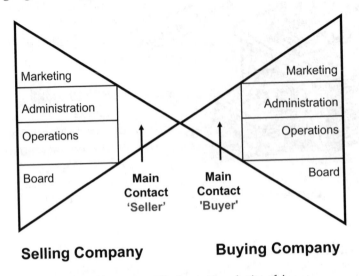

Figure 8.3 *The bow-tie relationship*
Source: From McDonald, M, Millman, AF, and Rogers, B (1996)
Key Account Management: Learning from supplier and customer perspectives, Cranfield
University School of Management, Bedford

The main benefits lie in its simplicity and its relatively high level of control; there are no surprises and both seller and buyer know what is going on. From there on the news is bad. There is no penetration of the snail, so limiting understanding and limiting the prospect for genuine added-value solutions. The relationship is perilously dependent on two individuals, and very open to competitor infiltration. Worse, the chance of managing any form of global supply through such a relationship is so small that no customer in its right mind would grant any kind of meaningful contract.

The problem for suppliers is that for much of the time it works, so removing the incentive to break away to something more ambitious, but what about when a new product, and so a new opportunity to supply, is being developed? By hearing about it so late in its development (and the buyer is rarely the first to know), the supplier might suffer several problems: they have little time to respond, competitors may be working on this already (particularly if they have managed their influencing strategy more effectively), most of the important decisions have already been taken, and the buyer only wants to talk about price. Selling value in such a circumstance is going to be difficult from the outset.

The supplier has to penetrate the snail, so much is clear, but reality presents them with several obstacles:

- The buyer doesn't want them to, and acts as a gatekeeper (sellers who get to meet other people get to learn stuff, and that reduces the buyer's negotiating power).
- The seller doesn't want to; it's 'not their job' to go looking beyond the buying office…
- The other people in the snail, and their functions and departments, may be situated in different countries (and guess what: there's no travel budget).
- Why should someone from the customer's R&D want to see a sales professional in any case?
- Does the sales professional have the know-how to speak with someone from R&D, even if they do manage to track them down?

Given this list it's maybe not so surprising that sales people get stuck where they do. The solution is for sales professionals to stop thinking that they wear their underpants on the outside and get on with using *other* members of their account team to develop these contacts beyond the buyer. Who is better to match up with the customer's R&D department: a sales professional who struggles with the language and is keen to get back to the familiar ground of the buyer's office, or a technical person who has a genuine interest in the subject?

What I am advocating is the development of a cross-functional account team, matching disciplines with disciplines, expertise with expertise, as a means of observing, learning, concluding and influencing. It all takes time and must be managed carefully for there are many genuine difficulties:

- Throwing people at the customer like mud at a wall and hoping that some of it will stick is unlikely to succeed, or bring you many thanks from the customer.
- Going beyond the buyer, without their permission, is likely to land you in very serious trouble indeed.
- Sending unsuitably briefed people in to see the customer is likely to cause more harm than good.
- Giving up too early – the *comfort zone*.

The comfort zone

It is surprisingly easy to convince yourself that you have gone far enough with your penetration of the snail when in fact there is plenty more penetrating to be done; we might call this the comfort zone syndrome. Perhaps you have managed to secure that relationship with their R&D people; it all took a lot of time and effort but now you are there things have improved a good deal: you know more, and you know it earlier. And so we come to a rest, and yet R&D is not the real decision maker, nor do they represent the full picture of the customer's needs, for their project came to them from somewhere else...

Building *diamond teams*

The penetration process requires plenty of research, a good deal of patience, a certain amount of opportunism, but most of all, teamwork.

The snail is a simplification, and it is for the team to put the flesh inside what is in fact a mere shell, but it is a useful model as a point of reference and discussion, helping us to move on to the creation of those all-important touch points, through the medium of a *diamond team*. The reason for its name will be seen clearly enough in Figure 8.4.

Figure 8.4 *The* diamond team, *or partnership* relationship
Source: From McDonald, M, Millman, AF, and Rogers, B (1996)
Key Account Management: Learning from supplier and customer perspectives,
Cranfield University School of Management, Bedford

The example shown in Figure 8.4 is just that, an example. There is no need to replicate these labels in your own team (this example represents a typical B2B relationship in a manufacturing industry), or to match this number of contacts. I have known global diamond teams of three people, and global diamond teams of one hundred plus; it all depends.

Such 'partnership' teams will not spring out of nowhere, and nor should they 'spring' in any case. They will build over time, and with care, for if they 'spring', or worse, 'explode' on to the customer they can become very damaging things indeed.

The pitfalls…

Take another look at Figure 8.4 and wonder for a moment about all the disasters waiting to happen in a badly formed and badly managed diamond team.

First, people will not know what is expected of them and will doubtless do many foolish things. *Second*, customers are very good at taking advantage of suppliers who send coachloads of 'innocents' to see them; they often like the resultant supplier foolishness. *Third*, the more senior the people you allow to 'explode' on to the customer, the more costly the foolishness can be. *Fourth*, once the customer has encouraged the innocents to do all the foolish things they can think of, they will soon tire of the game and become annoyed by the mass of people crawling over and around their business, and before you know it, you're banned. *Fifth*, if you don't get banned, you may live to wish you had been. Putting unmanaged specialists in front of the customer is a sure-fire way of generating unnecessary work. New projects pop up aiming to cure diseases that never existed and it can get to be rather like the Chinese Cultural Revolution when a thousand flowers bloomed: all very expensive.

The benefits… (some)

The benefits are good, very good, but they will take a while coming. Always remember that this is an investment.

First, you penetrate the customer's decision-making snail and so learn more about their true needs and enhance your ability to influence their decisions. *Second*, you increase your security. The diamond relationship is like two strips of Velcro: almost impossible to be pulled apart in one go, it needs unpicking over time. *Third*, you become a part of the customer's operations, taking on tasks that give you lock-in (see service provision strategy below). *Fourth*, you increase your chance of being awarded key/strategic global supplier status. *Fifth*, the relationship develops into a partnership based on trust and mutual ambition. *Sixth*, information is shared, access to people is facilitated, systems are integrated, pricing is stable, profitability improves... do you need any more?

Managing the diamond team

Managed well, diamond teams will become the very heart of your GAM strategy, bringing you the benefits while avoiding the pitfalls, but *only* if managed well. One of the main requirements is that the members of such teams actually speak with each other, and act as a team. If all you produce is a series of bow-ties, each one an island to itself, as shown in Figure 8.5, then you may well have progressed *backwards* from what at least was the simplicity and control of the single bow-tie seen in Figure 8.3.

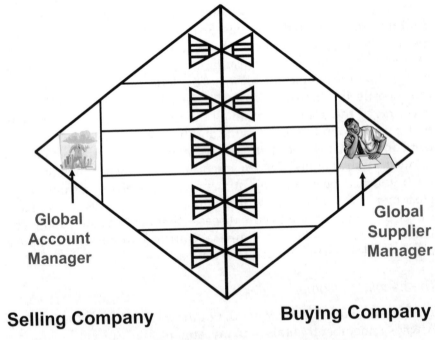

Global Account Manager

Global Supplier Manager

Selling Company

Buying Company

Figure 8.5 *The 'multiple bow-tie' diamond – the kind to be avoided*

Many *apparent* global account teams are in fact little more than this, a loose confederation of individuals with disparate ambitions, happy to pull in opposing directions if it suits their local goals. The supplier may think they have a diamond relationship, but they don't, and this is a very dangerous situation, courting all the disasters while their head is in the clouds of complacency. Perhaps the only good news is that the customer, out of sheer frustration, will start to point out your lack of form; it is at such times that they issue one of their more confusing requests: _'We just want one point of contact.'_ Rarely do they mean that they want to return to the single bow-tie, rather they mean that they want to be done with the randomness and chaos of the multiple bow-ties, and cannot one person pull it all together?

While dangerous in the wrong hands, the diamond team is at the same time an absolutely vital requirement of any successful GAM strategy. It is time to show how it can be made to work seamlessly and, from the customer's perspective, effortlessly, through the use of two very simple management tools. These will prevent your diamond teams from either 'exploding' on the customer or becoming undisciplined ragbags. The two tools are the _contact matrix_ and GROWs.

The contact matrix

	Account Manager	Your team member	Your team member	Your team member	Your team member	Your team member
Buying Director	XXX					
Their team member	XX					XX
Their team member					X	
Their team member	X			XXX		X
Their team member			XXX			
Their team member	X					XXX

(overlaid note box:)
Ken Reilly – John Smith
G – Secure global contract for …
R – Present solution …
O – Brief regional teams …
W – 3 July, London

Figure 8.6   _The contact matrix_

The contact matrix, shown in Figure 8.6, is a simple grid that aims to contain in one place the detail of _who is responsible for seeing whom_. This is information that almost certainly exists in other places – a CRM (customer relationship management) system, visit reports, and a great deal in various people's heads – but with the contact matrix anyone can see at a glance the whole picture, and that is its great value. It aims to avoid the confusions inherent in multiple contacts, and to guard against any particular customer contact being missed (often because everyone thought that somebody else was handling that one). It will guide people to whom they should speak with in their own team should they need information or advice. It is a convenient tool for both long-term influencing strategies and the shorter-term 'campaigns' such as new product launches where it easily maps out the order in which customer meetings should be scheduled. Overall, its aim is to bring order to what is undoubtedly a complex picture.

This is one of the most important of all the tools of GAM, and it should be reviewed regularly, and certainly every time that the GA team meets. Ask: what has changed, who has left, who has arrived, who needs particular attention, and who is the right person to give it?

GROWs

The contact matrix shows a named person in the GA team as being responsible for matching up with their opposite number(s) in the customer. The GROW adds to this the detail of what it is that they will be doing as a result of that contact.

GROW is an acronym:

G – Goal
R – Role
O – Obligation
W – Work plan

Every person that is part of a GA team should have a GROW. Why are they in the team and why do they have this particular contact (Goal)? What are they meant to do with that contact (Role)? What duty do they have to other members of the team, or to the customer, and are there any things that they must or must not do (Obligation)? What is their schedule of activities (Work plan)? Through this simple mechanism a GA manager can coordinate complex teams, across the globe.

The obligation part of a GROW is very important, especially if we remember that few (if any) of the team members will work for the GA manager, or respond to them in any formal management sense, and will have their own job with its own objectives to think about. Without such a discipline as this they might not feel under any particular obligation to do anything at all.

If you are the GA manager, get your team members to write their GROWs and send them to you. It is usually better that team members should do this for themselves rather than you issuing them with instructions. For one thing, they often know what they can contribute better than you do, and for another, it is a more constructive way of engaging their support and motivation. It should be noted, however, that there are some important cultural differences around the world in this respect, some cultures preferring 'the boss' to give them clear instructions, as discussed in Chapter 15, and this should certainly be taken into account.

If you use an Excel spreadsheet for the contact matrix it is easy to use the 'comment' facility as a means of adding the GROWs, as shown in Figure 8.6.

As with the contact matrix, this is something for regular review, and certainly at every meeting of the team.

The 'core' and the 'surround team'

On occasions, and ones worth celebrating, a team member will be able to say that they have achieved their goal. So what next, a new goal? For sure, but sometimes there will not be a new goal; the task is done, the project complete, and so that member of the team can withdraw from the active team until such time as a new goal does arise. This is important; GA teams must not become over large, and must not be composed of inactive people – that is a fast way to bring them to a dead stop.

You will normally be able to identify a relatively small number of team members who make up what we will call the *core team*. Who these are will depend on circumstances but they are usually the ones with the most permanent involvement or the most important contributions. The core team should aim to meet as often as it can, and should stay in close contact at all times. Beyond the core there will be a number of people whose involvement is occasional, and these we will call members of the *surround team*. To involve them in every meeting would become laborious and to keep them copied on every activity would be a burden.

From bow-ties to diamonds

Figure 8.3 showed the typical 1:1 relationship that we have to escape in order to achieve proper GAM, but how do we move from these bow-tie relationships towards fully formed diamonds? In most cases it will have far more to do with evolution than revolution; we have already seen the kind of difficulties that poorly managed or reckless leaps towards diamond relationships can cause.

There are five *critical success factors* that must be assured for the relationship to develop successfully towards the diamond, or partnership model:

1. management tools – the *contact matrix* and GROWs;
2. the customer's motivation – *value received*;
3. the possibility of mutual intent and trust – *strategic alignment*;
4. coaching skills;
5. avoiding workload overload.

We have already looked at the first of these, so let's move on to the second.

The customer's motivation – value received

The supplier already has a motivation to move beyond the bow-tie relationship, whether it be the desire for better information, greater security, improved influence, or the ability to better demonstrate their value. We might call this their strategic intent. Figure 8.7 illustrates the equal need for a customer motivation and strategic intent.

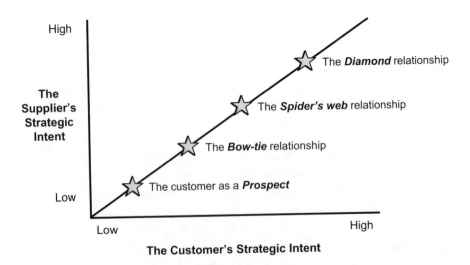

Figure 8.7 *The relationship development model*
Source: Adapted from McDonald, M, Millman, AF, and Rogers, B (1996)
Key Account Management: Learning from supplier and customer perspectives,
Cranfield University School of Management, Bedford

A supplier cannot impose a diamond team on a customer that only wants a bow-tie relationship. To attempt to do so will only lead to frustration and failure at best, and a mightily irritated customer at worst. Moving from bow-tie to diamond requires the same amount of change in the customer's attitude as was required to move them from a prospect to a customer. The buyer will perhaps be very comfortable with the status quo of the bow-tie; it usually gives them power, and the supplier will need to have much patience as they try to show the benefits of being allowed greater access. The customer's strategic intent will develop only if they can be convinced that they will receive something of value by expanding the touch points: no value, no expansion.

Often it can be problems that give you the first opportunities. The customer has a problem and to solve it you must engage the help of a team member, working alongside someone in the customer. The relationship advances from the bow-tie to the one shown in Figure 8.8.

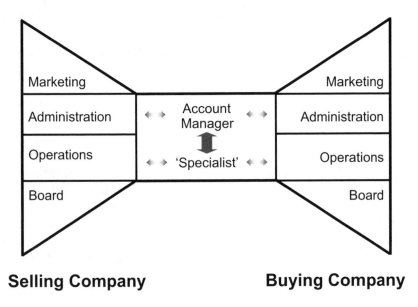

Selling Company   **Buying Company**

Figure 8.8   *Escaping the bow-tie*

Once the problem is solved, seek to continue with the new relationship gained; retain your team member, whether they be in the core or the surround team. Continue to look for opportunities to develop additional contacts, whether it be solving problems or bringing new value, but learn to be patient; forcing the pace will damage the customer's perception of you and set you back more steps than you move forward.

Mutual intent and trust – strategic alignment

For the relationship to continue to build and for greater access to be granted, supplier and customer will need to move closer to each other in terms of their ambitions. Long-term strategy will start to be shared (or at least discussed) and you will start to talk about aligning processes and activities. Trust will become a significant factor. Customers will happily do business with suppliers they do not trust, provided those suppliers are of no great significance, and provided that the relationship can be managed at arm's length. For a customer to allow a supplier the kind of access provided in the diamond / partnership model they would need to have a high degree of trust in that supplier. Much the same applies in the other direction; no supplier will be willing to put in the investment of time required to build such a relationship if they have any serious doubt about the customer's intentions.

Trust and expanding touch points must develop hand in hand, but here there is something of a dilemma: the greater the number of contacts, the greater the chance of doing something that lets the customer down, and so damages trust. I have heard at least one of my customers say that the beauty of the bow-tie relationship with a customer is that you can only offend them once. I can only hope they were joking, and can only encourage you to work hard to avoid the expansion of contacts becoming a problem in this way. The contact matrix and GROW tools are undoubtedly of great importance in this regard.

A good indication that alignment is developing, or at least that the customer has a serious strategic intention with regard to your position as a global supplier, will be the existence of a *global supplier manager* (GSM). If you look back at Figure 8.4 you will see that the global account manager is mirrored by a global supplier manager coordinating the customer's team on the other side of the diamond. The absence of such a person and role is one of the more serious hold-ups that you can face on your journey from bow-tie to diamond, for they play as important a role as the GA manager in forging proper and effective links between the two global teams. Who might they be? Well, just as a GA manager doesn't have to be a sales professional (see Chapter 10 for more on this discussion), so a GS manager doesn't have to be a buyer. And what if they don't exist? We might venture at some possible conclusions from this:

1. You are not considered an important enough supplier.

2. The customer is not truly global, at least not with regard to its suppliers. Perhaps they are a 'would-be global' (as defined in Chapter 1), and while they might have the intention to work with global suppliers they have not yet developed the appropriate infrastructure within their own purchasing organization to ensure a global capability.
3. They just don't do it that way.

The first and second of these you might be able to do something about (improving your proposal; encouraging your main contact to take on something of the task of a GSM), but if it is the third, then you had best just try to do it their way… or you could always give them a copy of this book…

Coaching

The contact matrix and the GROW will help you to manage a diamond team; the existence of a customer motivation and an increasing alignment will encourage the movement towards a diamond team; but none of this will actually make it happen. The only thing that will do that, the vital spark as it were, is the people. For all the systems and all the processes that can be applied to GAM, it remains in the end an intensely people-driven activity. The GA manager has a significant role to play in developing the individual capabilities of their GA team, through training and coaching (indeed it should be part of their 'O' for obligation to the team). One-to-one coaching is of particular importance (and should be part of their 'R' for role). More will be said about this in Chapter 10 when we will be looking at the capabilities and requirements of a good global account manager.

Avoiding workload overload

In time the relationship may well develop into something approximating that shown in Figure 8.9.

While this is progress on the bow-tie relationship, it is not a stage at which you should wish to linger for too long. Contacts are beginning to form, but so much of the communication has to flow through the GA manager (for purposes of permission and control) that there is a real danger of a workload overload. This is also almost certainly the most expensive stage in the development of the relationship; the people costs are rising fast but it is doubtful that you will have yet seen much return for your investment. It is vital that you progress through this stage and on to true diamond teams.

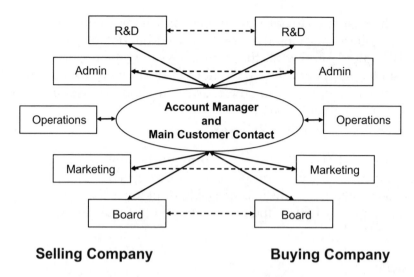

Selling Company   **Buying Company**

Figure 8.9   *'Workload overload' – the* spider's web *relationship*

Arriving at the true diamond team...

And how do you know when you have finally arrived at a true diamond team? (Not exactly a state of nirvana, but the closest you're going to get in GAM, I'm afraid.)

Here is a checklist, and one that you might just recognize:

- When everyone in the team knows clearly their purpose and *goal*; as a team member, and with the customer.
- When everyone in the team knows clearly what *role* they have to play.
- When everyone in the team understands the *obligations* that they have to the customer and to the rest of the team.
- When everyone in the team has a clear *work plan*.
- *And when you can say as much for the members of the customer's team.*

We are back with GROWs, of course, and the last point in the checklist points towards a worthy ambition: that your customer should think the same way in managing their own team. In a true partnership of genuinely mutual intentions you would expect this to be so, but I suggest that you don't hold your breath on this one; it happens in practice only very rarely.

From suspicion and doubt to confidence and clarity

GROWs work as the motive force of an important virtuous circle, and it is why the acronym GROW is in fact such an appropriate one. Let's start by recognizing the truth about why the bow-tie stage can maintain for such a long time:

1. Many a sales professional does not trust the capabilities of their colleagues enough to want to involve them directly with their customer (and sometimes they are right to be cautious).
2. Many a potential member of a GA team (particularly those from functions unused to customer contact) is afraid of the idea of direct customer contact, thinking 'selling' to be some form of black art (a view too often promulgated by the sales professionals themselves).

These may not be comfortable thoughts, but I urge you not to dismiss them too lightly, for this is where many GA teams start: mutual suspicion. Then we develop the concept of GROWs, a simple discipline that helps to give team members an objective clarity about what is expected of them, and so a boost to their confidence. The discipline also gives the GA manager the confidence they require in the team, even though at the early stages it may still be a grudging: *'at least it's written down what they have to do'.*

Out of clarity and confidence grows true capability, and so the GROWs are rewritten, and rewritten again, now with increasing ambition and precision. The GA manager's trust in their team continues to grow as they see its commitment and capability increase, and so they allow it greater freedom. Once the GA manager can trust the whole team to do the right thing without permanent supervision, then they might be getting close to a true diamond team.

Global diamond teams

Diamond teams on a global basis will clearly be more complex than the model shown in Figure 8.4, rather as the customer's decision-making snail grows more complex in a global scenario.

Figure 8.10 shows a possible global diamond team, but can I stress that the most important words on this figure are: *'depending, of course, entirely on the global structure of the customer'*. This is one of those cases where any kind of template for a team structure will be pretty much next to useless. It really does depend on the customer, and as they will probably have an ever-changing structure (and who doesn't these days?) it will be wise not to write yours in stone.

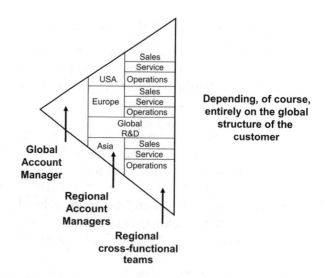

Figure 8.10 *A possible global diamond team*

The example illustrates a regional structure, with each regional account manager having a cross-functional team, but with one function, R&D, interacting with the customer on a global basis.

There are sales professionals in the regional teams, as in this case the customer determines its suppliers and purchasing standards centrally, but still operates through regional buyers.

Meetings

How often should the global account team meet? There can be no absolute answer to this, but plenty of advice:

- Define a core team (see above) and aim for that to meet to some regular schedule.
- The actual regularity can only depend on circumstances, but meetings will probably need to be more frequent at the earlier stages of forming the diamond team – mature diamond teams can meet less frequently.
- Don't meet just for the sake of meeting.
- When it does meet, have a clear agenda, with three 'must haves': review the contact matrix, review the GROWs, review the global account plan (see Chapter 14).
- When it does meet, aim to have some social side to the gathering, particularly useful in the pursuit of harnessing your cultural diversity (see Chapter 15).

- Aim for the core team to meet _with the customer_ to some regular schedule (quarterly?).
- In between meetings keep contact across the core team through all possible media.
- An annual meeting of the full core and surround team is desirable.

All of this will cost money, and there should be a budget held by the GA manager. Very mature teams may manage to meet 'remotely', by videoconference for instance, but with teams in the formative stages physical meetings are very important. It should not need saying, but trying to develop a GAM strategy and capability while also trying to cut travel budgets is an ambition unlikely to work out too well.

A reminder… look outwards, not inwards

With the significant effort involved in building, managing and coaching these global diamond teams it is easy for all of this to become something of an internal fascination: who _must_ I have on my team, who _can_ I get, and how can I get them? Let's just close this section by reminding ourselves of the purpose of such teams and so return our focus to a thoroughly customer-orientated one. They exist to enhance our knowledge and understanding of the customer (see Chapters 5 and 6), to exert influence, and to provide service. In order to do any of this effectively the form of such teams must reflect the form of the customer's organization and operations. With regard to their purpose as a means of persuasion and influencing, it is the analysis of the customer's decision-making process (see Chapter 7) that should be our guide in all cases, not the machinations of internal politics.

Global cross-business touch points

To add one last twist of complexity, how about managing the touch points in the case we have been discussing in Chapters 2 and 4: the supplier to the food, household, toiletries and cosmetics industries that is seeking to develop a cross-business GAM strategy with a particular customer. So far in this case we have considered the challenge of the different moneymaking logics across the business units; here we will consider how in a multiple business unit case the challenge of managing the global touch points can become a question of _value preservation_.

Different offers call for different touch points ...

There are five business units selling to the customer, and their offers are so different that the principal contacts at the customer, from the point of view of the influencing strategy, are equally diverse:

- Food ingredients = Buyer (and manufacturing)
- Food additives = Buyer and SHE/Regulatory
- Food flavours   = R&D and Manufacturing (and buyer)
- Fragrances   = R&D and Marketing (and buyer)
- Fine fragrances = Perfumers and Marketing

The DMUs are in fact quite separate and distinct for each business, and yet the customer is trying to draw them together through a global buyer. Something very important is at risk here; the diversity of the supplier's offers and the diversity of the customer's DMUs give the supplier security, and it gives them a chance to develop distinct value propositions. Might the global arrangement bring the relationships down to the lowest common denominator, the buyer? This would be no great change for the food ingredients people, but the fine fragrance account manager actually takes pride in not being able to recall the last time they had to visit the buyer.

... don't get dragged down to the lowest common denominator

Managing the DMUs as discrete entities while meeting the customer's requirement for a common touch point will be a delicate task, and will most certainly need careful coordination across the team. The need for very specific GROWs, with a good focus on the 'O' for obligation, will be vital. This is not a situation where the supplier can afford to have loose cannons in the team.

(To see how the case develops further, see Chapters 11 and 12.)

SERVICE PROVISION STRATEGY

The GA team's influencing strategy will necessarily be a dynamic one. Ever changing to match the circumstances, people will come and go as the strategy unfolds into practical application, and often in an entirely unpredictable fashion.

The service provision strategy must take a very different form. Rather than ever changing it will need to be stable. People cannot be seen to 'come and go' in the provision of service; long-term consistency is prized almost more than anything in this arena. And above all else, it must be entirely predictable.

Providing excellent service is about attending to the detail, and the touch points that matter in this regard will be the nitty-gritty of systems and processes as much as of people. Indeed, the customer's perception of excellent service is that they have no need to meet with people and are almost unaware of it happening; it's just what *does* happen.

I have mentioned it already, but one of my own client's definitions of GAM is very appropriate in this matter: '*GAM is what goes on between the supplier and the customer when the sales people are not there.*'

While the customer may not be aware of the people behind the service provision, their membership of the GA team is vital, and their understanding of the imperatives of service provision even more so. The GROW tool described in the section on the influencing strategy is very relevant here, and everyone responsible for providing service to the customer should have a fully developed GROW.

Where the people come into the frame is when something goes wrong. The first priority is to put things right, and once that is done the customer wants to be assured that the problem will not recur. Only people talking to people can assure them of that. The supplier has to demonstrate that they have learnt from the experience, and have taken appropriate actions to prevent its recurrence; such is continual improvement. While no customer is ever pleased at things going wrong, the supplier that responds in this way will win not only the customer's thanks but also their trust; two invaluable results of well-managed touch points.

Lock-in

The effect of the diamond relationship on the provision of service is that a number of links become established, each providing another anchor for the long-term security of the business relationship. It is very likely that the supplier will take on tasks previously performed by the customer for themselves; an outsourcing activity that builds 'lock-in'. 'Lock-in' is the idea that the customer finds it harder and harder over time even to think of dropping a particular supplier, on account of all the things done for them by that supplier. The supplier becomes an integral part of the customer's operational machinery, and to remove them would be like having to close down a department, or make people redundant. Such a supplier will have elevated their position upwards in the supplier-positioning matrix discussed in Chapter 6 (Figure 6.6).

Great strength though it is, a certain amount of care is required with this strategy. There are two lurking problems. First, the customer might grow nervous at their ever-greater dependency on the supplier and actively seek to find a way out, courting alternatives and seeking ways to sever the bonds that bind. Second, over time the number of service activities carried out by the supplier can grow large, and in a global account *very* large. Many of them may also become less significant for the customer, perhaps even no longer required, but because it is the supplier that is providing them, and not their own people, the customer accepts their continuation without complaint. The result is an expensive list of services that will drain the supplier's resources and depress their profitability. If you aim to practise lock-in, get into the habit of regularly checking the significance and cost of the services provided, and be prepared to withdraw them when they become obsolete.

THE INVISIBLE INTERACTIONS

The customer rarely tells you what they *really* think of you, and more is the pity. Their real thoughts are kept private, or shared around the staff canteen table: that's *their* canteen, not yours. Customer satisfaction surveys are worthy attempts to get to the truth, and should be encouraged, but they often obscure as much as they uncover. The real problem with such surveys is in the interpretation, and here we are all subject to the human weakness of wishful thinking. To borrow a phrase from David Ogilvy (guru of advertising and market research), too often the results of such surveys are used rather as a drunk uses a lamppost, for support rather than illumination.

We are dealing here with perceptions rather than facts. However good your product or your service may be, if the customer thinks it is poor then it is poor. This is a hard truth to accept for many people, particularly those devoted professionals who work hard to create excellent products and excellent service, but it is so.

One of the ironies of perceptions is that sometimes the more you do as a supplier the less the customer thinks of you, particularly if you spend a lot of time giving them what we might call *unwanted Christmas presents*. Figure 8.11 illustrates the syndrome.

Here are four true statements:

1. You are good at some things.
2. You are poor at some things.
3. The customer wants some of the things that you do.
4. The customer doesn't care about some of the things that you do.

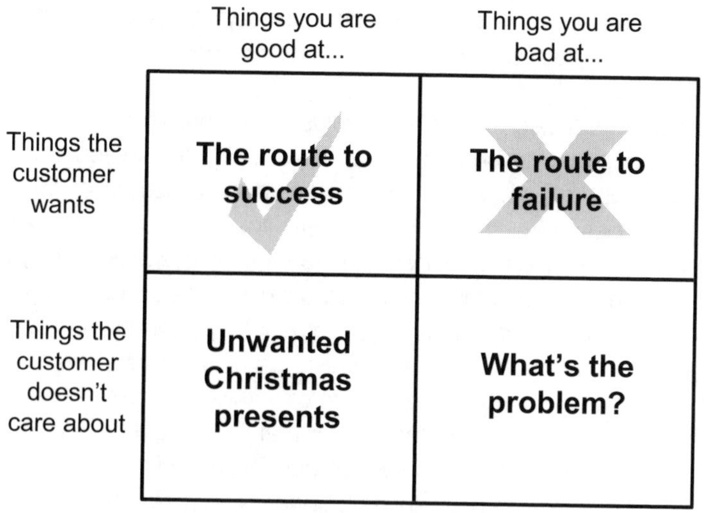

	Things you are good at...	Things you are bad at...
Things the customer wants	**The route to success**	**The route to failure**
Things the customer doesn't care about	**Unwanted Christmas presents**	**What's the problem?**

Figure 8.11 _Unwanted Christmas presents_

The way to succeed in business is to be good at things the customer wants. The way to go out of business fast is to be poor at the things they want. The way to increase your costs unnecessarily and damage the customer's perceptions of you is to be good at, and so keep forcing on them, things that they don't care about. What do _you_ think of people who give you unwanted Christmas presents? _'They don't know me, they don't care, they're just going through the motions.'_ Customers add one to the list: _'no wonder they are so expensive'_. If you indulge in such presents, drop them fast.

The task for the GA team is to manage the customer perceptions as well as to argue the facts, and to be sure that when the customer is discussing them (perhaps around that canteen table) the comments are good, not bad.

Many years ago I worked in a business that was one of the first suppliers to the retail trade to measure its own delivery performance, OTIF (on time and in full), and long before customers started to measure it for themselves. We were horrified to find that it was as poor as 35 per cent, and decided to do something about it. What we did was an act of genius, though I say it myself. In the space of two years we improved from 35 to 95 per cent, and all this while almost doubling our number of SKUs (stock-keeping units). With some pride we went to our customers to announce the good news. It was the first time that we had ever raised the issue with them and we expected nothing but unadulterated

It's not enough to be clever ...

praise. Of course, we were surprised and deflated when their response was: *'Well we should expect so too, and while you are here, why isn't it 100 per cent?'*

What had indeed been an act of genius within our own operations was nothing short of a disaster when it came to managing the customer's perceptions of those operations. What should have been a source of competitive advantage fast became a stick to beat us with (instructions were sent to store managers to start measuring our performance with an eye to achieving 100 per cent OTIF; something which anyone with any experience of such things knows to be a near impossibility, or else a hugely expensive possibility; and something that engendered a critical attitude towards us at store level (rather than a congratulatory one), and all because of the way it was handled).

... find a way for the customer to know just *how* clever ...

With bucket loads of hindsight it is clear that we should have approached the customer at the outset with news of our 35 per cent measure, and our plans to improve. At each significant step towards our target of 95 per cent we would then update the customer: *'great news, it's 50 per cent... a cause for celebration, it's 75 per cent'*, and so on. Had we done something like that, and made sure that all the people who needed to know got to hear the good news, then perhaps those invisible interactions at store level would have been a good deal more complimentary.

9

Getting the board *on board*

I have grown a lot braver in recent years. There was a time when if a customer asked me to train their sales team in GAM (global account management), I just said yes. Now that I am braver (and wiser) I have a rule, and that is that I cannot help the client unless they allow me first to speak with the board, or the management team. Unless I am certain that GAM is fully understood at this level, and supported, and that it will *continue* to be supported through thick and thin, there is little point running training workshops for sales teams. I know what is going to happen, I can even predict what will be said at around 14:30 on the first day of such a workshop: '<u>We</u> understand what you're saying, and <u>we</u> want to do it, but do <u>them</u> upstairs understand, and will <u>they</u> let us; really let us that is?' I like to be able to answer 'yes', and on all counts.

Senior management has three clear roles in making GAM happen:

1. as champions of the concept and enablers of the processes and capabilities;
2. as leaders: empowering and coaching;
3. as participants.

CHAMPIONS AND ENABLERS

Champions

There are so many minefields waiting in the path of the GA teams that without a very clear message from senior management that *'this is going to happen'*, progress will grind to a halt for fear of losing a leg. The board must give clear direction, and their blessing. An idea to be discussed in Chapter 11, that board members might act as mentors for global account managers and their teams (some have referred to them as fairy godmothers), is a great way of demonstrating this act of 'blessing' as fact.

Enablers

Organization

If there is need for any organizational change (see Chapter 11) then clearly this will need management from the top. A sure-fire killer of GAM is the internecine warfare that can go on in organizations that have been left to argue it out among themselves. And where the solutions don't lie entirely in organizational structures, but involve what in Chapter 11 we will call a 'persuasive process', it will be the task of the senior management team to navigate the subtleties of such a course. Whether through organizational change or persuasion, it is their responsibility to ensure that GAM becomes a cross-business, cross-functional, and cross-regional activity.

Systems

If there is a need for new systems (see Chapter 13) then the investment will have to be sanctioned at the top. Uppermost among such systems should be a means to measure account profitability, a means to manage the data and knowledge that will build and flow around the global accounts, and a means to manage the global communications. The responsibility of senior management does not stop with a signature on an investment approval form; they must also ensure that the right attitudes and disciplines are instilled in those who will use these new systems – a tougher task, and too often a sadly neglected one.

Processes

There will be key processes to be established, and some of them mandatory. Uppermost among such processes will very likely be the global account *selection process* (see below), the global account *performance measurement process* (see Chapter 12), and the global account *planning process* (see Chapter 14).

Tools and skills

This book covers a wide range of tools, both analytical and action focused, and it will be the task of a senior management team to select from these those most appropriate to their own circumstances, and to present these to the whole business as a *GAM toolbox*.

There will be the need to develop and enhance a wide range of skills, whether through recruitment, formal training, or coaching. As well as the particular skills of GAM, as described throughout this book, experience shows the following skills to be of particular importance:

- team leadership and team working;
- financial awareness;
- strategic influencing;
- problem solving and creative thinking.

Identifying and selecting the global accounts

This is a decision too important to be left to the sales professionals alone, and one too complex to hope that the regions or local businesses will come to a consensus unaided. It can only be done at the top, though the information required may well have to be fed upwards from the bottom.

Why not leave it to the sales professionals? Surely they know the customers better than the board? Perhaps, but asking sales professionals to classify their customers – whether as A, B and C, strategic or key, or local or global – has never been an entirely fair or reliable way to go about the task. Imagine that a business was heading towards a clear key account management strategy, and that non-key customers would be passed to distributors, then what sales professional wouldn't want to argue that their top customer was a key account? We should remember that turkeys rarely vote for Christmas. But within global businesses, some even odder things can happen...

Don't expect the regions to be open, practical, or even logical if asked to classify accounts

A global petroleum company established a customer classification system that graded customers as Platinum, Diamond, Gold and Silver. Silver accounts would be entirely local affairs, while Platinum would be entirely global affairs, and the Diamond and Gold accounts occupied the grey area between. The regional sales directors were asked to grade their customers and submit the resultant classifications to head office.

One region's return went back without a single Platinum account on the list. When the regional business director expressed surprise at their sales director's grading, they quickly found themselves in complete agreement with the answer provided: *'You see, boss, if we tell them we've got a Platinum account every last bugger from head office will want to get their nose in the trough.'*

The global account selection process

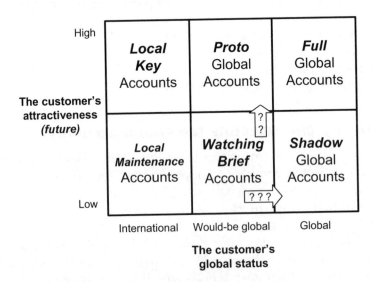

Figure 9.1 *Classifying and selecting global accounts*

You will recognize Figure 9.1 as a modified version of one seen before: Figure 1.2 in Chapter 1. There, we were trying to understand the balance between our global capability and a customer's global reality. Here, we are seeking to identify with which customers to apply the concepts of GAM.

The horizontal axis repeats our classification of customers across a spectrum from international, through 'would-be global', to global (purely locally based customers are ignored, for obvious reasons).

The vertical axis attempts to grade the customers by their importance to us, or their attractiveness. I have a preference for the word attractiveness, simply because 'importance' tends to focus minds on the here and now: _'Where would we be without Acme Rubber?'_ whereas 'attractiveness' tends to help us think about the future: _'Where might Acme Rubber take us?'_, and it is the future that matters in this selection process.

Now come the steps in the selection process:

1. Establish a small selection team of senior managers charged with the responsibility of managing the process.
2. Define what is meant by 'international', 'would-be global', and 'global'. Don't accept textbook definitions but aim for ones that are relevant in your own and your customer's markets. To get you started (and no more than that) here are the questions we asked in Chapter 1:

    *   Do they have needs that are consistent across different countries, and that require globally consistent solutions, measured by globally consistent standards?
    *   Do they have a global structure at some relevant operational level? For most suppliers this will mean that the customer has a global procurement operation, but depending on the nature of your offer, a global structure in the customer's R&D, manufacturing, operations, finance, or sales & marketing organization (or any other for that matter) might be equally relevant.
    *   Do they have, and demonstrate, the ability to implement global decisions (and in particular, supplier agreements)?

3. Assess your customers and place them on the matrix, left to right.
4. Identify a set of criteria by which you will rate and position the customers on the vertical axis. You will be wise not to let this list grow bigger than six or seven criteria; too many will dilute the analysis. This should be a list that can be used to rate all customers. (In multiple business organizations this can be difficult, and that may suggest that each business must identify its own global accounts, using its own criteria, at least as a first step.) The criteria might include things such as:

- growth potential
- profitability
- strategic fit
- geographic fit
- capability fit
- access
- market standing
- financial health.

5. Weight the factors; in other words, are some of these criteria of greater importance than others?
6. Rate your customer list against these criteria and place them on the matrix top to bottom. This part of the process will almost certainly require input from local businesses and local sales professionals, but take care if asking them to do the rating themselves (remember the petroleum company case study!); it is usually better to ask for data, not opinions.
7. Assess the resultant positions on the matrix: does it look acceptable? One aspect of 'acceptable' is how many customers appear in the top right box: just how many 'full' global customers will it be realistic for you to handle? Select too many and to some extent you pick none, as you will fail to make the necessary impact and progress that you might have made had you gone with a more sharply focused list. It is impossible to name a 'perfect' number, but in the vast majority of cases of my own experience the realistic number has always been in single figures.
8. Communicate your decision to those who will need to make it happen. It will be at this point that the management team will be pleased that they used a robust process and not their gut feel or the movements of the stars; pleased too that they didn't use too many criteria for judging customer attractiveness. The fewer the criteria, the more powerful and memorable the presentation. Never forget: you want people to do something as a result of all this rating and ranking.

(The details of a very similar process, selecting key accounts, are described in much fuller detail in Key Account Management (4th edition) *also by Peter Cheverton, and published by Kogan Page.)*

The customer classifications

The definitions and suggested actions given here against each customer type can only be generic, and can only be *suggestions*.

Overly precise templates are unlikely to fit your own circumstances and will very possibly be more damaging than they are helpful:

- **Full** global account – a customer where you will implement the full GAM package, in particular the creation of a cross-business, cross-territory, and multi-functional GA team.
- **Shadow** global account – a customer where you will implement only some parts of the GAM package, and probably utilizing a much smaller GA team. The extent to which you will complete the kinds of analysis that we have been discussing in this book will be determined by the time you are able to devote to this account, and that being less time than you will give to *Full* global accounts. This is a question of investment and return; these customers are not as attractive to you as the *Full* global accounts, and should receive a lesser investment as a result.
- **Proto** global account – a customer where it would probably be unwise to implement the full GAM package as the customer is not ready for it, and so you will implement only those parts that will best help the customer to progress towards a genuine global status. (The term 'proto' is used in the sense of the account being at a very early or primitive stage on its path towards global status, but with signs of it heading in that direction.)
- **Watching brief** account – a customer that may be moving to the right, and may also move upwards in your assessment as a result. Keep an eye on them, but don't expend the kind of investment that you are making in the *Full* and *Proto* global accounts.
- **Local key** account – a customer that is clearly worth an investment, but not on a global scale.
- **Local maintenance** account – a customer that should be maintained with a relatively low cost sales and service package, and managed by local teams.

Identifying the global account managers

Chapter 10 will look at the range of qualities and capabilities required in a top-class GA manager, and it will be the responsibility of the management team to select from this range those qualities and capabilities that will be vital to their own business success.

Finding the right people for the job is the next task, and don't limit your options by considering only sales professionals. We will debate this question at greater length in Chapter 10, but for now it is sufficient to say that success usually has more to do with getting the right capabilities than it has to do with the function from which the GAM comes.

In some cases I have known members of the board to be appointed as GA managers, and particularly in cases where there is a multi-business approach to the customer. If this is your inclination, take care to define the parameters of the job well, stating clearly what is *not* expected of them as well as what is. In such cases it is unlikely that you will be asking them to take on a sales role; there should be sales professionals in the GA team to handle that aspect of the task.

Global account mentors

More frequently, and I have to say more effectively in the long run (for it is hard for board members to find the time to carry out the role of a GA manager properly), a board member will be called on to act as a *mentor* for a particular global account. I have seen cases where it is expected of each board member, from whatever discipline or function they come, to take on such a mentoring role with one of the company's global accounts. This is certainly a great way to get the internal obstacles to GAM falling like autumn leaves, and so make things happen for real (nobody enables better than the self-interested).

LEADERSHIP, EMPOWERMENT AND COACHING

Leadership

GAM is a testing environment and requires high standards of leadership across a wide range of issues and questions. Here are just some of those questions:

- Are we heading in the right direction?
- Are we doing the right things?
- Do our customers prosper?
- Are we a key supplier?
- How are we different?
- Are we properly rewarded?

Figure 9.2 illustrates the breadth of the leader's challenge and shows how GAM fits into the overall aim to create value for customers and so be a winning business.

Figure 9.2 _The leader's challenge_

To make GAM happen, the leader must be able to promote and manage change. The _change equation_ discussed in Chapter 7 (Figure 7.5) will be a necessary starting point, but in addition the leader will have to understand the nature of people's behaviour in high-change environments, and as a _global_ leader they will need to understand the challenge of cultural diversity.

They must be able to manage the future, a challenge 'so simple' that we reduced it to another triangle in Chapter 1 (Figure 1.3). It does not understate the nature of this particular challenge to liken it to spinning plates, the resources being the plates, and the market opportunity being the number of sticks on which you can spin them (the objective being to get just the right number for a perfect act).

Empowerment

It goes without saying that the global account manager must be a highly empowered person, as must the members of their team, but this takes a great deal more than being told that you are allowed to do things. The only truly empowered person is the one who is first given the freedom to act and then helped towards the capabilities required for them to act effectively. It is an irresponsible management team that does only the first of these two things.

Coaching

Senior managers are often very good at telling people what to do, and for much of the time this is sufficient to keep things moving, but faced with the challenges of GAM, 'telling', however eloquently done, will not be enough to make things happen.

Coaching is much harder than telling, but it is also much more effective in the long term. Coaching is the skill of working *with* people to help them realize *their* full potential, and to achieve this *for themselves*. Chapter 10 goes into more detail on this vital skill but, for now, any leader might like to consider adding just one question to their conversations with those involved in GAM: *'What is it that you need, to do a better job?'*

PARTICIPANTS

To have a board member on a GA team, probably in the surround team, is hugely valuable for that team, and for the customer. First, the message that it sends out to all concerned is that we are in earnest. Second, they will be able to build relationships at levels in the customer's organization that are often beyond the grasp of the GA manager. Third, they will be on hand to clear the way of internal obstacles and to arbitrate on the inevitable disputes that will accompany the team along its journey.

As participants they should of course prepare their own GROW (see Chapter 8), and with particular attention to their obligation. Senior managers must take great care to have a very precise obligation to the team, as illustrated by the following case study.

Everyone needs GROWs, but *especially* senior managers

The CEO of a manufacturing conglomerate was visiting the main facility of one of their business unit's global distributors, in Pakistan. The business unit in question sold high-spec glass, an area in which the CEO had little expertise (he came from the chemical wing of the conglomerate), but that was of no great concern as this was more of a social call on the distributor. The glass was used, among other things, for building all-round-view squash courts. Squash is, of course, a big sport in Pakistan.

Over dinner the MD of the distributor suggested that having a real squash court of this type on their premises would be a great sales aid, and much better than the samples and brochures they currently used; could they have one, free of charge, please? It had been a pleasant dinner (and so unexpected to find such an excellent wine list in Pakistan) and the CEO readily agreed. The next day he sent a note to the distributor's global account manager, asking them to make the arrangements.

The squash court was certainly an aid, but unfortunately the CEO had been unaware of two facts.

First, he didn't know that the cost would run to close on a hundred thousand pounds (and this is a tale from many years ago).

Second, he didn't know that the distributor had been asking that self-same question for many months, and had been receiving the following answer from the global account manager: _'When you pay your bills on time, and stock our full range, and meet your sales targets, and employ two new sales reps, then we will happily split the costs on the materials for a squash court.'_

The boss had committed the sin of pulling the rug from underneath the GA manager's feet. So whose fault was it that they gave away a fully equipped squash court and got nothing in return? Well, of course the CEO should have known better, but in truth, wasn't the global account manager equally responsible for not ensuring that the boss was properly briefed? That is their job after all, managing the complex of touch points with the customer, from top to bottom.

Rather than ascribing blame, shouldn't we ask how the whole sorry mess could have been avoided in the first place? The answer is a simple GROW, with particular attention to the 'O' for obligation. What might it have said?

How about: _'You will be asked for a free squash court, and you may offer to split the costs of materials if they agree to pay their bills on time, to stock our full ranges, to meet our sales targets and to employ two new sales reps…'_? This is better than handing over a free squash court without any return, but I still don't like it, largely because it still pulls the rug from beneath the GA manager's feet, and in the worst way possible: by taking their job away.

Better might be something like: _'You will be asked for a free squash court, and I would like you to say: "That's an interesting idea, but I am not nearly important enough to agree anything like that with you, you will have to speak with our GA manager…".'_

You can imagine that the CEO would have to practise this line a few times, but then it's a long flight to Pakistan…

10

The global account manager
– rarest of breeds?

How do you spot a global account manager? Aren't they the ones whose wallets bulge with airline gold cards? Aren't they necessarily single, for surely the amount of time away from home would break even the strongest of marriages? And aren't they those multilingual genii, switching at the drop of a hat from Spanish to Mandarin? There they sit, on the plane (business class, of course, with their gold card upgrade), without a care in the world for the home they won't be seeing for weeks, and happy with whichever newspaper they are handed by steward or stewardess: *'Le Soir, Madame? Frankfurter Allgemeine, mein Herr?'* It's all the same to them.

Would it surprise you to learn that the good global account managers, that is to say the ones that do their job most effectively, spend only 25 per cent of their time, *at most*, with the customer? They are not super-reps whose sales area just happens to be the world. At the close of this chapter we will ask whether they even have to be sales people (by background) at all.

The global account manager must be a good delegator, a good motivator, a great coach, and above all else, a leader. Those global account managers that attempt the task of GAM on their own will be lost from the very beginning. A huge part of their task is internal: clearing the obstacles, enabling the infrastructure of systems and processes, persuading the barons (see Chapter 3), and developing the tools and the solutions.

THE SKILLS FOR THE TASK

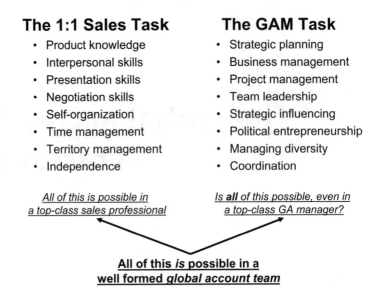

The 1:1 Sales Task

- Product knowledge
- Interpersonal skills
- Presentation skills
- Negotiation skills
- Self-organization
- Time management
- Territory management
- Independence

All of this is possible in a top-class sales professional

The GAM Task

- Strategic planning
- Business management
- Project management
- Team leadership
- Strategic influencing
- Political entrepreneurship
- Managing diversity
- Coordination

*Is **all** of this possible, even in a top-class GA manager?*

All of this *is* possible in a well formed *global account team*

Figure 10.1 *Some of the skills needed for the GAM task*

Figure 10.1 shows two lists of skills, the first being those required for the traditional 1:1 sales task, and the second those skills required (or at least some of them) for the GAM task.

It is possible to find top-class sales professionals who will have all the skills on the first list, and so their independent streak is to be regarded as a bonus, not a problem. What about the list for the GAM task; do you think it is possible to find any one individual capable of all these things (and a good proportion of those on the first list)? And if you did find them, do you think you would be able to afford to keep them?

Of course, some people really are this good, and maybe you are one of them, but the solution to the problem is actually much easier than setting the HR department to find these rare and beautiful creatures; it is to realize that all of these skills need to be present in the GA team, not an individual. Indeed, the last thing that you want is a jack-of-all-trades GA manager who dabbles (and meddles) in all areas.

The vital few?

Perhaps then there is a vital list of skills that any good GA manager _must_ possess? Sorry to be difficult, but even this is going to be hard to pin down, because it depends so much on the circumstances. Consider just two: the first a case where the GA team has existed for some time, serving a long-established global account – we might call this the **mature** stage of GAM; and the second where the team is only just beginning to form, in pursuit of a newly recognized global account – we might call this the **start-up** stage.

Mature stage GAM

In the mature stage the requirements that stand out will be the ability to think strategically, the ability to lead a complex team, the ability to influence at a high level, and the ability to manage projects. _'What comes next'_ must be a question ever on their mind, even before the current _'what'_ has been fully formed. Such foresight calls for an understanding of the customer's business, their drivers, their ambitions, their capabilities, and the dynamics of the market in which they operate. Plus, they must have an equal understanding of their own business, its drivers, ambitions, capabilities, and all the rest, so that an appropriate match can be built. The projects that ensue are likely to be as complex as any in the business; their global nature almost guarantees that to be so. A vital requirement will be the ability to navigate and 'negotiate' such projects through their own and the customer's organizations, calling on the combined skills of persuasion, influencing and project management.

Start-up stage GAM

In the start-up stage little of the infrastructure exists, and the organization is probably still predominantly locally focused. Real projects may be some time off yet. Winning a consensus across the global business must be the first task, and the one skill or attribute that stands out above all others is the one we introduced in Chapter 4, and have called _'political entrepreneurship'_ (my thanks again to Kevin Wilson, Nick Speare and Samuel J Reese for coining the phrase _'political entrepreneur'_ in their book _Successful Global Account Management_, published by Kogan Page, 2002).

Political entrepreneurship

Perhaps not the most precise definition of a skill, but then GAM is not the most precise of tasks. Who knows what obstacles may exist, and who knows what is required to clear them? Is it changes to processes or changes to attitudes? Is it changes to structures or changes to skills? Is it about listening or telling? Is it about influencing the troops or the bosses? Political entrepreneurship is about knowing in the first place that these are the vital questions, and then being able to pilot a course through the potentially troubled waters ahead.

So how do you know if someone has political entrepreneurship? Look at their track record. Are they a bruiser, or a facilitator? Bullying might *just* work within their own business unit, but don't even think of it in the big wide world beyond.

Are they sales people or strategic persuaders? Don't sales people persuade? Of course they do, but within closed environments and with a short-term focus, while the strategic persuader must have an eye on the wider environment, with all its bear traps, and the longer-term implications. The 'political' part of the skill is to be seen in this wider vision; knowing what is likely to be possible, knowing when to compromise, knowing when to stop... for now.

Do they insist on being *given* authority, or do they realize that they must create their own authority through their actions, and through their ability to consult with all involved? The entrepreneur doesn't wait for the job specification to be written.

Do they recognize that just as people are different, so are cultures, and that recognizing this diversity, without building stereotypical pigeonholes, is the route to making culture work for, and not against, you?

Do they understand how organizations work? There are organizational cultures every bit as much as national and ethnic cultures, and the GA manager that doesn't interest themselves in such things is likely to come unstuck before too long.

Are they yes men or yes women, or are they mavericks? This last choice is perhaps not as obvious as the others. Mavericks might have difficulties in winning the consensual support required, but the yes man or woman will soon be in bigger trouble; there are too many bosses to say yes to them all in a global organization. GAM is the proverbial omelette and eggs must be broken from time to time. It is here perhaps more than anywhere else that the political and the entrepreneurial skills of the global account manager will be most thoroughly put to the test.

MANAGING TEAMS

Teams are just one problem after another, and yet they remain the single best way to solve problems, to progress projects, and to work with global accounts. Global account teams are tougher than most: just consider four problems particular to GA teams, seen from the GA manager's point of view:

1. Few if any of the members work for the GA manager.
2. Some of the members are senior to the GA manager.
3. All of the members are 'smarter' than the GA manager when it come to their own speciality.
4. Most of them are 'out there somewhere'…

Getting GA teams even to meet can be a huge challenge, especially when you consider the cost of travel and accommodation, let alone the cost of people's time. And when they do come together?

Some of the problems

The following lists some of the main reasons that teams fail to work:

- poor leadership *(too assertive, not assertive enough…)*;
- poor team management processes *(time wasting, indiscipline, poor attendance)*;
- poor scheduling *(too often, too rarely, too erratically)*;
- wrong size team *(too many, too few)*;
- unclear or ambiguous team purpose *(what's it all about?)*;
- individual goals coming before the team's goals *(local issues versus global)*;
- clashes of values across the team *(saints and sinners)*;
- clashes between dominant members *(ever watched a troupe of baboons?)*;
- a blame culture *(you knew it was your fault…)*.

Forming, storming, norming, performing

A well-known model of team development is the one illustrated in Figure 10.2, and shown here in the form of a team development 'clock'.

Teams will develop through a series of steps, if they are to succeed, or they might just stay at step one, in which case they will almost certainly fail. If you have a GA team already, you might like to

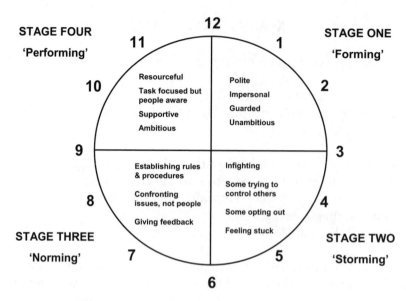

Figure 10.2 *The team development 'clock'*

consider at what time on the clock you think you are, and where would you like to be in six months' time?

Forming

At the forming stage all is politeness on the surface, but underneath are suspicion and watchfulness: *'Why are we here, and why aren't I somewhere else, doing something useful?'* In the GA team context there are some inevitable suspicions, particularly to do with the conflict between global and local interests.

Storming

The storming stage may seem a bad place to be – who wants conflict? – but it is a necessary step forward and should not be feared, but nor should it be prolonged any more than is absolutely necessary. Unfortunately, it is here that the majority of teams stall, and then burn themselves out in ever-decreasing circles of infighting.

Norming

To arrive at the norming stage will feel like things are really starting to happen, with agreement on rules and procedures and the desire to tackle real issues, but don't stop here – rules and procedures are for a purpose.

Performing

Few teams reach this final stage, true **performing**. I heard one guru of team leadership and team working say: *'It must feel great to be here, I know I never have been'*, so don't feel too despondent if this is still some way off.

Turning the hands of the clock

How then do we ensure that our team proceeds through the steps?

1. Make sure that the team understands the forming, storming, norming and performing concept. Ask each member to place the team on the clock, as they see it today, and then ask them to say where they would like it to be in six months' time. This is an exercise to repeat and repeat, pretty much every six months…

2. Identify the particular problems that beset your team (use the list given above as a guide only – you may have plenty more than these!), and set plans to overcome them.

3. Start to establish rules and procedures, but take care if you are not yet at six o'clock not to impose those rules on others; if they don't like them they will simply opt out.

4. Try your hardest to focus on tasks and issues, not the people. Don't get into arguments over who is to blame, but do have discussions (and the occasional argument if you must) over what isn't happening.

5. Understand that there is more to a team than the collective functional specialities of its members. Contributions to a team by each team member can and should come in two forms; what we will call their contribution to *content* and their contribution to the team *process*. By 'content' we mean the functional knowledge and capability that they bring. By 'process' we mean the way in which they help the team to function.

Belbin team roles

Belbin team roles are concerned with understanding how a team functions. Figure 10.3 shows the nine different team roles identified by Dr Meredith Belbin.

Each role is quite distinct (though team members can and will play two or three all at the same time) and each role has a valuable contribution to make to the successful working of the whole team. The 'ideal' team might be said to contain all roles. This does not mean that

Figure 10.3 *Belbin team roles (from the work of Dr Meredith Belbin)*

every team must have nine members; remember that team members can play more than one role each.

Why the need for such diversity? Well, a group of 'perfectly cloned statistically minded analysts' might get on very well together, but they will never complete the task in hand. Similarly, a room full of 'hard-driving objective-led extroverts' might make a lot of appropriate-sounding noise, but come to an agreed conclusion? No chance.

Each role has its positive qualities, and each has what Dr Belbin calls its allowable weaknesses, allowable because to remove them would probably also remove the positive contribution of that particular role. There are, however, some things to watch out for and guard against in each role.

Figures 10.4 through 10.12 summarize the roles. As you look at each role in turn, you might like to consider a series of questions:

- Which of these roles exist within your team?
- Are the people in your team aware of their team role, and are they aware of the value of their contribution?
- Which role(s) are you yourself most likely to play?
- Which role(s) would you expect the GA manager to play?
- Which roles are likely to be most valuable when working with the customer?
- Which roles are missing from your team, what are the implications of that, and what can you do about it?

THE *COORDINATOR'S* CONTRIBUTION

- Coordinates the way the team moves towards group objectives
- Makes best use of team resources
- Recognizes team strengths and weaknesses
- Maximizes the potential of each team member through encouragement
- Acts as a focal point for group effort in tough times

POSITIVE QUALITIES

- Welcomes all contributions on their merit
- Listens without prejudice, remains focused on the main objective
- The team's ringmaster

ALLOWABLE WEAKNESSES

- Is unlikely to be the most creative member of the team

WHAT TO WATCH OUT FOR

- Obstinacy vs. determination

Figure 10.4   *The Coordinator's role (from the work of Dr Meredith Belbin)*

THE *RESOURCE-INVESTIGATOR'S* CONTRIBUTION

- Explores and reports on ideas and developments outside the team
- Creates external contacts
- The best person to set up external contacts

POSITIVE QUALITIES

- Capacity for contacting people and exploring anything new
- Enthusiasm and a source of external ideas
- Ability to respond to challenge
- The team's detective

ALLOWABLE WEAKNESSES

- Low boredom threshold, needs stimulus of others, may spend time on irrelevancies

WHAT TO WATCH OUT FOR

- Too much involvement in own ideas rather than those of the team

Figure 10.5   *The Resource-Investigator's role (from the work of Dr Meredith Belbin)*

THE *SHAPER'S* CONTRIBUTION

➢ Directs the way in which team effort is channelled

➢ Focuses attention on objectives and priorities

➢ Results oriented and competitive

➢ Pushing through change

POSITIVE QUALITIES

➢ A readiness to challenge politics and inertia

➢ Tough on complacency and self-deception

➢ The architect of the team

ALLOWABLE WEAKNESSES

➢ Prone to provocation, irritation and impatience

WHAT TO WATCH OUT FOR

➢ Arrogance and pushiness

➢ Steamrolling colleagues into a course of action

Figure 10.6 *The Shaper's role (from the work of Dr Meredith Belbin)*

THE *COMPLETER-FINISHER'S* CONTRIBUTION

➢ Ensures nothing has been overlooked

➢ Checks details

➢ Maintains a sense of urgency

➢ Invaluable where accuracy and deadlines are important

POSITIVE QUALITIES

➢ Capacity for follow-through

➢ High standards in quality and delivery

➢ The team's workhorse

ALLOWABLE WEAKNESSES

➢ Tendency to worry about small things

➢ Reluctant to let go

WHAT TO WATCH OUT FOR

➢ Getting bogged down in details

Figure 10.7 *The Completer-Finisher's role (from the work of Dr Meredith Belbin)*

THE *IMPLEMENTER's* CONTRIBUTION

➢ Turns concepts and plans into practical working procedures – does what has to be done

➢ Carries out agreed plans systematically and efficiently

POSITIVE QUALITIES

➢ Organizing ability, practical common sense

➢ Self-disciplined, hard-working, trustworthy

➢ The process controller of the team

ALLOWABLE WEAKNESSES

➢ Lack of flexibility, unresponsive to new or unproven ideas

WHAT TO WATCH OUT FOR

➢ Criticizing others for their lack of pragmatism

➢ Getting stuck in a rut

Figure 10.8 _The Implementer's role (from the work of Dr Meredith Belbin)_

THE *MONITOR-EVALUATOR'S* CONTRIBUTION

➢ Analyses problems, evaluates ideas and suggestions

➢ Enables the team to take balanced decisions

➢ Checks and balances

POSITIVE QUALITIES

➢ Judgement, objectivity, discretion, hard-headedness

➢ The team's conscience

ALLOWABLE WEAKNESSES

➢ May lack inspiration and ability to motivate others

➢ Can appear aloof and even negative

WHAT TO WATCH OUT FOR

➢ Criticizing others too frequently

➢ Lack of awareness of the big picture

Figure 10.9 _The Monitor-Evaluator's role (from the work of Dr Meredith Belbin)_

THE *TEAM WORKER'S* CONTRIBUTION

- Supports other team members
- Builds on suggestions
- Compensates for other team members' shortcomings
- Fosters a team spirit
- Ensures internal communications are kept up

POSITIVE QUALITIES

- Ability to respond to people and situations
- Enthusiasm
- The team's 'glue'

ALLOWABLE WEAKNESSES

- Indecisive, especially under pressure

WHAT TO WATCH OUT FOR

- Stress, especially within internally competitive teams

Figure 10.10   *The Team Worker's role (from the work of Dr Meredith Belbin)*

THE *PLANT'S* CONTRIBUTION

- New ideas and creativity
- A creative approach to problem solving
- Challenging the status quo

POSITIVE QUALITIES

- Lateral thinking
- The 'spark' of the team

ALLOWABLE WEAKNESSES

- Inclined to disregard processes and protocols

WHAT TO WATCH OUT FOR

- Handling criticism badly – switching off
- Becoming an ivory tower

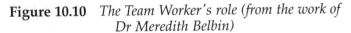

Figure 10.11   *The Plant's role (from the work of Dr Meredith Belbin)*

THE *SPECIALIST'S* CONTRIBUTION

➢ Specific skills and work-related capabilities

POSITIVE QUALITIES

➢ High level of functional skill and knowledge

➢ Professional standards

➢ Commitment

➢ Pride in their work

ALLOWABLE WEAKNESSES

➢ Lack of interest in others' roles

WHAT TO WATCH OUT FOR

➢ Can become too single minded

➢ Slow to change if their specialization is threatened

Figure 10.12   *The Specialist's role (from the work of Dr Meredith Belbin)*

I suggested that you consider a number of questions as we walked through these roles; let's just go back to a few of them:

● *Are the people in your team aware of their team role, and are they aware of the value of their contribution?*
Make sure that they are by taking the team through a Belbin team roles session (see Chapter 16 for more on this).

● *Which role(s) would you expect the GA manager to play?*
There is no absolute match to the task, but a mixture of *Coordinator* and *Shaper* is likely to succeed well, while a mix of *Monitor-Evaluator* and *Specialist* could spell problems. It doesn't have to: the real key as a GA manager is to identify your own preference and ensure that those roles less preferred by you are well represented in the team. Trying to be what you are not can only lead to stress, poor performance, and the downward spiral that inevitably ensues.

● *Which roles are likely to be most valuable when working with the customer?*
Some of these roles are more outward looking than others, the *Resource-Investigator* being the most obvious (a typical sales

professional 'type'), but a better approach might be to ask: who will we be working with inside the customer's teams, how do *they* behave as team members, and what roles could we usefully contribute to *their* team?

- *Which roles are missing from your team, what are the implications of that, and what can you do about it?*

  It is possible to compensate to some extent for a missing role, through being aware of how it would contribute naturally and making sure that you formally make time for that missing contribution; for instance, if there was no *Monitor-Evaluator* in the team (and especially if you have an abundance of *Shapers* and *Implementers*) you might like to pause at regular intervals and ask: '*Are we doing the right thing, have we considered everything, have we looked at all sides of the question?*' Better, however, to look for new team members that will contribute the role naturally.

Managing virtual teams

The most obvious challenge of global teams is physical distance, and the problem of gathering with any regularity. Facing the facts, most teams will fail to meet as often as would be liked, and will have to rely instead on alternative means of communication. Technology has come to the aid of the GA team, but only to some extent. Videoconferencing, and in particular the style of conferencing that allows live access to presentation materials and data, is of tremendous value, but problems remain when trying to address the 'people issues' of team management through such means.

New members of the team tend to remain outsiders, despite months of videoconferencing, until such time as they meet their colleagues face to face. The social element of the team is important and the simple fact of putting personalities to the names and the faces is hugely beneficial.

Only the loudest of personalities transmit with any force through the flickerings of a videoconference, and it is far too easy for the loudest personalities to dominate proceedings, a noticeable phenomenon when watching Americans and Asians at work with this medium. When the plugs are pulled, what do the parties go away thinking?

Once the team has moved through storming and into performing, the new technologies are very powerful indeed, but hoping to travel that path without physical meetings is, I'm afraid, just wishful thinking.

The earlier you can arm the team with an awareness of their cultural preferences (see Chapter 15), a knowledge of their team roles (see Belbin, above) and a clarity on the team's and individuals' purpose (see GROWs, Chapter 8) – and all of this through physical meetings – the better use you will make of the remote meeting technologies. Imagine tackling a problem by videoconference, and there is a lull in the proceedings, with no contributions from anyone (it is very easy to 'hide' during these sessions). It can be very helpful for someone to be able to say: *'Carl, you're our Plant, what do you think?'*

Saved by the e-mail…?

E-mail remains easily the most used tool for global communications, and it is hard to imagine GAM without this piece of technology, but that it is still abused as much as used is undeniable. Even after long years of experience it remains both servant and master. Does the rush to equip 'global executives' with the magical BlackBerry®, allowing us instant access at any hour and in any place, show the value of e-mails, or our ever-growing paranoia at being away from them for a moment? Both for sure.

How many messages do you have when you return from a week away? (Going away for a fortnight is now just too daunting!) But let's be clear, it wasn't the system that sent you this headache, it was people. What are needed are some rules, or what we might call the team's communications charter.

The GA team's 'communications charter'

Start by recognizing that some people prefer the telephone to e-mail, and some prefer physical meetings to either. E-mails require a certain ability with the written word, and many people are happier expressing themselves in the spoken word. At the same time, e-mails, because they allow time for thought, can be much friendlier to those whose command of the 'team language' is a little shaky, certainly compared to a telephone call that can put them on the spot.

Next, recognize that different communication media have different pros and cons for certain tasks. E-mails are wonderful with time zones, for instance, but hopeless for negotiations. There is a rule in my own company: never ask anything by e-mail where the answer 'no' will be unacceptable. E-mails cope with details well, while face-to-face meetings excel if you are seeking agreement to a broad sweep. Follow these agreements up with e-mails to confirm the details. Telephone calls work well for those occasions when you 'just want to check something...' and when a physical meeting would be excessive. Videoconferences are wonderful for bringing groups together easily, but can so easily exclude the more retiring members. Anything that *can* be misunderstood *will be* with e-mails... and so it goes on. All of this may seem rather obvious but you would be amazed at how many teams struggle on for years with inadequate communications and just because nobody raises the issues – too obvious...

Beware the e-mail monster ...

A GA manager was worried that one of the sales professionals in their team was a bit 'rough' with customers, and sought the advice of their HR department on how to help this individual develop a softer approach. They struggled with the words of their e-mail for some while – they were rough round the edges, they lacked sophistication, they were like a pit bull terrier – but none of the phrases sounded right, and then they had it: 'Helmut lacks polish'. The return e-mail suggested a self-learning course of Linguaphone cassettes...

And then, agree the rules on a series of nitty-gritty issues, such as the following:

- *Address groups* – do we want all communications shared across the whole team or will the unthinking use of address groups lead to overload?
- *Confirmations* – when someone asks for something to be done, must the recipient reply to say they are doing it, or can it be taken as read?
- *Attachments* – take note of the fact that users working from hotel rooms can end up with massive bills if they have to receive large and complex PowerPoint presentations, and the like, as attachments.
- *Length of messages* – messages should be edited ruthlessly. Don't send long rambling 'streams of consciousness'. Of course, this takes time. George Bernard Shaw once sent a long letter to a friend and closed it with an apology: *'I am sorry for sending you such a long letter, I didn't have time to write you a shorter one.'* I like in particular the reply of one of my clients to anyone in their team who sends an over-long message: *'I couldn't see your signoff on the screen...'* The team knows what this means – great rule.

Finally, a piece of advice from Lord Chesterfield to his son in 1747: _'Do as you would be done by.'_ He wrote a letter, of course, but such brevity would have made him a natural for e-mail.

COACHING

I once listened to a CEO praising their top GA manager.

'She's great with the customer,' they said, _'she's great with the team, and she's got plenty of that stuff you're always going on about, what do you call it – "political entrepreneurship" – and by the bucketful. And do you know what's the icing on the cake?'_ I waited with interest. _'We've discovered that she's a great coach.'_

I had to disagree there: _'That's not the icing,'_ I said, _'that's the cake.'_

The GA manager that cannot coach is going to struggle. To bring together a diverse group of people with varying talents, and to mould them into an effective team, will require patience and application in any event – just think of the challenge of moving from a bow-tie relationship to a diamond team relationship (see Chapter 8) – but coaching will help speed things enormously.

Coaching is a process and a skill, and a state of mind. The state of mind part is about a belief, a belief that people will perform better when they are motivated, and that self-motivation is better than any other kind of motivation. Self-motivation comes out of confidence, and the satisfaction of seeing that your good performance is the result of your own talent and efforts. The process of coaching then is to help the individual work out for themselves, as far as is possible, their own solutions, using the knowledge and the ability that is already inside them. Coaching is less about putting things in (_your_ ideas, _your_ solutions) and more about getting things out (_their_ capabilities). It will be no surprise then that the skill of coaching has very little to do with telling and everything to do with questions and listening.

Coaching technique

This is such a fundamental process and skill (the cake, not the icing) that it is worth taking a little while to expand further. Let's consider the process and attendant skills in two circumstances, coaching someone who is having difficulties, and coaching someone who is about to do something for the first time. The process may seem a little laborious, as a written process, but remember that in reality this will have the flow of a conversation. Coaching is not a lecture, it is a conversation, and one in which you should aim to use that famous piece of advice to all persuaders and counsellors: *'God gave you one mouth and two ears, aim to use them in that proportion.'*

Coaching the problem holder

1. Identify the problem or issue:
    i   Introduce the subject in a non-threatening way.
    ii Ask questions to help clarify the problem or concern.
    iii Ask how they feel about things not working out as hoped.
    iv Identify the obstacles, internal and external, personal and non-personal.
    v   Ensure that they continue to own the problem and that it doesn't pass to you to resolve.

2. Establish the desire for a solution:
    i   Discuss the consequences of not solving the problem or not rising to the challenge.
    ii Discuss the rewards of solving the problem or rising to the challenge.

3. Work towards a solution:
    i   Seek their ideas, by asking questions:
        a. How might things be improved?
        b. What might you do differently next time?
    ii Listen actively (which means demonstrating that you are listening, through body language, through eye contact, and through references to what they are saying).
    iii Ask if they would like your own thoughts.
    iv Offer suggestions, don't impose them:
        a. How would it be if...?
        b. Have you thought about...?
    v   Build on their ideas wherever possible.
    vi Ensure where there are options that choices are made.
    vii Agree an action plan, with a date for review.
    viii Ensure that they continue to take responsibility for the problem.

4. Follow up:
    i   Ask how things have been going:
        a. Ask what has gone well.
        b. Ask what has not been going well.
    ii Ask why they think things have gone as they have.
    iii If necessary, return to point 2 above, and continue the loop.

Coaching the first timer

1. Ask how they feel about the prospect ahead.
2. Ask what concerns they might have.
3. Ask them about their current plan or approach.
4. Ask if they would like your help.
5. Offer suggestions, don't impose them.
6. Build on their ideas wherever possible.
7. Agree an action plan, with a date for review.

A health warning

There is a danger with coaching, and one that lurks in wait to catch out the inexperienced. In discussing the problem so fully and openly, the problem can slowly shift from being theirs to yours. Maybe you have heard people talk about problems as monkeys sitting on the problem holder's back? Well, the idea is not to let that monkey hop on to your own back if you are the coach, otherwise it becomes *your* monkey. At all times make sure that the problem holder retains ownership and responsibility.

AUTHORITY

It goes without saying that the GA manager is going to need a high level of authority, but what will be the source of that authority? Authority can be *given*, through a job title, through a position in a hierarchy, through the signals sent from bosses, or authority can be *earned*.

For the GA manager, '*given* authority' will only go so far, and can even be destructive rather than constructive, especially when used as a whip, or a particularly efficient machine gun. It is to the sources of '*earned* authority' that the wise GA manager must look.

Sources of earned authority

Authority is earned, or dissipated, as a result of your behaviour and your example. It builds slowly over time but can be lost in a moment. It is more than respect and more than trust, but must involve both of those things. You will know when you have successfully earned sufficient authority for the job, when people start to do what you wish them to do, *willingly*. Here are some typical behaviours, to aspire to and to avoid, that given the right mix will earn you authority:

- Demonstrating that you have knowledge or experience...
  ... but being honest about what you don't know, or have not done before:
  - Don't bluff.
  - Don't be unduly innocent.
  - Consult openly with the specialists and the experts.

- Demonstrating that you have confidence...
  ... but be realistic about the challenges ahead:
  - Don't boast, and don't boost.
  - Don't despair about the impossibility of it all...

- Demonstrating concern for the views of others:
  - Seeking diverse opinion.
  - Explaining your decisions clearly.
  - Don't try to please everyone all the time.
  - Encouraging and welcoming feedback.
  - Giving feedback openly and constructively.

- Communicating your plans openly:
  - Demonstrating the structure of your thinking.
  - Showing that you have thought about the implications.
  - Sharing the global account plan.

Too much, or too little?

GAM can fail when senior management is unwilling to give or allow sufficient authority to the GA managers and their teams, but their reticence is sometimes well founded: are the global account managers up to the task?

Rather than issuing charters at the outset, and declaring bold new roles and responsibilities with new lines of reporting and authority, sometimes it is better to allow things to develop more naturally; authority building alongside experience. The time for charters is when the facts already match the aspirations – or are getting close enough for the charter to cement them.

In time, every GA team gets the authority it deserves, with the key determinants being its observed professionalism, its ability to communicate outside the team, and yes, its endowment with political entrepreneurship.

THE GLOBAL ACCOUNT MANAGER – *A SALES PROFESSIONAL?*

GAM is no place for super-reps; the moment the GA manager thinks they can win every deal and make every presentation they are lost. Most GA teams will have sales professionals as active members, so why are so many GA managers sales professionals themselves? The answer is history.

Because most global customers have evolved slowly from international customers, and before that from local customers, the local sales professionals have often grown with them; rather like sitting on the acorn. The 'best' sales people, or the most experienced, got the jobs, and most regarded it as promotion. Being the 'best' might mean many things, of course, and unfortunately in the past too often this meant being the best 'hunters'.

Hunters and farmers

The hunter is a loner, good at spotting an opportunity, and good at chasing it down. They are invaluable people in any sales organization, but are they the right people to be put in charge of complex global accounts? They tend to be short-term, relishing the quick win, and then moving on to the next opportunity fast.

The farmer is a planner, thinking of next year's crop while planting the seed of this year's. The farmer has to coordinate a range of activities and must stick at some of them patiently and with resilience. Sounding more like a global account manager?

But would these farmers have been recognized as the 'best' sales professionals, in a traditional sale force focused on 1:1 relationships? Probably not.

Look for farmers for this task, and keep the hunters hunting down the shorter-term challenges such as winning new customers and launching new products. A farmer GA manager will probably be pleased to have some hunters in their GA team, provided they can be reined in when required.

Capabilities not function

Sales professionals can make great global account managers, of course they can, but if they do then it will be because of their wider capabilities, not because of their functional background. Look for the capabilities first and you will find that all sorts of people from all sorts of functions can make good GA managers.

171

A sales professional with all the broader capabilities will probably have the edge on anyone else, but only very marginally. The biggest test for them is ensuring that they avoid the super-rep syndrome, as illustrated in Figure 10.13.

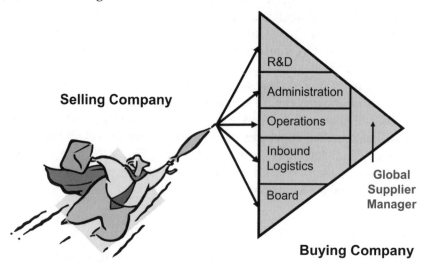

Figure 10.13   *The 'super-rep' syndrome*

I remember hearing a world-renowned concert violinist explain why he thought he had never been as good a conductor as he had been a violinist. So often, he said, when hearing the violinists playing: *'I couldn't help looking at them and thinking – I could do that so much better...'*

Business managers

Throughout this chapter a picture has been developing – the GA manager as business manager. For many if not most newly appointed global account managers this will be the first time they have taken on a role with such breadth of scope, both territorially and functionally. It is a role that offers the true challenge of business management, and probably relatively early in the jobholder's career. After this experience, it can be a problem letting go. I have met several GA managers that have been reluctant to move on to another job after their time in GAM, precisely because the reduced scope of their new role was going to be such an anti-climax.

This is great when trying to attract the best people into the role – the prospect of true business management – but if you want to keep them there, the prospect must be met with the reality of resources, responsibility and recognition. Any business manager worth their salt will want to be able to measure their effectiveness, and in the case of GAM one vital measurement will be the profitability of the account, a point that will be taken up in earnest in Chapter 12.

11

Making it happen – structure and the *persuasive process*

Remember the 'there are no rules of GAM' rule? Well, it is in the subject matter of this chapter that it applies most stringently. Organizational structure is too complex a thing to be boiled down to a template, and so for the next few pages you will find nothing more assertive than observations and some tentative guidelines.

The 'right' structure is the result of so many 'it depends' that you should be very wary of 'borrowing' anyone else's, however successful it may have been in their situation. That there are more 'wrong' structures than 'right' is a certainty, and here at least we might start by looking at a template, just to see how wrong it can get.

The wrong structures

Starting with the easier challenge of KAM, Figure 11.1 shows what I call the 'no chance' structure, where the company's key accounts are buried deep in the bowels of the sales department, and separated by regional and business unit structures.

Should one of those key accounts be a potential global account, or, tougher challenge still, should it be a potential cross-business global account, then for the sake of this particular firm I can only hope that their competitors are just as badly served by their organizational structure.

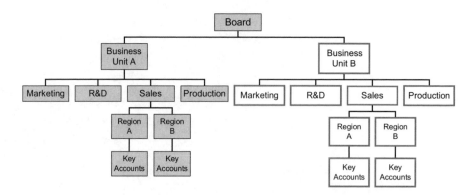

Figure 11.1 *The 'no chance' structure*

Some of the earliest research into the world of key account management, by the Cranfield School of Management, came to one particularly pungent conclusion with regard to structure: '*The customer will not forgive any organizational structure in the supplier that has no relevance or benefit to them.*' In the realm of global suppliers this is an observation to be magnified tenfold. Global customers will grow very impatient with suppliers that bury them in the depths of regional or functional silos. Any buyer looking at a chart such as that in Figure 11.1 would fast conclude that this is not a supplier that will be able to meet their global needs.

So, what to do? Well, if your structure chart *does* look something like this, don't show it to the customer. And if they ask? Start showing them how you would *like* to work with them, how you would like to be able to make things happen for them, and you know what, slowly but surely things begin to look that way for real. We should be thinking of evolution rather than revolution, and an evolution based as far as is possible on the customer's own structures.

There are plenty more structural faux pas; here are just three more examples. First and most common, setting the global account manager and team up with two or more sets of bosses; a global boss and as many local bosses as you like. To whom do they report? From whom must they seek approvals? What does the customer make of the continual '*I'll just have to check that with someone*' refrain? Will they ever manage to do anything meaningful ever again?

Then there is the kind of Soviet-style centralism that attempts to run the whole show from head office, complete with five-year plans. Local structures are either ignored or subverted. If this *really* is how the customer is formed, then fine, but otherwise it is one to be avoided.

Finally, and just as bad, is a loose federation of island sites that encourages maverick behaviours. Again, if this is what the customers want, then fine, but in that case are they really global accounts?

SOME 'GUIDELINES'

These are not rules, perhaps not even guidelines as such, but simply some observations based on real experiences of what has worked and what has not worked. Feel free to disregard them if they do not suit your own circumstance, but if you do so, may I suggest that you ask yourself the following in each case: are you ignoring them because it would not work for the customer (good!), or because that isn't how things get done around here... (questionable at best).

- Aim to understand the customer's structure first, and see how far you can match theirs with yours. Of course, if you have very many global customers, and if they are themselves diverse, there is a point at which this aim becomes unreasonable (but you might just question the *number* of global customers you are targeting before giving up entirely on the notion).
- Evolution not revolution. Since such things shift almost permanently in any case it is rare that a single and wholesale change is the best thing to do (unless you are in crisis, in which case take a look at the contact details in Chapter 16).
- We are not only dealing with sales structure, of course. Ask yourself: which functions deliver value to the customer, and aim to include those at least in your thoughts on structure.
- Set up a GAM steering committee with the task of evaluating the options, identifying the obstacles, determining the critical success factors, and navigating the course towards a practical and successful application (for more on this see the 'persuasive process' case study later in this chapter).
- Structure should clarify and facilitate the authority of the GA manager (but see also the debate on given versus *earned* authority in Chapter 10).
- Consider creating global account *mentors* (a role to be performed by senior managers, as discussed in Chapter 9). To some extent the appointment of such mentors is a recognition that structure is not the cure to everything (see below) and that from time to time *people* will be required to intervene, perhaps superseding the normal demarcation lines.

- GA teams should aim to work *through* local organizations rather than attempting to replace or bypass them.
- Local organizations should recognize and contribute towards GA objectives.
- Local management should be involved in GA teams.
- Performance measures should be both global and local (see Chapter 12).
- Nothing must compromise the effectiveness of local service and application.
- GA team budgets should be held globally, by the team, and not shared across functions or business units, or regions. As an example, if the team wishes to organize a global meeting, with all the costs of travel for people from different functions, then that must be something they can decide for themselves, rather than being at the mercy of some other department's travel budget.

The inevitable matrix

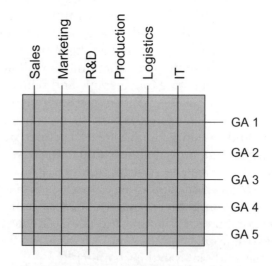

Figure 11.2 *The inevitable matrix*

Figure 11.2 shows the idea of a matrix 'structure' with, in this case, global accounts working across business functions.

The variability of customers forces the supplier to take this more flexible approach, and with all its attendant ambiguities. (Ever since a French colleague of mine told me that we were all 'working in a mattress' I realized that structural organization could never again be about hard and fast lines.)

The matrix approach has long been the norm for the practice of KAM, but Figure 11.3 shows the additional variability that arises from the practice of GAM.

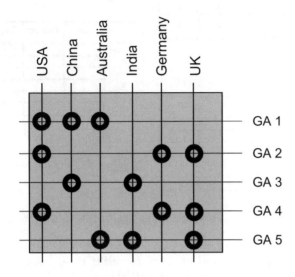

Figure 11.3 _The inevitable matrix_ – countries

What are the possible results of such diversity – confusion? Conflicts of interest? All of these will be very likely to result if the matrix is just allowed to 'happen'. The best way to ensure clarity is to start by recognizing the problems and to discuss them openly. Then, recognize the diversity; don't attempt to shoehorn it into a template solution.

Each global account will be different, and so the structural solution must to some significant extent be allowed to vary as appropriate. But don't create 10 different templates; such revolutionary spirit can only end in tears. Instead, by listening to your customers, and by discussing them within your own business, and by actively involving the relevant functions with the customer, so the 'right' structural solutions will evolve.

Evolution

Figure 11.4 is not a prediction, but simply an illustration of how organizations can evolve over time.

We start with a structure based on national units. Perhaps business units do exist, but they are very much secondary to the national structures. As far as customers are concerned, there will be a series of national sales offices headed by their all-powerful national sales

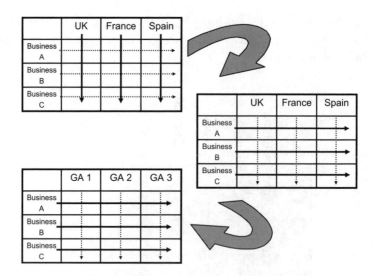

Figure 11.4 *Structural evolution*

directors. This picture will be very familiar to anyone who worked for a multinational company in the 1960s and 70s.

In time, perhaps the need to develop better product propositions and more market-focused strategies might see a swing towards the business units as more important entities, and at some point their rationale becomes the dominant focus, replacing the national units (the second box in Figure 11.4). When such things happen it is not unusual to find the country managers trading in their roles to head up the newly dominant business units, an act of HR planning that might go some way to ease the pain of transition.

Perhaps in time the national entities fade away from the scene, the sales offices are closed, and we see the development of global account teams, their GA managers reporting to the business units, or perhaps even to a global head office. We have arrived at the third box in Figure 11.4.

And what next? If the global customers are also cross-business customers, might the GA teams develop into the next dominant force? Might we find HR directors encouraging heads of business units to consider trading in their jobs for the role of a global account manager? We might, and indeed it has happened already in some cases, while in other cases there has been a shift back towards national structures, or regional ones. The shifts happen for a complex of reasons, but companies will be well advised to make sure that uppermost among those reasons should be the nature of the customer; *their* structure, *their* markets, *their* needs.

GA teams – a rock to cling to?

Organizations are in a permanent state of change, and while that may be a necessity if they are to keep pace with a changing world, it does also tend to encourage the inefficiencies of instability. One benefit of strong global account teams can be that they provide a longer-term and so more stable feature in the ever-shifting landscape.

And what happens to account managers as these changes occur? At first they are part of a national team responding to a national sales manager, and then they are part of a business team, and perhaps a team that develops a key account management strategy with its key account managers responding to the business unit manager (the artfully named BUM). Perhaps some of those key accounts become global accounts, and perhaps also cross-business accounts. At this point, do the GA managers continue to respond to the business unit they started in, or must a new structure be developed to cope with their global and cross-business role? As you may have already guessed, there are no right answers to this, but with all this change going on, surely the greater the stability that can be built around the global account team itself, the better?

MAKING IT HAPPEN – *THE 'PERSUASIVE PROCESS'*

Is making GAM happen going to be about structure in the end? 'In the end', quite possibly, but even then it should be recognized that organization and structure are not going to be able to solve every problem. And at the beginning? Faced with the prospect of making GAM happen in your own business, it may seem that there is no feasible or practical structure possible, at least, not to do what you need.

At such a point something else must take the place of structural solutions, and something that might just in any case be a more effective way of handling the challenge. We have already seen some hints of what this might involve with the discussion around GA mentors, and the idea of a GAM steering committee. These are not structural solutions but have more to do with process and persuasion. Perhaps what we really need to get GAM moving is not so much organizational change as a *persuasive process*?

In Chapters 2, 4 and 8 we have encountered a supplier to the food, household, toiletries and cosmetics industries that is trying to organize its approach, as a cross-business team, to a global customer. Let's continue the case study by looking at how the company chose to work through a *persuasive process* rather than seeking the solution in structural change. It should also be noted that the principal skill required by the project leader in this case was just the kind of *political entrepreneurship* that we discussed in Chapter 10.

The *persuasive* process in action ...

Let's begin with a quick summary of the case. The potentially global supplier is made up of five independent business units: food ingredients, food additives, food flavourings (all three selling to the food manufacturing industry), fragrances for toiletries and household goods, and fine fragrances for the perfume and cosmetics industries. Each one of these businesses currently deals with the same global customer, though each on a rather different basis (some globally, some locally) and each with rather different ambitions. The customer appears keen to work towards a genuine global agreement, but with the supplier as a whole, not as separate business units. The supplier is aware of the opportunity but there are some significant internal problems, largely resulting from the fact of each business unit's very different *moneymaking logic*. The food ingredients business seeks large orders to fill its manufacturing capacity, the additives business is not interested so much in volume but is very keen on secure forecasts, the two fragrance units prefer to cherry pick high-margin opportunities, and the food flavourings business sits somewhere in between. Each business fears that a global offer might compromise their own proposition and so endanger the source of their profitability.

The five business units agreed to work through a particular process (summarized here in a much simplified format) in order to arrive at an actionable plan. This intentionally *persuasive process* involved six distinct phases of development:

The six phases

1. establishing a steering committee;
2. information gathering;
3. opportunity analysis and the setting of objectives;
4. establishing the cross-business team and determining the internal operating procedures;
5. developing the customer plan;
6. implementation.

Dividing the process into six distinct phases was important as it thereby involved a formal 'signing off' by each participating business unit at the end of each phase. This was deliberate, in order to ensure that there were no surprises, and no regrets. As a result, both trust and a collaborative spirit were engendered.

Phase I – the steering committee

A representative from each of the five businesses was identified to form the steering committee.

A member of the parent company board was nominated as a project mentor (it was realized that there would be occasions when heads might need either stroking or knocking together) and took a lead role in helping to agree the project/committee leader.

The agreed project leader came from the fine fragrance business, but they were selected not because that business had any greater share, or was more global (in fact they were one of the smaller and more regional players), but because it was seen that they possessed the necessary skills of political entrepreneurship: they understood the realities of the different moneymaking logics, they appreciated what was possible and what was not, they did not wish to play with organizational structure (at least not at this early stage), and they also possessed a customer-focused drive. In addition, they represented the business that potentially had the most to lose from a global agreement, so helping that business unit to engage their support for a process that they might otherwise have boycotted. There was of course a risk to this politically motivated strategy, that their business unit's 'natural opposition' might lead them to wreck the committee through poor leadership. Fortunately their personal profile would not allow for such an unprofessional act, fortunately the mentor was well aware of that profile, and fortunately the skill of political entrepreneurship was alive and well at a senior level in this company.

People and politics – ignore either at your peril

Each representative had to have sufficient authority and status to have full access to any data required and to be able to commit their business as agreed at the end of each stage. They also had to have an existing relationship with the customer, not necessarily in a sales capacity, but it should be a close and knowledgeable one.

A good deal of time was spent by the project leader reassuring the steering committee team that the purpose of the process was to build confidence and that nobody was going to be sucked into anything against their interests. Time was also spent making it clear that the customer's wishes should drive their decisions as much as possible and that any failure to collaborate would be seen by the customer as a failure to serve their needs. Political entrepreneurship must always combine the carrot and the stick.

Phase II – information gathering

- Sales data: history, current and forecast, by business unit, by customer entity (ie the separately operated parts of the global customer), and by region.
- Revenue/profit data: history, current and forecast, by business unit, customer entity, and by region.

183

- Current contacts (including a commentary on the nature of those relationships; good/bad, deep/shallow, locations involved, functions involved, etc) – create an initial *contact matrix*.
- Any existing account management procedures and especially any existing account plans.
- Current contractual arrangements, including terms and conditions.
- Is there already evidence of a cross-business approach? (It was found that this was most evidenced at a local level and largely through the customer's insistence.)
- An analysis of the customer's business, including financial performance, business strategy, main markets, etc.
- To what extent does the customer or its constituent parts operate on anything approaching a global basis?

Phase III – opportunity analysis and objectives

- Where are the opportunities for growth?
- How do these opportunities sit with each business unit? Do they fit with the existing strategy and moneymaking logic?
- Are there any opportunities best avoided, as being damaging to any individual unit's interests?
- What are the dangers of a global team approach simply resulting in bigger discounts, and how can this danger be avoided?
- What benefits are there to the customer of receiving a managed approach from the five businesses units, and can those benefits be quantified, and in the customer's own terms?
- What are the customer's expectations and how must we manage them?
- Does a cross-business team approach give us competitive advantage?
  - Are any of our competitors able to match this breadth of offer?
  - Do any of our competitors have a truly global relationship?
- Define the objectives for the total group.
- Define the objectives for each business unit.
- What will be the impact on profitability, for the group and for each business unit, if we succeed with these objectives?
  - What is the investment required?
  - What are the expected rewards?
  - Is this better than working as five independent units?

Phase IV – the cross-business team and internal operating procedures

- What are the internal obstacles to operating as one team in front of the customer?
  - Performance management?

- Value drivers?
- Reward?
- How will these obstacles be overcome?
- Who will be the members of a cross-business GA team?
  - Prepare first-draft GROWs.
- Who will be the GA manager?
  - What authority do they require?
  - Who will they report to?
- Create a global customer profit & loss account.
- How will costs and rewards be allocated to individual business units?
- Identify the GAM toolbox:
  - Which tools/processes will be mandatory?
- Ensure an adequate cross-business knowledge management and communications system.

Phase V – developing the customer plan

- Prepare a cross-business global account plan.
- Draw up a global contact matrix with GROWs.
- Agree procedures for customer interactions from the GA team and from each business unit.
- Agree procedures for sharing data and experiences across the GA team.

Phase VI – implementation

- Review at regular intervals, and almost certainly not longer than a month in the early stages:
  - Continually ask: is the cross-business and global approach succeeding where a solo business and local approach could not have done?
  - Continually ask: what obstacles are we encountering?
  - Continually ask: are we creating any new problems?
- Be prepared to learn fast from experience, and make changes as appropriate.

(To see how this case develops further see Chapter 12.)

The particular *persuasive process* laid out in this case study is, of course, just an example, but shows how the way in which the approach to GAM is undertaken is every bit as important, and probably more so, than questions of structure. Indeed, trying to tackle organizational structure in this case would almost certainly have had the five business units going their separate ways at a very early stage.

Consulting with the local operations

While this persuasive process was under way, one other activity was in evidence. The debate was largely a cross-business one, but once it came to implementation the full support of the local operations was going to be essential, and in circumstances that would be rather different from those they had experienced before. In order to 'make things happen' a high degree of consultation was essential.

Too often such consultation is put off to the last moment, the excuse being given that it is pointless to discuss things before it is clear what is likely to happen. Such laziness (or is it cowardice?) is only likely to store up problems. If you expect the local operations to have any apprehensions about the changes required to service global accounts, then the sooner you uncover these apprehensions the sooner you can do something about them.

It should be no surprise that the local operations will have concerns and questions, but don't allow these to obscure something else that will also be present: their enthusiasms. You will be discussing customers that they have dealt with for some time, and with which they will have built relationships and loyalties. The earlier you discover their enthusiasm for these customers, the sooner you can harness their energies.

Engaging the customer

When to engage the customer in your thoughts and plans? Be guided by the advice given in Chapter 1 and summarized in Figure 1.2, but on the whole the answer has to be the sooner the better. How else could you properly gather information? How else could you properly assess opportunities? How else could you start to formulate a plan?

In the case study discussed in this chapter, the formulation of the steering committee was an integral part of engaging the customer because each member was someone with an existing customer relationship. They shared two responsibilities: to the process and to the customer. Such a dual responsibility is important when we consider the real challenge: to involve the customer with your own journey but to do so without raising expectations in their minds that may not subsequently be met, and without setting too many cats among the pigeons within your own business. This will be a narrow path, a veritable tightrope at times, and once again we see the importance of that skill so necessary for any successful GAM leader or GA manager: *political entrepreneurship*.

12

Performance and reward

One of the most testing issues for GAM (global account management) is the business of matching activities with rewards. Failure in this regard will lead to continual arguments, which at best will occupy a great deal of time and sap the energies of all concerned, and at worst result in the encouragement of patently stupid, often spiteful activities (or, more commonly, a *lack* of activities).

Let's consider a particular global supply situation, and compare two different outcomes, both of which were regarded by those involved as resulting in inequitable rewards for the activities carried out.

A company that you sell to has operations in five European countries and has been pretty much an international customer (as defined in Chapter 1) for the 10 years you have done business with them. For each of those last 10 years you have sold through a team of five nationally based sales professionals, each with their own targets and each with their own preferred methods for growing the business. Three of them have done well, and in France, Germany and Italy your business thrives along with the customer's. They have established a secure base, are trusted and respected by the customer, and can regard themselves as key suppliers. All of this is the result of years of hard work and they see their reward in the booming sales statistics. In the other two countries, Spain and Holland, the sales professionals have made only the smallest of impacts on the customer. They don't regard this as a failure on their part; they have simply had better (and bigger) fish to fry.

Now for the two outcomes, and as you read them you might like to ask yourself: which is the worse of the two?

In the first outcome the customer decides to move to central purchasing, and chooses Holland as the place from which to operate the new regime. The Dutch buyer is keen to win a big discount for purchasing in bulk and although there is no actual increase in volume across the whole company, by agreeing with your sales rep in Holland to place one order per month, for delivery to their central warehouse in Holland, and invoiced to the Dutch office, they manage to make it look as if they have hugely increased volume and so justified a 'global discount'. They will of course look after distribution to the different parts of their European business. The Dutch rep is delighted; from a customer of little consequence has suddenly sprung a huge order, and one that will be repeated each month. The discount is of no concern to them; it is amply justified by the size of order received. And the other four sales professionals? The Spanish rep shrugs it off as no great loss, but the sales reps from France, Germany and Italy have just seen 10 years of consistent investment disappear from their sales statistics.

In the second case, the same customer chooses to centre their purchasing operation in France, and your French sales rep works hard to coordinate an order that will be suitable for all five countries. They contact each of the other four sales professionals and make sure that their needs are represented to the French buyer. They are pleased to take on the task, the anticipated order easily justifying the extra work, another example of the excellent return on their investment in this customer. At the final meeting, with the order about to be signed, and in return for a substantial 'global discount', the buyer asks that all deliveries should be made locally, and that all invoices should be sent, as before, to the local operations. After weeks of work, your French sales rep sees the anticipated reward for all their efforts disappear into the sales statistics of their German, Spanish, Italian and Dutch counterparts.

So, which is the worse of these two outcomes? If you are tempted to say: *'What does it matter, in both cases our company has benefited'*, then can I urge you to look ahead a little further? Certainly it is true that in the first outcome you will have saved substantially on the cost of logistics, and in the second you have secured an order that ensures supply to all five locations, but by ignoring the psychological consequences of these outcomes you risk consigning yourself to the consequences of your own complacency.

In the first case, a splendid order is credited to your Dutch sales organization, and the sales reps for the other four countries see their sales disappear. And how do those four sales professionals react? They lose interest, they stop calling, and local knowledge and influence disappear. The relationship with your customer becomes a head office one based on volume and price, and on such a basis alone the future can only be troubled.

In the second case, something that would have happened anyway – five local deliveries – has happened at the extra cost of the 'global discount'. Worse is to follow. How much effort will your French sales rep be prepared to put in for the next time around? Very quickly you run the risk of suffering the worse of two worlds, a central discount but no central incentive.

Perhaps you think there _is_ a central incentive for your business as a whole, what you might call the 'common good', but unfortunately the existing performance measures and reward structures are not designed to take account of such a noble concept, they are all local.

RIGHT PERFORMANCE, RIGHT REWARD

In both of the outcomes discussed above, the problem has resulted because of what those involved see as an inequitable reward for their efforts. Of all the CSFs (critical success factors) listed back in Chapter 4, this is perhaps the toughest one to get right. There are so many competing interests, egos and power structures involved that you can be sure of one thing: whatever you contrive, you will never satisfy all of the people all of the time.

Let's at least start with an important principle: that the methods chosen for measuring and rewarding performance should aim to match the globality of the challenge. If the customers are truly global then a plethora of local measures is going to get in the way, but if the customers are largely local or international, then global measures risk being meaningless. Given that the measures used to measure and reward performance will themselves drive that performance (another important principle), it is important to get this matching process right.

When my own business decided to open an office in AsiaPacific our reasons were very clear – we had customers in Europe that also wanted our help in their AsiaPacific operations. Unfortunately, and in our innocence, we established the

When rewards drive the wrong behaviours, performance is bound to suffer

AsiaPacific office as a separate profit centre. If one of our European-based team went out to run a training course for one of our global customers in India or China, the revenue was credited to the AsiaPacific P&L. The problem with that was that all the time the European team member was in Asia they were failing to contribute to the European P&L, and it was that P&L that paid their salary.

We wanted to serve global customers but we designed a performance measurement system that encouraged us to ignore them if it called us out of our home territory. Fortunately for us, all of that is now long in the past.

Assuming a reasonable globality in the challenge, there are three places to start in the search for solutions to this problem:

- a global P&L (profit and loss account);
- measuring the 'assists';
- reward structures.

A global P&L

If the customer is global then there must be a global profit and loss account, measuring the revenue across the whole business and allocating all the costs, central and local. There is no huge problem with continuing to run local P&L accounts for the customer (though it has to be said that in the majority of instances this is an academic issue in any case as there is no P&L *by customer* at all, whether globally or locally), but increasingly the global P&L should be the one seen as the more important, and the one that should drive performance and provide the basis for rewards.

Measuring the assists

We can learn from professional basketball in our pursuit of the right measures and the right rewards. Players in a basketball team are measured on a number of things, but the two most prominent measures are: how many times do they put the ball through the hoop, and how many times are they involved in a play that ends with the ball being put through the hoop? This second measure is called the 'assist' and is an important concept in the realm of GAM.

So many functions and departments are involved in the GAM task, and some with a considerable investment of time and effort, that it becomes important to measure their contribution. These functions already have their performance standards, but it is possible, perhaps even likely, that these existing standards will not meet the requirement for measuring their contribution to GAM.

Take the plant, as an example. They are probably measured on some form of 'occupacity' – how well utilized are the manufacturing assets? Such a measure may actually conflict with the goal to work with an important global customer, who might want some short runs of products, to local specifications, so damaging the plant's occupacity rating. So what to do? Change the plant's performance measure to one of customer satisfaction? I don't see many plant managers buying that one, and frankly I don't blame them – such a thing is too 'loose' and too distant from their own arena.

The answer is in measuring how well they 'assist' the GAM effort. A better measure might be how quickly they can switch from one line to another, a measure of their manufacturing 'fleetness of foot'.

Reward structures

There are plenty of options, the 'right one' being dependent very much on the nature and culture of the business, and almost certainly being a combination of elements. Let's just consider three of those possible elements.

Recognition of the global team

If the customer is global then there must be a global account team, and they must operate as a unit, be measured as a unit, and be rewarded as a unit. In the case introduced at the start of this chapter there are five sales professionals in this team. Some take orders, some provide services, some bring information, and some are engaged in influencing, whether at a local or global level, and they are all as important as each other: they are a team.

Identify these teams, praise them, and encourage them to gather (perhaps at a suitably exotic location?) on a reasonably regular basis. Such intangible rewards are very important, as well as meeting the practical needs of team management.

Salary and bonus

This is, of course, a very complex area, and there are no 'templates' that will fit the bill. One piece of advice, however: if rewards are to be financial it is important to ensure that they are transparent, that is to say, it is clear how they will work out _in advance_ of activities, as opposed to arbitrary awards after the event. It is very likely that the global profit and loss account will form an important point of reference, and it hardly needs to be said that measuring success by profit rather than revenue is to be preferred in most cases.

GROWs

GA teams are likely to be cross-functional, and therein lies another problem for measuring performance. The members of cross-functional teams will already have their own objectives and reward mechanisms, as members of their own individual functions. Will the performance measures related to those objectives drive the right kind of performance against a particular global account? Maybe not, and it is just as likely that the functionally based reward structures will provide no means of rewarding individuals for their involvement in the GA team.

GROWs, as described in Chapter 8, provide an excellent mechanism for setting performance objectives in cross-functional teams, and provide a basis for determining rewards (by whatever means) beyond individual functions.

The global P&L and the common good?

I have often heard people (usually senior managers) say: *'It's their job and they should just get on with it without all this whinging about rewards.'* Such comments indicate a strong belief in the idea of the 'common good', that the health of the many outweighs the problems of a few. There is nothing intrinsically wrong with the idea, provided it is worked out through appropriate performance measures, and a certain amount of management subtlety.

What if arguing the 'common good' …

We have been tracking the progress of a supplier to the food, household, toiletries and cosmetics industries as they attempt to become a cross-business global supplier. In Chapter 11 we looked at the *persuasive process* they used to work towards that goal. Part of that process was to determine how the rewards might work out and how they should be allocated to the individual business units.

A global P&L is, of course, a must, combining all of the business units involved and measuring the common good, but it would be naïve to assume that each business unit will not be concerned to examine their own part of that whole, and to compare it to what went before, and in this case particularly so, given the very different business models involved.

How would it be if the global P&L showed an overall improvement, a victory for the common good, but the nature of the global deal pushed the supplier towards high-volume products matched by discounts? The food ingredients business unit is going to be happy, this is right up their street and just more of the same as far as they are concerned.

The fragrance business unit on the other hand might start to feel that they had lost out on the deal, and not for the most immediately apparent of reasons. Let's suppose that the fragrance unit is encouraged to take on significant new volume. It looks good on the global P&L, but now that the fragrance unit's manufacturing capacity is stretched to the limit by the extra volume they are denied the opportunity of snapping up the smaller but highly lucrative contracts in the way they used to do. In netting the big fish, all the little ones have got away, and considered as a whole it was the little fish that made this particular business thrive.

... hurts in unpredictable ways?

So how about the fragrance business (who have done rather badly from the deal) _charging_ the food ingredients business (who have done rather well from the deal) what they might call a 'lost opportunity charge', to compensate for all that they would now miss? It's the kind of thing that happens, but it is 'funny money' and to be avoided. The truth is that the business might look healthy on paper, but deep inside it will be getting sicker and sicker as it continues to operate 'untrue to itself'.

... makes you 'untrue to yourself'?

So how about just telling the fragrance business to get on with it, for the common good? If the financial mathematics is compelling enough then perhaps this will be right, but the management of this business should take care not to mistake short-term benefits for long-term health. Which is likely to be the more reliable in the long term, a proven business model or a powerful global customer? That may sound a terribly customer-phobic thought, but we are in the real world and our customers do not always have their supplier's health as their number one priority.

What we see in this case is not the 'end of the road' for a cross-business global supply strategy, but rather an instance of 'a bridge too far'. Perhaps the two fragrance business units should be taken out of the equation for the moment, so leaving the global deal to the relatively uniform food trio? They do, after all, speak with a different part of the customer (see Chapter 8) and so it may be possible to keep the customer happy 'in stages'. Perhaps the fragrance business units could frame their own global arrangement? The answer to this can only lie in the nature of the customer; are they really as uniform in their requirement as they sound? And so we are right back to our very first test: how to define a truly global customer, and how to respond.

... forces you into a 'bridge too far'?

If you ever find yourself suggesting that one part of your business should suffer for 'the common good', then whatever the merits of the suggestion, don't be surprised when the sufferer fails to contribute of their best. And if that is likely to cause problems, particularly with the customer, then you may be wise to think of ways of mitigating their pain.

MEASURING THE REWARD – *CUSTOMER PROFITABILITY*

We have spoken of the need for a global profit and loss account for each global customer, but it has already been noted that the measurement of profitability by customer on a national basis, let alone a global one, is still a rarity for most businesses. Plenty of excuses are made (and the only one that I have much time for is: *'Our margins are so huge we have no need to measure; we know we are making a mint!'*), but can I urge that before getting too far into GAM you should establish a process and system for measuring whether the venture was good for you or bad for you.

The costs of GAM

When the customer puts all their purchases together in one pot, the 'global order', then they expect a discount. In Chapter 6 (Figure 6.1) we looked at the relationship between volume, discounts and gross margins, and discussed how easy it is to erode profits by miscalculating the additional volumes required for relatively modest discounts, but this is only the start. The costs of GAM can often be substantial lower down the P&L – the overheads as opposed to the directly allocated costs. How many businesses measure true net profit, and how many are *marmaladers*?

To 'marmalade' is to spread your costs (usually the fixed costs, but sometimes also the variable ones) across all customers, with no regard to the actual costs involved in servicing those customers. Figures 12.1 through 12.3 show the perils of such an activity, particularly if important decisions such as which to invest time in and whom to remove resources from are made based on the analysis.

Customers:	A	B	C	D	Total
Year I					
Revenue	100	80	60	50	290
Costs	60	60	60	60	240
Profit	**40**	**20**	**0**	**(10)**	**50**

Figure 12.1 *The perils of 'marmalading' (part 1)*

This business has four customers, and shows a good profit overall, but the *marmalading* of costs indicates a loss-making customer – customer D. The decision is taken (perhaps not surprisingly, based on this analysis at least) to cease doing business with customer D. Unfortunately, the costs do not reduce immediately by the 60 that had been allocated to customer D. Why should they, as these are largely fixed costs? Perhaps they go down by 30 (and that's ambitious), and people give themselves a slap on the back for a smart decision.

Customers:	A	B	C	D	Total
Year I					
Revenue	_100_	_80_	_60_	_50_	_290_
Costs	_60_	_60_	_60_	_60_	_240_
Profit	_40_	_20_	_0_	_(10)_	_50_
Year II					
Revenue	100	80	60	XX	240
Costs	70	70	70	XX	210
Profit	**30**	**10**	**(10)**	XX	**30**

Figure 12.2   *The perils of 'marmalading' (part 2)*

The company is still in profit, but customer C is now a loss-making customer, and the troubled board meet to decide action. *'Concentrate on profitable customers'*, they say, and customer C is quietly dropped, but unfortunately, the costs once again do not reduce in line...

Customers:	A	B	C	D	Total
Year I					
Revenue	_100_	_80_	_60_	_50_	_290_
Costs	_60_	_60_	_60_	_60_	_240_
Profit	_40_	_20_	_0_	_(10)_	_50_
Year II					
Revenue	_100_	_80_	_60_	_XX_	_240_
Costs	_70_	_70_	_70_	_XX_	_210_
Profit	_30_	_10_	_(10)_	_XX_	_30_
Year III					
Revenue	100	80	XX	XX	180
Costs	90	90	XX	XX	180
Profit	**10**	**(10)**	XX	XX	**0**

Figure 12.3   *The perils of 'marmalading' (part 3)*

I think you can guess what happens next.

The decision to manage a customer as a global account will have an impact on the costs related to that customer, and very likely the costs related to other customers. Investing in the few usually implies a level of disinvestment from the many, perhaps not to the point of dropping them altogether (as in the example discussed in Figures 12.1 through 12.3), but enough to change the shape and nature of costs and profitability. Plan to measure the impact of these changes, as they can sometimes be more dramatic than at first expected.

Customer retention, lifetime value, and GAM

Given the costs involved in winning new customers (almost always higher than you think), retaining customers is usually an activity with a more immediately positive impact on the bottom line. Plugging the holes in the 'leaky bucket' of customer 'defections' is a high-value activity, and one made all the more so in the face of so many 'supplier reduction programmes' (see Chapter 7). And there is more. The longer a customer is retained, the more experienced the supplier becomes in servicing it, and so the lower the costs involved (that's the theory, at least, of the 'experience curve'). A good example might be an improvement to forecasting based on that increased experience, improvements that are to the benefit of the whole business.

The importance of retention brings us to the one significant downside of the global P&L: this is the simple fact that a traditional P&L measures performance based on a single year. Customers that remain customers over long periods have a 'lifetime value' to the supplier: the true measure of the return on your investment.

Figure 12.4 shows how the longer you retain a customer (or put another way, the more you reduce customer defections), the better the lifetime value.

This is neither complicated nor surprising mathematics, that to halve your defection rate doubles the lifetime value of those retained, but for all its simplicity it is not a measure or a consideration high enough in the minds of senior management. One of the strongest arguments in favour of GAM should be that it has a beneficial effect on reducing customer defections, by reducing the incidence of local defections.

Customer Defection Rate	Average Customer Lifetime	Annual Profit	Profit over a Customer Lifetime
40%	2.5 Years	1,000	2,500
20%	5 Years	1,000	5,000
10%	10 Years	1,000	10,000
5%	20 Years	1,000	20,000

Figure 12.4 _Calculating lifetime value_

The financial benefits of global 'diamond relationships'

Good relationships win customer loyalty, and long-term loyalty is a very valuable thing. Some suppliers will even calculate the premium won from the customer as a result of such loyalty, so measuring the reward for their investment in the diamond relationship.

The financial value of the diamond relationship can be demonstrated further, when considering the costs of the wasted efforts that result from less ambitious customer relationships.

Figure 12.5 shows how the better knowledge brought by global diamond teams, when compared to the uncertainty of detached bow-tie relationships, can result in lower costs, less wasted effort, and faster, more effective responses.

The separate bow-tie relationships lead to a situation where each location chases their own opportunities and establishes their own projects, often with wasteful duplication (reinventing the wheel), often with conflicting outcomes (one chases a low-cost option, another an added-value premium solution). The result is a great deal of sub-optimal performance. The coordinated and managed diamond approach will probably see more opportunities in the first place but will also do a much better job of selecting the priorities, editing out the 'no-hopers' and devoting a more focused attention on to the winners. The benefits are clear: less time is wasted on projects that will be going nowhere, development costs are reduced, there

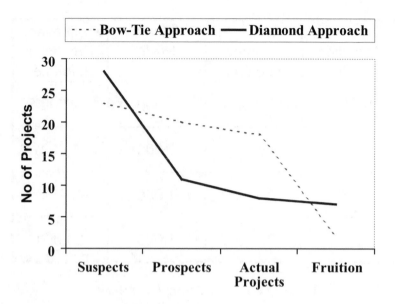

Figure 12.5 *Global diamond teams and 'doing the right things'*

will be a higher success rate, and those successfully completed projects will be on line much faster.

Such considerations are beyond the scope of a global P&L, but are of great importance when calculating the rewards from the practice of GAM.

13

Getting *IT* right

You're just stepping off the plane after a long-haul flight and the pilot is at the door saying his goodbyes.

'Great flight', you say.

'Thanks, but after 12 hours at the controls I was so dog-tired I just had to put it on autopilot for the landing.'

How does that make you feel?

It's the wrong way round, of course; the autopilot is for the dull bit at 35,000 feet, the landing is when you want a human touch at the controls. Much the same goes for GAM (global account management) and the use of IT (information technology).

The complexity of GAM demands some fairly sophisticated IT solutions and a plethora of systems has grown up to meet the need. Some simply log information, some help you to work with that information across a global team, some aim to ease the problems of global communications, and some even claim to manage the customer relationship for you. These last ones are to be avoided. Managing the relationship is rather like landing the aeroplane: something best left in the hands of human beings.

BP's self-designed 'Platinum' system, based on Lotus Notes and used in its Specialized Industrial Business Unit, provides the global account teams with a full range of support, including:

- customer data, and not just the figures, but including details on their needs, motivations, purchasing styles, and key drivers;

BP: managing its systems, not being managed *by* them

- a smoothly oiled system *(what else would you expect from a lubricants specialist!)* for setting actions and monitoring activities across global account teams;
- performance measures, including the all-important cost to serve data and the resultant measurement of account profitability.

One of the most impressive parts of the system, perhaps the most important, is the way in which individuals can sponsor changes and improvements to the system found through its use in practice, changes that can then benefit all users, worldwide.

Adding value through IT

Where IT can add the most value is through systems that will:

- help capture information in an *easily* inputted and *easily* retrievable way (there are still too many tales of account managers spending three to four hours a day simply *inputting data*);
- help share that information across the global team;
- help in the analysis of that information;
- track progress, particularly with complex global projects;
- prepare vital reports, such as customer profitability (the idea of a live global customer P&L at the press of a button is no longer just a dream);
- help manage the complexity of communications that can so easily swamp a global account team;
- manage the global touch points (see Chapter 8), facilitating open relationships between supplier and customer while preserving the clarity of 'who does what';
- provide an interface with the customer's systems. How far this interface should go is discussed below.

The customer interface

Chapter 6 discussed how buyers position their suppliers, with the aim of determining their expectations from, and their management style with, those suppliers (see Figure 6.6, the supplier-positioning matrix). This gives some clues as to what kind of IT interface might be required and valued by the customer. Going much beyond their expectations is not likely to gain you much credit, and may even give the customer real difficulties.

Figure 13.1 takes the supplier-positioning matrix and overlays it with the kind of IT interface that might be expected.

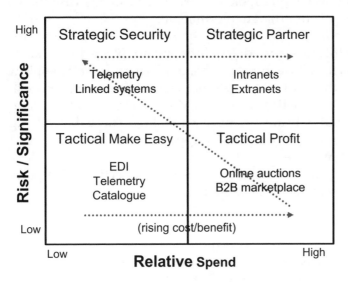

Figure 13.1 *Supplier positioning and expectations for systems interfaces*

We can see how the solutions increase in their complexity, and their likely cost, but also their hoped-for reward as the supplier grows in their scale and significance. They move from simple transactional tools focused on cost saving, through more ambitious trading tools focused on price reductions, and on to systems in the upper two quadrants that provide logistical security and pooled knowledge.

It is also plain to see how the more complex IT interfaces will require a high level of partnering from the supplier, not to say investment.

Data protection – just what can you record?

There is only one safe piece of advice here – take advice. You will certainly already have done so in the individual markets you work in, but the age of the global customer brings an additional challenge. Keeping uniform records and databases across the whole customer organization might just find you infringing individual national regulations.

Getting the attitudes and disciplines right

This is no place to discuss the merits or otherwise of any particular system. Developments move at such a pace that to do so would risk making this chapter look a dinosaur, and in any case there is something more important to recommend.

Before investing in any IT system, take steps to ensure that the right attitudes and disciplines are in place to be able to take advantage of its features and benefits. There are still people willing to debate whether CRM (customer relationship management) systems are in fact a benefit or a burden. Most will now say that it is a genuine benefit, but only after years of grumbling. Those that still regard it as a burden are probably still trapped in attitudes that prevent them from seeing the benefits, and are very unlikely to develop the necessary disciplines to make it work effectively (so perpetuating their view of its nuisance status).

The ROI from your system depends on the people, not the system

Two similar companies decided to install a CRM system at much the same time. The first company had it up and running in weeks and sent its staff on very thorough training courses on how to make it run. The second company delayed installation for six months but spent that time discussing among the users what the system would be able to do for them.

The first company was surprised to find a great deal of opposition among the users, despite the training, largely over the amount of time it was taking to input the data required.

The second company was delighted with the positive responses from users eager to get their hands on the long-awaited system and its promised benefits.

The first company waited three years before beginning to see a return on its investment. The second company was reaping the rewards within six months of installation.

If IT systems are intended to help people do their jobs better, then it is well worth the extra time and effort to prepare those people for the benefits they are about to receive, and this takes a good deal more than training in what buttons to press…

Global accounts demand global IT

In the context of GAM there is another thing to get right, and that is the universal availability and application of the IT solutions. Traditionally, large companies have rolled out their new IT platforms on a regional basis, typically starting with their home territory and proceeding by measured steps around the globe. This makes great sense from the IT manager's point of view, but presents some real problems and frustrations for the members of the global account teams (not to mention their customers). Indeed, many of these new systems find themselves redundant (and so unused) until they are available to everyone within the GA team.

This places an additional challenge in front of the IT function, and calls for a different planning approach. Of course, what it really calls for is the recognition that IT specialists will be important members of any global account team.

14

The global account plan

'*Beware imitations!*' and '*Accept no alternative!*'. That's what it used to say on bottles of patent medicines at the end of the 19th century, and much the same should go for global account plans. There is only one correct content and format for a GA plan, and that is the one you create for your own business circumstances. To echo a point from Chapter 11, no generic templates will do, and don't even be tempted to steal; this one has to be created by you and for you.

There are three key reasons for this:

- Everyone's circumstances are different: the nature of their customer, their starting point or phase of GAM development, their ambition, their resources and the level of investment intended.
- In many businesses, and perhaps your own, it will be decided that the style and format of GA plans should be mandatory for all (the appropriateness of this, or otherwise, will be discussed below). A borrowed template is unlikely to meet the exact need, and will almost certainly have a number of irrelevant elements. Designing it for yourself is the best way to save a lot of people from the pain of pointless box ticking.
- The act of deciding the necessary content and preferred format for such a plan is one of the single most effective ways of focusing the mind on the challenge of GAM *as it impacts on your own circumstances*. You will need to sort a mass of issues and

potential questions into three categories: the vital, the interesting, and the irrelevant. Those listed under 'interesting' deserve a second sort into 'interesting and useful' and 'just interesting'. Discard the latter category; there will be quite enough to occupy you and your team without becoming bogged down in the 'just interesting'.

Purpose

First, decide the purpose of your GA plans. There are many things that they might be expected to achieve for the business, the GA team and the customer:

- establishing goals, strategies and action plans;
- ensuring the GA team has a common understanding and a unified approach;
- winning support from senior management;
- winning support from local operations and teams;
- winning support from support functions or other business units;
- getting things done to set standards and schedules;
- turning strategy into action;
- a performance review mechanism (possibly related to reward);
- focusing internal functions and resources on to market and customer needs;
- demonstrating commitment to the customer (and at the right stage of maturity, why not share your plans with the customer?).

There are many more, but taking just these few ambitions we might group them in two categories of purpose: getting things done, and getting things communicated. And there we have it, the fundamental purpose of the GA plan. Remember these two simple ambitions when deciding the format and the content required; they will keep you focused on the 'vital' rather than the 'interesting', they will help you steer clear of the *four-box matrix* syndrome (filling your plan with 'worthy' charts that show you have swallowed a textbook), and they will stop you creating a Frankenstein's monster.

This has to be a task for a senior management team, or a GAM steering committee if one such exists. Given that the plans must work across functions, regions and businesses, and given that at least their core content is likely to be mandatory, then it is clear that their design can hardly be left to the GA managers alone. In reality, a good example is sometimes spotted, perhaps the work of a particularly talented GA manager, and it is held up as an example to all. This can work, and is better than stealing from the outside world, but take care that it does not represent too parochial an approach – perhaps the approach of the sales professional alone?

Top down or bottom up?

Perhaps you are trying to create for the first time a GA plan for a customer where there have existed for some time a variety of local or regional account plans. That GA plan has to be more than the sum of those existing plans. As such, there is certainly a top-down aspect to the process, setting the direction and the approach for the global team. Arriving at such a set of decisions, however, is only likely to be possible after considering the opportunities and realities of each local entity. In this regard the process is likely to be bottom up.

Format... the choices...

This may seem rather pernickety, but which of the following formats is most suitable for a GA plan: a Word document, an Excel spreadsheet, or a PowerPoint presentation? (There are, of course, others, but let's just compare these three in order to make what I think is an oft overlooked but very important point – and I should confess to a definite bias here....)

Word is great for 'telling stories', but therein lies its problem, the danger of your GA plan turning into _War and Peace_. I have seen documents of over 50 pages, and who has the time to wade through such a thing? In creating such a plan the team can so easily find themselves bogged down in questions of prose style and even grammar; hardly good use of their time. Worse, when it comes to amending or rewriting such a plan the task looms like a monster and gets put to one side. Result: one dead plan.

Excel is great for all kinds of analysis, but have you ever had to sit through one of those presentations where one indecipherable spreadsheet after another is flashed across a screen? They just don't communicate, at least not to anyone but their author.

If the prime purpose of the plan is to get things done and to communicate your intentions to those who need to know, then surely the PowerPoint presentation wins every time? By forcing you to think in bullet points it helps to avoid the fluff and the flannel that creep into such things, and by taking a presentation style it helps you to focus on what you wish your audience to know, and what you want them to go away thinking. There is a danger with PowerPoint presentations that they can become 'lazy', by which I mean facile bullet points, unsubstantiated assertions, and the kind of objectives that say 'grow the business'. We need a much tighter discipline than that; grow the business by how much, by when, and how?

Excel is, of course, the best for any kind of number crunching, and indeed I also recommend Excel for the contact matrix, but I would rather see these parts imported from Excel into PowerPoint.

Perhaps the clincher for me, if there is still any debate over the format, is that PowerPoint is the most collaborative of the formats, and that is an important aspect. The plan is a team effort, and should be easy for a team to review and revise. Word and Excel tend to be 'solitary' formats.

Core content

Regard the following list with care; it is certainly not meant to be prescriptive, and add and subtract as you see fit to design your own global account plan:

- The global account team – *core and full*
- An executive summary – *one slide maximum*
- The profit plan – *current profitability and future target (globally and by regions if appropriate)*
- Opportunities and objectives – *driven by:*
  - *the customer's ambitions, projects, problems and locations*
  - *competitive activity*
  - *the potential return on investment*
- The contact matrix and GROWs – *(see Chapter 8)*
- The value proposition – *products, services, and the measured impact of your proposition on the customer's business* – and your planned reward
- Projects – *project teams and milestones*
- Resources required – *actions required by management to commit resources*
- Implementation timetable – *including review*
- Appendices – customer analysis *(see Chapter 5)*, customer information, and historical data

That's it, and if you can keep it to less than a dozen slides (the GROWs can run to several slides in a large team, so maybe excepting those), then well done. Get into the actions fast and leave the history, the analysis and the detailed information to the appendices. The plan is a document to make things happen, not a doctoral thesis or a glorified telephone directory.

A mandatory style and format?

Everyone's circumstances are different, and doesn't that include the customers themselves? Can one size fit all? Is the desire for a uniform plan in terms of content and format a customer-focused or an internally focused desire? It is almost certainly the latter, but with some good reason. We have seen how a vital requirement for successful GAM is a supporting cross-business and cross-functional team. Imagine for a moment that you are a member of the R&D function, and are called on to work with three separate global accounts. How easy will it be for you to be as supportive as you would like to be if you are faced by three very different teams, working in three very different ways, and to three very different planning processes?

On the other hand, if your customers are starkly different from each other, and your realistic ambitions equally different, how can it be helpful to force them all into the same planning approach?

Try to find the point on the spectrum from 'absolute uniformity' to 'anything goes' that suits your own complex of circumstances. In most cases the answer will be found in a mandatory *core* plan in terms of content, and probably a mandatory format, with scope for each GA team to add their own variations as required.

Start-up or mature: the same plan for both?

Of course not. For one thing, in a start-up situation you are unlikely to have anything like the same data as with a mature case, and for another, your focus will quite rightly be on some of the basics, things that have long since been resolved in the mature customer situation. Projects will be in place in the latter case, while in the former it may still be about getting to know the right people. Even the driving purpose of the plan will differ; the 'start-up' plan will perhaps be about winning support from others, while the 'mature' customer plan will be concerned with working the projects. How can a one-format and mandatory-content plan help you in such diverse circumstances?

The answer will again most probably be found in a mandatory core; there are some things that will just be absolute musts regardless of the customer, your phase of development, or whatever else. Agreeing that list is one of the most valuable ways to focus the mind of the business on to the *real* GAM challenge, that is to say, the one that impacts on *your* business.

Communicating the plan

There have been plenty of 'ifs' and 'buts' in this chapter, so let's close with something rather more definite. A key purpose of any GA plan is to ensure that the whole business understands the objectives and the requirements, and is united in pursuing them. Communicating the plan far and wide is an important task for the whole GA team. The team is, in a sense, the customer's champion, their PR agency or their 'promoter'. So, don't stamp the plan 'Top Secret' and restrict it to the chosen few; aim instead to have its contents broadcast to all who need to know. Don't just post it on a website and expect everyone to seek it out; get out and present it to people (we're back to the PowerPoint format, of course).

And finally, make this a communication of substance, not meaningless hype and razzmatazz. The people you have to persuade, whose support you seek to gain, are usually smarter than the razzmatazz merchants give them credit for....

15

Harnessing the strengths
of cultural diversity

What breaks more global account teams than any other thing? What causes more frustration within those teams than any other thing? What is the cause of more sub-optimal performance with the customer than any other thing? Failing to come to terms with the cultural diversity inherent in a global relationship and in the global account team.

This is an important chapter, but for a far better reason than the potentially negative impact of a poor appreciation of the challenge. The aim is to help you to harness the positives of cultural diversity, and so ensure that what at first might have looked like a problem becomes in fact one of the main sources of your competitive advantage. The purpose is to go much further than simply making you aware of something with which – if you have attempted any form of GAM before – you are already very familiar. The true aim is to challenge your thinking, for the first instance of self-questioning is to be celebrated as the first instance of cultural awareness. To harness the strength of cultural diversity you must start by assessing your own cultural preferences, and understand why they are as they are. From there you can move on to assess other people's preferences, and in the same way understand why they are as they are. And at this point we are very near the breakthrough point, which is to recognize that nobody's set of preferences is better than another's, but that they provide a rich source of motivations and inspirations to get things done; a source from which you can select the best to suit the circumstances.

Missing the trick

Imagine that two people from different cultures meet as part of a global team. One thinks their own set of cultural preferences to be better than the others, and because they have some form of seniority or authority in the team they impose those preferences on the other. It is easy to see why so many global teams are sub-optimal if this is how they aim to work together; one aims to dominate and the other has to submit if the team is to get anywhere. The result of such a sum is one and a half at best; one fully motivated and inspired person and one half-motivated and uninspired person. This is a great shame because by approaching the issue in another way it would have been entirely possible for the sum to arrive at two.

CULTURAL PREFERENCES

I have used the phrase 'cultural preferences' a good deal already and it deserves a short explanation (to be expanded on later in this chapter). Our culture is the set of preferences that we have for dealing with life, for making decisions and for solving problems. There are ways that we like to go about doing things, and for the most part we will consider these the 'best way' of doing things. That is fine so long as we work solely with people who share those preferences, that is, people from the same culture. The problems start when we find others working by different preferences. The problem, I should stress, is not in the fact of the difference, but in the response it causes in the culturally unaware; *'I'm right and they are wrong'*, or worse, *'I'm right and they are dishonest.'*

Culture and how we prefer to learn

Consider how different cultures like to learn; it is something that you will need to think about if you want to develop the talents of a diverse global team through formal training. To make some sweeping generalizations that will have a long line of philosophers turning somersaults in their graves, much of the West has developed its ideas on learning from the thoughts and teachings of Socrates, while much of the East looks to Confucius.

212

The Socratic approach to learning is bound up with debate, with discussion, with argument. In New York, the trainer's ideas are tested in the fire of classroom debate: all very noisy, all great fun, and all very Western. In Shanghai, the same training workshop will be received quite differently. The Confucian approach to learning is to listen to the guru. The result is a much quieter ride, and to an inexperienced Western observer the result might have them fearing the worst: this is all very polite, but they don't understand, they don't care, they're not going to do this...

The truth is rather different, as I have learnt myself from happy experience. One of the first training workshops I ever ran in Asia was in Taiwan, where the delegates were just as I described, quiet, polite, and very attentive. It was the first day of a three-day workshop and I was suffering. There were none of the raucous discussions I was used to in Europe or America, and getting anyone to volunteer an answer to my questions was hard work, bordering on the impossible. The day finished very quietly and I went to my bed that night determined to 'shake them up' the next day. Fortunately for all involved, we began the next day with a short session on applying our learning to the real world, and I was amazed at the extent to which the delegates had clearly gone away to think, and had come back full of practical thoughts and suggestions. Nobody challenged the theory, that would have been disrespectful, but the nature of their application of that theory clearly showed a talent for modification!

I began to wish that people behaved like this when I ran workshops in the United States where all is noisy enthusiasm at the close of the day and next morning it has been quietly forgotten... but then I realized that there were advantages to the Americans' approach to learning, and if only people would combine the two... at which point I realized I was heading nowhere!

In a global account team you will certainly have to cater for both preferences, and more, though the danger is for one preference to dominate, often the account manager's or the trainer's, and even more often the noisiest! And it isn't about wishing that the people in your team would merge into one cultural compromise – that would neuter the very strengths of diversity you want to harness. It is about recognition and understanding and respect, and about openness. Don't assume that everyone will want to learn and be developed the way that you would like for yourself. Try asking them...

There is probably more misunderstanding, more fear, and as a result more avoidance of this issue than any other. It is the issue that everyone wishes would go away, to the extent that I have known at least one company populate its entire global sales team with people from the same nationality, in the fond hope that this would 'solve the problem'. (From other experiences and examples this appears to be a particularly Scandinavian solution: the company in question was Danish.) Of course, while this 'solution' ensured that there were no 'cultural misfits' within their own team, it bedevilled the relationship with the global customer!

Many companies provide cultural training for their staff, but in a lot of cases it is a superficial gloss; what we might call the 'traveller's guidebook' version of cultural understanding. You know the kind of guidebook advice I mean: four pages on the minutiae of certain customs that passes for an explanation of a culture. Cultural diversity is something far more complex than the fact that people in the West and people in the East hand their business cards to each other in different ways (but let's just develop the point for a moment, to see where it might take us). Anyone who has done business in the East will know that the card is usually presented with both hands, and should be taken in the same way. It might not be realized that the greatest sin at this point, having successfully received it, is to put it away in your case or pocket. You should read it, taking care to note not only the name but also the position, and so the status, of the person you are meeting. Ideally you will place it on the table before you and take care to note its presence there throughout your meeting. And don't ever forget to produce your own card. If you do forget, then it won't be taken as modesty or deference; it will be taken as not caring. Getting this piece of cultural awareness right or wrong is like getting a tactic right or wrong in a negotiation; neither mistake will kill the relationship, but it would, of course, have been good to avoid the error all the same. What matters more, however, is the strategy, and the card ritual is only one clue to what that involves, a clue about the importance of status, a clue about the significance of recognition, and a clue about the importance of relationships themselves.

But I am already committing a sin by talking of East and West. There is often a fascination with East and West in such matters, and it is true that some of the boldest contrasts can be painted in the comparison (I have already taken advantage of that), but it would be most unwise to talk of an Eastern or an Asian culture, as anyone who has watched a team of Japanese and Indians working together would recognize, just as it would be misleading to talk of a Western culture with preferences as diverse as those held by the Italians, the Russians, the French and the Greeks.

The 'double-whammy' challenge

It might be thought that the practice of GAM throws up two parallel challenges, so making the task even harder than that facing most 'ordinary' global teams. There is the challenge of diversity within the account team, and then the challenge of the customer's diversity. Is this apparent double-whammy such bad news? In fact, managed well, it will be the diversity of your own team that goes a long way to helping you handle well the diversity of the customer (that Danish mono-cultural team really did shoot itself in the foot). In addition, we are luckier than some global teams in that GAM provides us with a working rule, and this in an area where there are very few rules indeed. The rule is that, wherever possible, the cultural preferences of the customer should be our guide.

WHAT GOES WRONG?

There are a hundred examples, but I will take just one (loosely adapted from one related by Penny Carté and Chris Fox in their splendid book, *Bridging the Culture Gap,* of which more a little later). It is an illustration of how misunderstandings lead to wrong assumptions, which can lead to unfair or misplaced judgements, and so on until the eventual destruction of trust and any chance of genuine collaboration.

Assumptions without understanding ...

A Western-owned and globally active business draws up a code of conduct for managing its suppliers, and issues it to all purchasing professionals around its many local operations. One of the key points is that no supplier should be allowed to represent more than 50 per cent of any business's purchasing budget, or of any critical project or product. A buyer in China is found to be ignoring this guideline, and is in fact giving more than 80 per cent of their business to one local supplier. Worse is to follow when it is discovered that the local supplier is owned and run by the buyer's brother.

... judgements without enquiry

The immediate reaction at headquarters is that the Chinese buyer is indulging in costly favouritism, inappropriate activities, and almost certainly fraud. The riot act is read. The Chinese buyer is surprised, and asks if the people at headquarters wish him to do a bad job for them and for his own company.

'Who is more likely to give me the best price,' he asks them, 'my brother or a stranger? Who is more likely to get out of bed at two in the morning to help me through a problem, my brother or a stranger? Who is more likely to extend me credit, my brother or a stranger? Who is more likely to wish to see me succeed, my brother or a stranger?'

He had a point, but company policy was company policy, and the contract with the buyer's favoured supplier was closed; just as he predicted, prices went up, service got worse, quality dropped, and a bad job was done all round. So who was right?

And here's another thought: how many Eastern-owned businesses would send a directive to their Western subsidiaries insisting that all suppliers should be related to the purchasing staff?!

Bad assumptions

There is a discussion around this example that could go on for days, so let's cut straightaway to the issue of assumptions, and not the details of the case. The most damaging assumption of all is that how *we* think about the world, how *we* make our decisions, what *we* believe to be right and wrong; that all these things are absolutes, and so (it follows) absolutely right. Anyone who thinks differently is either plain wrong (at a dangerous best), or plain dishonest (at a relationship-busting worst).

Of course, people around the world do think differently, and do have different versions of right and wrong, and this isn't just about the 'big things' like politics and religion, it is just as much the case in the world of business, as we can see in this example. The task is to find the right ground between such differences.

Does this mean that GAM will be a series of compromises, with all the dangers of fudge and sub-optimal performance that such compromises might imply? Absolutely not. Does it mean then, to go to the other extreme, that the global account manager must decide which end of the spectrum of preferences will triumph (most likely their own) and consign the other end of the spectrum to a 'like it or lump it' existence? You will recall how this kind of one plus one sum adds up to only one and a half.

The answer lies neither in compromise nor in dominance; it lies in selecting the best from the choices available.

WHAT MUST GO RIGHT?

There are four crucial steps, and they do come in this order:

1. An open mind (and heart).
2. Be self-aware.
3. Develop your knowledge of others.
4. Be practical (but not superficial).

An open mind (and heart)

The mind is like a parachute; it works best when it is open. There are, however, plenty of things that might conspire to tamper with your ripcord, the most serious of them being the matter of prejudice. Prejudice is an ugly word, perhaps the ugliest in the language, and the business professional will do well to equate it with two cardinal sins, and sins that would see their career come to a dead stop should they be seen to exhibit them: stupidity and poor judgement.

If you have five minutes to waste, take a piece of paper and list all the music-hall stereotypes of peoples and nations around the world. Then, having compiled your list, tear it up and throw it away. The danger of these stereotypes is that from time to time you meet someone who lives up to everything you had ever thought or expected, and so this 'sample of one' confirms you in all your more generalized prejudices. Remember: stupidity and lack of judgement...

Having an open mind means that all involved should take the effort to see the world through the eyes of others. It doesn't mean they have to agree with everyone else; that would be open-mindedness to the extreme of empty-mindedness. Proper openness of mind often leads to pleasant surprises; a realization that someone else's way of doing something might actually be good, maybe even better, so allowing you to select the best preferences from each party, as they suit the particular circumstances. And where compromise is necessary, even where one party has to submit, getting that person to do something that they are culturally uncomfortable with is all the easier if you have gone to the effort to see the world through their eyes in the first place.

Be self-aware

Aim to understand the nature of your own preferences for dealing with life, for taking decisions and solving problems. What do you believe to be the 'the right way' to do things, and how does this translate into your behaviour and attitudes? Later in the chapter we will work through 16 'preference scales' designed to help you assess _how_ you behave and, even more importantly, _why_ you behave that way.

Each member of the team should aim to develop this same self-awareness, and in doing so you make a huge leap forward as a team, towards the goal of using cultural diversity as a tool of competitive advantage.

Develop your knowledge of others

Study the nature of other cultures' attitudes and behaviours, and so build an understanding of *their* preferences for 'the right way'. The same 16 scales will help you to assess *how* others behave, and *why* they behave that way.

Again, each member of the team should aim to develop this same ability to observe and understand. The best way to do this is to gather, and discuss, and listen. In practice you may need the services of an expert facilitator, at least to begin with. A good indication of a team's developing cultural awareness is its ability to manage such things for itself.

Be practical (but not superficial)

There are eight guidelines for success in your team's pursuit of a practical application of its newly developed open-mindedness, self-awareness and knowledge:

1. Recognize that when two cultures meet it is not necessary for one to dominate and one to submit. Compare notes on preferences, not with the intent of declaring a winner, but in order to select the best (in the particular circumstances) from both parties.
2. Try hard to be guided, not by the preferences currently held by your head office, nor the preferences held by the GA manager, but wherever possible by the preferences held by the customer (though, of course, this being a global customer, their preferences will themselves be subject to some degree of cultural diversity).
3. Decide which preferences (exhibited as attitudes and behaviours) must become uniform across the global account team in order to match the customer's expectations.
4. Recognize the discomfort caused for some, where the chosen standards might work against their cultural preferences, and seek to actively explain the purpose behind these standards. Keep the focus on the customer's needs and preferences, not as a means of apportioning blame, but as a genuine explanation of why the choices that have been made are so.
5. Instigate this uniformity as a set of standards and guidelines (using the word 'rules' is an open invitation to rebellion).
6. Strenuously coach the application of these standards. Please note: the word used here was 'coach', not 'police'. It is true that coaching is harder work, but ultimately it is far more successful and fulfilling.

7. Decide which preferences (exhibited as attitudes and behaviours) must be local, and again, based on the customer's requirements. (Note, I didn't say what *can* be left as local, rather, it is what *must* be local. In other words, this is a positive choice, not a reluctant admission of defeat.)
8. Instigate the resultant diversity with a full awareness (and celebration) of the value of that diversity within the global team.

CULTURAL PREFERENCES – *THE 16 SCALES*

I have already mentioned the book by Penny Carté and Chris Fox: *Bridging the Culture Gap*, published by Kogan Page. The greater part of what follows is based on the models and advice to be found in that splendid book, and the 16 *'preference scales'* we will work through are taken wholly from it (for which, many thanks to the generosity of Carté and Fox). I have taken the liberty of applying an occasional twist to their approach, in order to relate the question to the particular challenges of GAM.

The purpose of these scales is to help you in your efforts towards self-awareness and in the observation of others. The more you look and listen, and with as open a mind as possible, the more you will learn about these 16 preferences. Over time you will be able to place your customers on these scales, and then your colleagues, just as they will be able to do the same for you. Discuss your placements; have you observed each other correctly, and if not, what is it that has stood in the way of a better observation? Or perhaps they have observed you better than you have observed yourself? It happens, and when it does your capacity for open-mindedness will be tested to the full!

The reward

All this observation and discussion is for a purpose, so let's turn to the payback for all your efforts.

Discuss as a team the implications of different positions, between team members, and between your team and the customer. What is the potential for misunderstanding? What is the potential for conflict? (You may just explain a few old battles and missed opportunities as you go.) Most importantly of all, how does this new awareness help you to do a better job of selecting the right people for the right tasks, and adopting the best behaviours for each and any circumstance? This is where you will find yourself able to harness the strengths of your cultural diversity, presenting a team to the customer that has immediate competitive advantage, and not just because of *who* you are, but because of what you *know* about being who you are.

The scales

Each of the 16 scales (as shown in Figures 15.1, 15.2, 15.3 and 15.4) considers a particular aspect of a person's behaviour, with two widely different preferences noted in each case. Explanations for those different preferences and outcomes are to be found in the person's collected beliefs, opinions and attitudes; in other words, their culture. The 'scores' on each scale are intended only to help you identify the relative magnitude of a preference held by yourself or by someone that you wish to better understand.

A health warning

In fact, *two* health warnings before we start. The first is that where I have indicated particular cultures as examples of positions on these scales, it has not been possible in the space available to say more about the subtlety of these positions (please refer to Carté and Fox's book if you want more about this). Please can I urge you therefore to avoid the use of these scales as an exercise in labelling or pigeon-holing? It is about understanding, which is rarely black and white, and if we are not very careful pigeonholing can be worryingly close to, indeed, just a short step away from, prejudice...

The second health warning concerns the advice given and suggestions made on how to deal with people at the opposite end of the preference scale to your own position. Again, space allows only this polar-opposite treatment, whereas in reality you will be working with people at all points along the scales, and needing to observe a great deal more subtlety than my tips might suggest.

The scales are divided into four groups, and displayed in the following figures:

Relationships	Figure 15.1
Communication	Figure 15.2
Time	Figure 15.3
Truth, meaning, and decision making	Figure 15.4

Relationships

Individualist						Group-orientated				
My first duty should be to myself						My first duty should be to the group to which I belong				
50	40	30	20	10	0	10	20	30	40	50
Flat hierarchy						**Vertical hierarchy**				
Leaders should share power						Leaders should hold power				
50	40	30	20	10	0	10	20	30	40	50
Acquired status						**Given status**				
People should be judged on what they do, not who they are						Other factors – such as family, class, nationality, race, education, age, sex, religion – should also be taken into account				
50	40	30	20	10	0	10	20	30	40	50
Functional						**Personal**				
We need to focus on business first and personal relationships later in order to do successful business						We need to build a personal relationship first in order to do successful business				
50	40	30	20	10	0	10	20	30	40	50
Physically distant						**Physically close**				
I prefer people not to come too close to me physically						I think physical closeness and touch are reassuring				
50	40	30	20	10	0	10	20	30	40	50

Figure 15.1 *Cultural preference scale* – Relationships (with thanks to Carté and Fox, from their book *Bridging the Culture Gap*, Kogan Page, 2004)

Individualist–group orientated

The first scale considers a culture's preference towards the individual (US, British, French, Dutch) or the group (Asian, Arab, African).

If the customer displays a strong preference towards an individualist culture then your response must be tailored accordingly; introduce yourself as 'you', not simply a representative of the collective, deal with them on the same basis, stand up for yourself, say what you think, be prepared to challenge and push back.

Such behaviour with someone from a more group-orientated culture may have you in trouble almost before you get started. Here you should aim to represent your company, and regard them as doing the same. Involve others in presentations and negotiations, show teamwork and encourage them to do the same. Avoid displays of internal friction, aim to promote harmony, and make use of the social side for genuine business discussions.

It becomes easy to see the cause of so many misunderstandings, such as how what *you* thought was a straightforward enough reward structure for GAM fell foul of a mixed preference team.

Needless to say, because group-orientated cultures will value teamwork highly, they also tend to be better at it – a strength and a preference worth remembering when trying to form a global account team.

Flat hierarchy–vertical hierarchy

Observing how people use authority, and watching how others respond to that authority, points up one of the most marked of cultural differences. Scandinavians in particular are to the left of this scale, expecting leaders to share power with subordinates and expecting those subordinates to take full responsibility, where they have expertise. Arguments with superiors are not only expected, they are encouraged, provided the subordinate really is taking responsibility for their case. When there are problems with colleagues you are expected to sort them out yourselves, not run to the boss for help at every obstacle.

Selling to customers with this preference requires careful analysis of the decision-making units to find the experts, and to understand who will respect whose views. Just selling to the boss and expecting things to happen is likely to end in tears.

Selling to a customer dominated by a vertical hierarchy culture is in some ways a little easier, at least with regard to the analysis of the decision-making process (as discussed in Chapter 7). You might expect to find a much closer correlation between the structure chart organigrams and the actual decision-making process than you would in a customer dominated by a flat hierarchy culture.

Managing a GA team composed of people with a flat hierarchy preference will involve a good deal of consulting, empowering and coaching; fine if that is your own preference but hard work if you come from the land of 'tell'.

In Chapter 8 we discussed the GROW tool, urging that wherever possible team members should be encouraged to write their own. This methodology would be only as expected in a flat hierarchy culture, but might cause some significant discomfort and even suspicion in a vertical hierarchy culture. The reluctance of someone from the right of this scale to provide their own GROW should not be read as dissent or a lack of commitment; it is far more likely that they are confused by your motives in asking. Equally, the left-sider who leaps to volunteer their GROW to a team dominated by a vertical hierarchy culture might just found themselves chastised rather than thanked.

Scandinavian managers can find it tough working in France, Latin America, India and China, where power and authority are held in very few hands, just as a culturally unaware French boss can be regarded with dismay by a group of Swedish workers.

Cultures that prefer vertical hierarchies make their decisions at the top and don't encourage debate among subordinates either before or after those decisions are made. Bosses will keep information to themselves, and subordinates will show great respect to those decision makers. The rule of selling to a customer with these preferences is clear: get to the top, but don't ignore the lower levels that will be charged with implementing the decisions taken.

If you manage a GA team composed of people with these preferences then the advice is again clear: be autocratic, even if it offends your own preference for debate. If you fail to tell people clearly what you wish to happen then don't be surprised when it doesn't. This isn't insubordination; they simply didn't think you really meant it, and were doing you a favour by not embarking on something you were so half-hearted about.

Acquired status–given status

Spain, India, China, Japan and the Arab world tend to be 'given status' cultures where who you are and where you come from can have high significance. This can be one of the more alien-sounding preferences if you hail from an acquired status culture such as the United States where not only do age, gender and race have nothing to do with it, they are increasingly legislated out of the equation.

Selling to a customer from a given status culture takes much diplomacy for an acquired status person. Show respect for age, for length of service, and don't be shocked by paternalistic attitudes either towards you or towards subordinates in the customer's business. In fact, focusing on people is more important than focusing on their jobs.

Selling to a customer from an acquired status culture requires you to analyse the decision-making unit based on functions first, and then the people.

Managing teams composed of mixed preferences on any of these 16 scales is a challenge, but particularly so in this case. Those to the left want you to value and reward their performance, while those to the right will show loyalty to you if you take a paternalistic approach. This may work out OK when working with individuals on their own, but the combined team presents a problem, and may have you 'found out' for double standards. It is safest by far to agree the rules in advance.

223

The British have an interesting perspective on this preference scale; it is not so long since we lived in a thoroughly class-based society where people knew their betters (and by and large genuinely respected them), but now we live in a much more meritocratic society (where, for some, respect appears to have gone out of the window). Perhaps we are able to look both ways along this scale, understanding the two extremes, and perhaps that is why a British manager finds it easier than an American manager to be placed in *either* Mumbai or New York.

Functional–personal

The first time I ran a KAM workshop in China I spent a whole morning on the virtues of diamond teams and the importance of relationships, and to a very polite audience, only to be told at lunchtime that I really was preaching to the converted. The idea of *guanxi* is well rooted in this *personal*-orientated culture. Guanxi is about connections and their importance; don't try to do a deal in China if you don't have the time to respect and develop the relationship. Of course, a *guanxi*-motivated seller, working in a functionally orientated culture, might be surprised at the little return they get for their lengthy overtures and efforts to build personal relationships, and yet, in the long term their efforts may well pay off in comparison to the functionally orientated seller, and don't forget: GAM is a long-term game.

Those from cultures where the *functional* preference is more pronounced should take care not to jump to the wrong conclusions when encountering such *personal*-orientated cultures. Working in mixed GA teams can be a difficult experience for, let's say a German, who is frustrated by the amount of time their colleagues from, let's say southern Italy or Egypt, put into socializing and small talk: *'Can't they just get on with it?'* is a common enough response, *'and are all those little gifts quite the right thing?'*

Perhaps of all the preference scales and their diverse behaviours this is the one where, for the successful application of GAM, I would encourage the team to learn from each other's strengths. A genuine combination of behaviours, not a compromise, but an ability to recognize when to be personal and when to be functional, will be a huge strength in any long-term, team-selling pursuit.

Physically distant–physically close

This one may sound more like a tactic than a discussion on a deep-seated preference, but it is as deep and real as any of them. Northern

Europeans sit more or less in the middle, with the southern Europeans and the Turkish to the right, and the South-East Asians very much to the left.

Mixed teams of long standing will have learnt to cope with the differences in preference here, perhaps making a joke out of someone's reluctance even to shake hands and another's urge to kiss everyone on both cheeks before the meeting can start. It is in the newly forming teams where these things can be awkward, embarrassing, and possibly even the source of longer-term frictions.

Working with customers, eye contact is very important; not too much to a left-sider, but plenty for a right-sider – it indicates your sincerity, your confidence, and your resolve.

Communication

Low context						High context				
Business relationships are complicated, so communication needs to be frank, explicit and direct						Business relationships are complicated, so communication needs to be diplomatic, implicit and indirect				
50	40	30	20	10	0	10	20	30	40	50
Reserved						**Effusive**				
I think you should talk only when you have something relevant to say						Lots of talk indicates warmth and interest. Silences should be avoided				
50	40	30	20	10	0	10	20	30	40	50
Written						**Spoken**				
For serious issues I prefer the written word						For serious issues I prefer oral communication				
50	40	30	20	10	0	10	20	30	40	50

Figure 15.2 _Cultural preference scale_ – Communication (with thanks to Carté and Fox, from their book _Bridging the Culture Gap_, Kogan Page, 2004)

Low context–high context

By 'context', we mean: how much more is there to what someone is saying beyond the words? A low-context speaker means what they say; the message isn't wrapped up in any extra 'cultural clothing' (Germans, Finns, Dutch). The high-context speaker expects the listener to understand that what they say comes clothed in some very definite cultural values (Chinese, Japanese, French). These extra meanings are usually communicated through tone, body language, or eye movements.

You can see straight away how the low-context 'left-sider' may easily think the high-context 'right-sider' less than straight, while the high-context speaker will be frustrated at the low-context listener's inability to get their meaning. The British use of irony places them towards the right, as high-context communicators, and the scope for misunderstanding when working with a low-context German or American is too well known for further comment.

When working in a low-context culture, expect frank exchanges and take them as they are usually intended: constructive (even if they might not sound so!). What the customer says, they mean. In a high-context culture listeners must exercise more subtlety; in short, they must listen better. If a Japanese customer says it is 'difficult' they may well mean it is 'impossible', and your attempts to overcome the difficulties will be wasted, and probably regarded as foolishness. Listening 'better' means several things: watching as well as listening, asking questions to confirm and check understanding, staying patient, and avoiding assumptions.

In the world of GAM so much communication is bound to be by e-mail that there is even more scope for misunderstanding here than usual. E-mails are notoriously bad for correctly conveying things such as British irony or the Gallic shrug of the shoulders, yet these things are there, behind the words. The moral of the story should be: if the conversation is important, and if there is any risk of misunderstanding, try to have it face to face. It is noticeable how the airlines have picked up on this issue when trying to persuade us that, despite the technological revolution, physical meetings are still of vital importance in doing business.

Reserved–effusive

Watch an American and a Japanese in conversation and count the number of words spoken by each. Care to guess who says more? The same test can be done watching the Italians and the Germans, the British and the Finns...

Reserved cultures will tend to wait their turn to speak, with conversations worked through in orderly packages. Effusive cultures will interrupt, reading interaction as a good thing. Sellers have a reputation for speaking too much in any case, but an effusive seller working with a reserved customer is going to have to do a lot of tongue biting if they want to avoid being thought of as rude, pushy, or even dishonest.

Good relationships grow from feelings of rapport, whether between colleagues or between supplier and customer, and rapport can be killed very quickly by ignoring this particular preference. While the effusive speaker will do well to bite their tongue to build rapport with a reserved listener, the reserved listener will do well to listen 'actively', with occasional nods of the head, and reasonably frequent '*I see*'s, and the like. With this preference scale, meeting in the middle may well be the best course of action, and that is what will happen as rapport develops, and the '*I see*'s become '*Well that's interesting because...*'s, and the tongue biter gets to avoid drawing blood.

For the culturally unaware and unthinking team member there can be a particularly unfortunate outcome. An effusive American may be inclined to think their reserved Thai colleague uncommitted, or dull, or even stupid. The Thai may conclude that the American is arrogant, or shallow, or even dubious. In both cases the fault lies with the beholder, of course, but such assumptions can bedevil effective team working. This is one to get out into the open at the earliest opportunity. I have run sessions for Chinese employees of an American company where they have been asked to 'be American' for the day, and where the American team members have been asked to practise the reserve of the Thai. The discomfort is palpable, but the experience is almost always for the good.

Written–spoken

Between suppliers and customers the most important aspect of this scale is probably the preference for a written contract, or letters of intent (American), versus the hope that our word is our bond (Middle Eastern).

Within teams it will manifest itself as some people wanting formal confirmations of meetings and agreements, and others just wanting to get on with it after a phone call. Both sides can be suspicious of the other's motivation: does the left-sider want it written down because they don't trust me; does the right-sider just want to get on with it because they want to do it differently? This is one where the team will be well advised to decide on a rule; what gets written down, and what doesn't.

Time

The minefields are spread wide here, between suppliers and customers and within GA teams. Playing it the customer's way is usually the best advice, while within the team there is a need to agree the rules well in advance.

Monochronic						Polychronic				
I prefer to deal with one task at a time in a structured fashion						I prefer to have several tasks running at the same time				
50	40	30	20	10	0	10	20	30	40	50
Speed						Patience				
Too much analysis leads to paralysis						Taking my time helps me make the right decision				
50	40	30	20	10	0	10	20	30	40	50
Short-term						Long-term				
I prefer to focus on the here and now						I need to see beyond the horizon and plan accordingly				
50	40	30	20	10	0	10	20	30	40	50
Future						Past				
Tradition gets in the way of progress						Change needs to respect tradition				
50	40	30	20	10	0	10	20	30	40	50

Figure 15.3 *Cultural preference scale* – Time
(with thanks to Carté and Fox, from their book *Bridging the Culture Gap*, Kogan Page, 2004)

Monochronic–polychronic

The Swiss are known for their timekeeping, and their time management, their precision extending to the niceties of life just as much as the big things. Events are ordered, the day sliced up into sections that follow on from each other in a neat linear fashion. This monochronic view of time is also common to Anglo-Saxons and Scandinavian cultures, though perhaps with a little less vigour.

The polychronic view of time is that it is the servant and not the master. The Italians, the Hispanic United States and Indians share this view, regarding relationships as more important than time-keeping.

A polychronic sales professional hoping to impress a monochronic buyer will have to adopt some uncomfortable disciplines – and these have to be absolute rules across a GA team selling to a monochronic customer. Fix appointments well ahead of time, send agendas for meetings, don't be late, and keep to agreed agendas.

In the reverse situation – a monochronic seller and a polychronic customer – it isn't about throwing the clock out of the window, rather that other things might take priority. Try to stay relaxed, and don't look at your watch every five minutes.

Speed–patience

This scale is not a carbon copy of the monochronic–polychronic. The polychronic Spanish may appear to allow their meetings to ramble, but when it comes to making a decision they will act with great speed, often perplexing the monochronic Germans who were eager to complete just one more analysis.

When negotiating a global deal this is the scale that can lead to the most frustration and nervousness. Should the seller force the pace? Not if the customer sits to the right of this scale (Mexican, Japanese). If they sit to the left, perhaps an American position, then expect them to want to get on with it.

Within the GA team the different preferences are liable to cause agitation unless they are recognized, and again, some rules set. This is definitely a case of learning from others and choosing the best preference for the circumstance. From time to time there will be projects that really do demand some serious analysis, perhaps not a job for the _speed_-orientated members of the team? And if the project needs to be actioned fast, don't make life difficult for yourself and the individuals concerned by giving it to those of a more _patient_ orientation.

Short-term–long-term

The Japanese are famed for taking the long-term view, their investment strategies in new markets reflecting this well. In theory, this should make them good at GAM; the management of a long-term investment. The Americans have a tendency to want the payback a lot sooner, and in theory, this should make GAM rather a challenge, or at least, a frustration. Is this true? From my observations, I think yes to some fair extent. So how to teach the Americans patience? A genuinely diverse GA team might go some way to achieving this.

Future–past

If there is a problem in the GA team, perhaps a project has failed, those team members with a future preference may wish to leave it behind and get on with the next thing. Their 'past focused' colleagues may read that in an unfortunate way; a lack of sincerity, an inability to learn from past mistakes? Of course, the 'future focused' members may read an equally unfortunate inference into their colleagues' concerns; a lack of dynamism, an inability to handle failure? Recognize the dangers and aim to avoid them through modified behaviours.

Truth, meaning, and decision making

Fixed truth						Relative truth				
There are clear rights and wrongs						What is right and wrong depends on the circumstances				
50	40	30	20	10	0	10	20	30	40	50
Analytical						**Intuitive**				
What I value most is logical, comprehensive and consistent argument. Even if I instinctively feel a proposal is right, I need to test every step of the argument before I can commit myself						What I value most are creative and intriguing ideas that appeal to the emotions. If I instinctively feel a proposal is right, I don't need to test every step in the argument before I commit myself				
50	40	30	20	10	0	10	20	30	40	50
Theoretical						**Empirical**				
I like using abstract concepts to solve problems						For me, concrete experience is more important than theory				
50	40	30	20	10	0	10	20	30	40	50
Choice						**Destiny**				
I am in charge of how I live my life						Forces beyond my control determine what happens in my life				
50	40	30	20	10	0	10	20	30	40	50

Figure 15.4 *Cultural preference scale* – Truth, meaning and decision making (with thanks to Carté and Fox, from their book *Bridging the Culture Gap*, Kogan Page, 2004)

Fixed truth–relative truth

This one can get you into deep trouble, not only with customers and colleagues, but also with your legal department, and even the law. Those cultures that hold to an idea of fixed and absolute truth will tend to favour procedures and processes as a way of ensuring a uniform observation of those absolute rights and wrongs. This could be seen as an unnecessary and bureaucratic restriction by those in the team from a relative truth culture, where they want the flexibility to determine their actions based on the actual circumstances. Of course, should this latter group act on this preference, they could find themselves breaking procedures, and perhaps even breaking the law (though typically it will be *someone else's* law).

A 'fixed truth' customer may not appreciate the 'flexibility' of a 'relative truth' supplier (they'll do anything to get the order, like the plumber who is keen to be paid cash and won't give you a receipt), while a 'relative truth' customer will certainly grow frustrated at the 'inflexibility' of a 'fixed truth' supplier that seems to have its head in the rule book. How to avoid this bind?

How about the rule suggested earlier in this chapter: we should aim to match our behaviours to the preferences displayed by the customer. Fine, but what if our business exists predominantly in a 'fixed truth' culture and we have a customer in a predominantly 'relative truth' culture; won't this rule risk putting us in conflict with our own internal procedures, perhaps even in conflict with our business ethics?

There are lines to be drawn in the sand here, and perhaps more so than for any of the other scales. If your business wishes to behave in a 'fixed truth' way, then there will have to be limitations to your dealings with a customer living in a 'relative truth' world, and limitations that will have to apply across your team. Should this even apply where some of your team members share that 'relative truth' culture? Only you can decide, but doing business while being untrue to yourself is rarely a happy circumstance.

There is a complication here when your customer, being global, displays both preferences in different locations. Let's say the head office is of a 'fixed truth' persuasion, while some of the local sites are far more 'relative truth' orientated. The best advice here is to discuss the issue openly, at as senior a level as possible. How does the customer wish you to proceed? Presumably they will also want to be drawing some lines in the sand?

Does this suggest that a supplier from a 'relative truth' culture may have the advantage over a competing 'fixed truth' supplier; a flexibility that allows them to duck and dive more freely? Perhaps so, and most likely to be the case when the two competitors are chasing a 'relative truth' customer. Some customers are always going to be harder to work with than others, and perhaps in a 'fixed truth' world that will be one of the ways of determining the really key global customers. Reverse the customer's preference and much the same dilemma faces the 'relative truth' supplier.

Analytical–intuitive

This preference scale can guide us when deciding how to present a case, whether within the team or to the customer. The analytical preference suggests a case well supported by facts and solid evidence. The intuitive preference suggests a need for more creativity in the approach. So, faced with a mixed team, as in a GA team, do you throw in a bit of each, to keep everyone happy? Inside your own team this is one to discuss openly and recognize that different presenters will have different comfort zones. It is up to you to decide whether you want people to work outside their comfort zones, in pursuit of a more uniform team style, or whether you allow people their own style, with the rest of the team knowing where it comes from. The French, Germans and Swiss will fall to the left of this scale, the Americans somewhere in the middle, and the British towards the right.

Theoretical–empirical

Isn't this the same as the previous scale? For the French, perhaps yes, with a positioning to the left in both cases. For the British, perhaps yes, leaning to the right in both cases. But the Germans and the Finns, while having a clear preference for logical analysis, will combine this with a preference for empirical experience rather than abstract theory. If you want to make sure your case really hits the mark, especially when presenting to a customer, you will need to consider both of these scales together.

Choice–destiny

Whether consciously held or not, religion and philosophical ideas play a vital role in a culture's view of how things get to be how they are. Philosophers have debated the self-will versus determinism argument for centuries, and we find it still in global business today. Consider a supplier that has just lost to a competitor a big contract with a global customer. Those in the GA team to the left of this scale (Americans, British, Germans) will look for reasons, and often find them in something that they, or the team, did wrong. This is an exercise (usually) not in self-flagellation but in wanting to get it right next time. Those to the right of the scale (many Asian cultures, but not all) will reflect that how it turned out was 'how it was meant to be'. This happened in my own business, and I thought that my Asian colleague who expressed this view was simply trying to soften the blow for me, but in fact it really was his view, that we were not meant to get that contract and would find that our resources were now freely available for something more suitable. And do you know what: he was right!

The experience has not converted me to a believer in destiny, I still think that I can make things happen despite the circumstances (I'm British, and that's our dominant culture), but it has made me more open to listen to the views of others, and helped me to engage in much more fruitful debates than *'We lost it, and it was your fault.'*

FORGING A COMPETITIVE ADVANTAGE

The 16 cultural preference scales discussed here are not, of course, the 'last word' on cultural diversity, but they do provide the GA team with an opportunity to understand each other better, and so work together more effectively. Figure 15.5 shows how you might use a diagram to draw out the cultural 'footprint' of any individual.

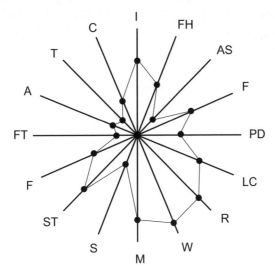

Figure 15.5 _A cultural 'footprint'_

Each leg of the diagram represents one of the preference scales (from Figures 15.1, 15.2, 15.2 and 15.4), always with the left-hand choice to the outer edge, and the individual's own 'scores' marked by the black dots. By joining the dots you create a shape that is then easy to compare to the footprints of the other team members. Look for similarities and for strong contrasts and then ask the all-important question: what does this mean for us as a team?

By taking the time to discuss your preferences in this way you give your team the opportunity to select or to modify particular behaviours to suit particular circumstances, both within the team and with the customer. This flexibility will be of huge importance and value when working on a global stage. So it is that the enhanced performance of your team, through its recognition of cultural diversity, turns that very diversity into a source of competitive advantage.

Before long, not only will you appreciate the benefits of discussing the diverse preferences within the global team, you will also be recognizing the imperative of having those different preferences in the first place. Successful global account teams are more than cross-functional groups armed with a set of processes and procedures. Where such 'limited and self-limiting' teams do exist it is usually the result of the 'dominant and dominating' cultural preferences of the lead members. The best teams, and the rarest teams, will consider the people, and their motivations, and their behaviours, and then seek to find the best mixes of those things for each circumstance. Achieve this maturity and the customer will notice it, and there lies your competitive advantage.

Let's close with a quick summary of the vital guidelines, and this time with an additional fifth item:

- Be open-minded.
- Be self-aware.
- Develop your understanding of others.
- Be practical.
- Make sure it all works to the customer's benefit.

16

Next steps, and getting further help

Throughout this book I have tried to focus on the practical and the real world, the aim being to help you move by measured steps towards the implementation of a successful GAM (global account management) strategy. By the time you have arrived here, I hope that you will have already gone a long way to developing your own plan of action. But there is always more help on offer.

VALUE PROPOSITIONS

You may be wondering why there was no chapter on the *value proposition*, or on *value selling* as a skill and activity. Space is always a good excuse, but a better one is that the purpose of this book was to look at GAM as it is different from KAM, and while both value propositions and value selling will certainly form a part of most GAM strategies, they also form a part of most KAM strategies, and were covered in such depth in my earlier book, *Key Account Management*, 4th edition, published by Kogan Page, that I would rather recommend that you find them there. However... a very short summary of the main points may whet your appetite for more!

In the eye of the beholder...

The most important thing to say about any value proposition is that value is in the eye of the beholder: value is received, not given. Value has nothing to do with your costs, or the efforts you have put in, and should not be calculated in those terms. It is only about what the customer receives, and even more importantly what they perceive that they receive, and can only be measured in their terms.

This is a challenge in the context of GAM, because only the most thoroughly global customer (by my definitions) is likely to perceive value in the same way across their many locations. This is a genuine problem for the value seller, as it tends to dilute the potency of their value proposition, and so make it easier for the global buyer to buy on price. The difficulty of dealing with the 'would-be globals' will be most apparent in this matter. A possible solution is to stress that while certain things can be standardized globally – terms, products, price(?) – value propositions are inherently local and should be discussed, valued, and rewarded in their local context. The global buyer may not go for this, but it might be your best shot!

Identifying your value

Figure 16.1 proposes a tool that can be used to identify the value created by your offer, and also the potential for new value (a tool covered in very much more detail in *Key Account Management*).

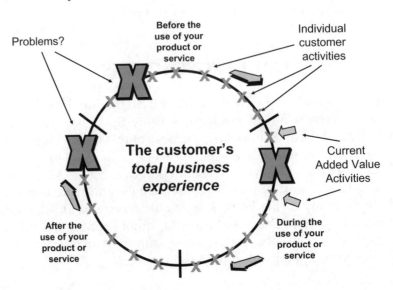

Figure 16.1 *The customer's activity cycle, and total business experience*

It asks you to trace out the customer's activities in doing business with you, from start to finish, and looking at every small interaction. The next step is to place your existing customer-focused activities against the steps in their journey, to see what positive impact they have on the customer's experience – or to put it another way, the value that they already receive from you. Next, look for where things can or do go wrong, and ask what actions you could take to correct or improve – more instances of potential value received.

Once you have identified the elements of your value proposition, try to calculate the value received by the customer, and in their terms. If your product or service helps the customer to make a more uniform product, with reduced downtime on their plant and fewer complaints or recalls from the market, then try to work out what you save them, and then consider what premium they might pay for these savings. If your product or service helps them to remove an activity from their own operations, again, try to calculate what have you saved them and consider the appropriate premium.

In a global context this can get very complicated indeed, as the costs and savings involved in the customer's different locations may vary considerably, but undertaking the task will help you to understand the relative potency of your own value proposition in each location, and so help you decide whether you are better off discussing and negotiating your reward centrally or locally.

INSIGHT MARKETING AND PEOPLE

My own business specializes in helping clients with their KAM and GAM challenges, and we will be happy to discuss your needs with you whether you are looking for advice, consultancy, coaching, or formal training.

INSIGHT is a global firm, working in the Americas, Europe, Africa, the Middle East and AsiaPacific. We have particular experience working with customers in the following industries/markets: financial services, fast-moving consumer goods, information technology, pharmaceuticals, retail, speciality chemicals, telecommunications and transport.

Your challenge – our response

In Chapter 9 we discussed the challenges faced by leaders wishing to implement a GAM strategy (Figure 9.2), and Figure 16.2 shows

237

- Leading Change
- Multicultural Leadership
- MTBI® – *Myers Briggs*
- Coaching – *The Masterclass*
- Strategic Influencing Skills
- Right Team, Right Purpose

STRATEGY & LEADERSHIP

Are we going in the right direction?
Are we doing the right things?

- Strategy Into Action:
  Facilitating Your Strategy
- Peer Reviews
- Corporate Profitability
- The Marketing Workshop

The Creation of Value...

...to be a Winning Business

- True Value Propositions
- Value Pricing & Value Selling
- Customer Service
- Branding & Brand Management
- Creativity – *The Masterclass*
- Delivering Value – *the financials*
- Pricing – *The Masterclass*

How are we different?
Are we properly rewarded?

VALUE PROPOSITIONS

Do our customers prosper?
Are we a key supplier?

GLOBAL ACCOUNT MANAGEMENT

- KAM – *The Masterclass*
- The KAM/GAM Programme:
  Alignment, Selection, Application
- Global Account Management
- Customer Distinction Strategies
- Sales Workshops

Figure 16.2 *INSIGHT's response to your challenge*

INSIGHT's response to that challenge: a suite of training work-shops designed especially for those taking on the KAM or GAM challenge.

- Our _KAM/GAM Programme_ will take you and your team through the whole process discussed in this book. In particular:
  - The _KAM/GAM Masterclass_ provides an opportunity for engaging the full understanding and support of the senior management team, and has a particular focus on identifying their own role in making KAM and GAM happen.
  - The _GAM Selection_ workshop from the _KAM/GAM Programme_ will help you to identify your global accounts, as discussed in Chapter 9.
  - The _KAM/GAM Team_ workshops from the _KAM/GAM Programme_ will help your team to identify the Belbin team roles discussed in Chapter 10.
- The _Coaching Masterclass_ will help you to develop the coaching skills discussed in Chapter 10.
- The _Multicultural Leadership_ workshop will help you to harness the benefits of cultural diversity as discussed in Chapter 15.

You can contact us at:

Website: www/insight-mp.com
E-mail: customer.service@insight-mp.com

Insight Marketing and People	INSIGHT Asia Pacific SDN
Lidstone Court	BHD
George Green	Kelana Business Centre
Uxbridge Road	513 Block A
Slough	97 Jalan 7/2 Kelana Jaya
Berkshire	47301 Petaling Jaya
SL3 6AG	Selangor
United Kingdom	Malaysia
Tel: +44 (0)1753 822990	Tel: +603 7880 7740

FURTHER READING

Carté, P and Fox, C (2004) *Bridging the Culture Gap*, Kogan Page, London

Cheverton, P (2006) *Key Account Management*, 4th edn, Kogan Page, London

Cheverton, P (to be published 2006) *Key Selling Skills*, Kogan Page, London

Cheverton, P, Foss, B, Hughes, T and Stone, M (2004) *Key Account Management for Financial Services*, Kogan Page, London

Wilson, K, Speare, N and Reese, SJ (2002) *Successful Global Account Management*, Kogan Page, London

Index